The Natural History of
NORTH AMERICA

The Natural History of
NORTH AMERICA

in association with the
AMERICAN MUSEUM OF NATURAL HISTORY

by
EDWARD RICCIUTI

CRESCENT BOOKS
NEW YORK · AVENEL, NEW JERSEY

CLB 4548
© 1995 CLB Publishing, Godalming, Surrey, England
All rights reserved

This 1995 edition published by Crescent Books, distributed by Random
House Value Publishing, Inc.
40 Engelhard Avenue, Avenel, New Jersey 07001

Random House
New York • Toronto • London • Sydney • Auckland

A CIP catalog record for this book is available from the Library of
Congress.

Printed and bound in China

ISBN 0-517-12164-6

8 7 6 5 4 3 2 1

ART EDITOR	Stephen Bitti
DESIGNERS	Paul Oakley
	Ruth Levy
PROJECT EDITOR	Carolyn Pyrah
EDITORIAL ASSISTANT	Heather Collins
PRODUCTION MANAGER	Siân Jones
PICTURE RESEARCHER	James Ricciuti
CHIEF CONSULTANT	John Farrand Jr.
CARTOGRAPHERS	Euromap Limited
ILLUSTRATORS	Kevin Maddison
	Carol Buckman

To Greg Tremper for days in the grouse woods and
Tom H W Emanuel for patience

CONTENTS

FOREWORD

The poet William Blake felt a person needed sublime innocence
'to see a world in a grain of sand'. For a reader to see the whole
natural panorama of the USA and Canada in a single book is
almost as demanding.
Like a pointillist painter, an author can fill the canvas species
by species with the continent's flora and fauna. But these bits
need to be laid down under broader brush strokes of background
geology and evolutionary time. Both of these techniques are
applied in this book and augmented by splendid
color photographs.
Of course, on one level any book must fail. So wondrous a world
cannot be captured on pages. But this book should succeed
admirably in inspiring the reader to pursue the subject further.
This can be done by following the leads in the ample
bibliography and stepping outdoors to see nature face to face.
With its parks, reserves, and vast public lands, North America
welcomes the curious traveler.
I hope this book and the trips that it inspires will turn readers
into further advocates for nature. As the philosopher William
James said, 'Scenery seems to wear in one's consciousness better
than any other element of life.'

Alan Ternes
Editor, *Natural History* magazine
The American Museum of Natural History

The EVOLUTION *of a* CONTINENT

The continents we know today, including North America, began to form about 225 million years ago. According to the theory of continental drift, all the present continents originated from one immense land mass, called 'Pangaea', which covered somewhat less than half of the earth's surface. The rest of the earth's surface was ocean. Approximately 225 million years ago, this supercontinent started to fragment and the pieces, which were to become our continents, began to drift away from one another. According to the theory, continents continue to drift and in the far distant future may once again merge as a united land mass.

The rugged face of the Big Sur Coast in Los Padres National Forest, California typifies the rough surf-eroded rock of the Pacific Coast. Large cut-off rock areas sometimes form haystack-shaped islets, like the one that can be seen in the distance, upper right.

BEFORE the supercontinent fragmented, North America was attached to Europe, and South America to Africa. As North America and Europe separated, the ever widening gap between them became the Atlantic Ocean. Slowly, North America assumed its present shape until about 5 million years ago it was close to its present configuration.

The theory of continental drift was first proposed in 1912 by Alfred Wegener, but seemed too fantastic to believe. However, the theory has gained credence in the last few decades, supported by additional theories about movements deep within the earth causing the continents to travel, if only at a rate of a few inches yearly. The continents are carried on colossal slabs of the earth's outer skin, or lithosphere, which is composed of plates.

PLATE MOVEMENT

The plates are made up of the earth's crust and the upper layer of the mantle. The mantle is the region between the crust and the core of the planet. The cooler upper part of the mantle is solid, while nearer the core it verges on melting point, and is plastic. The plates ride upon the flexible inner mantle, carried, scientists believe, by the flow of convection currents. In the same way that warm air rises and cool air sinks, the hot, malleable rock deep within the mantle rises towards the top and the cooler upper rock sinks to the bottom. The descending cool rock heats as ascending hot rock cools in a never ending cycle.

As the plates glide over the lower mantle, they pull apart, collide or scrape against one another. Such interactions at plate boundaries are the cause of the greatest natural upheavals on earth, including earthquakes, volcanism, the creation of mountains and, ultimately, the shaping of continents. Land masses carried on plates can stick together or ride over each other when the plates collide. When plates bearing continents collide, the crust of the earth can be crumpled upward. This process, known as folding, is one of the ways in which mountains are formed.

Volcanic mountains and earthquakes can be produced by the colossal friction and pressure that results when two plates meet and one slides under the other. (If the edge of one plate is sea floor and the other continent, the continental plate will

This area near Bakersfield, California, clearly shows the San Andreas Fault zone. The fault is the result of the collision between the Pacific and North American plates. The Pacific Plate is sliding north-westward past the North American.

EARTHQUAKES

THIS map illustrates the North American portion of the so-called 'Ring of Fire'. The Ring extends in an arc around the Pacific rim and is an area where volcanoes are abundant and earthquakes frequently occur.

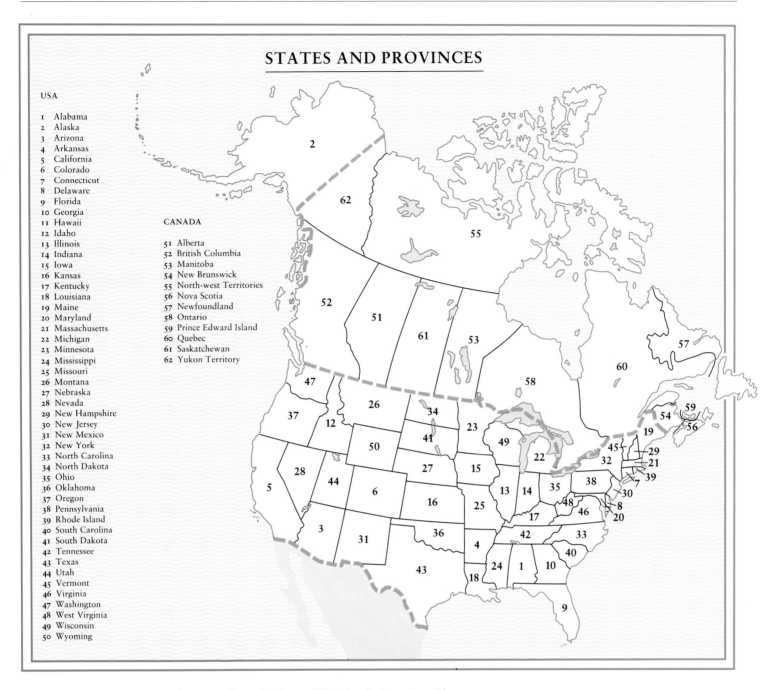

STATES AND PROVINCES

USA

1 Alabama
2 Alaska
3 Arizona
4 Arkansas
5 California
6 Colorado
7 Connecticut
8 Delaware
9 Florida
10 Georgia
11 Hawaii
12 Idaho
13 Illinois
14 Indiana
15 Iowa
16 Kansas
17 Kentucky
18 Louisiana
19 Maine
20 Maryland
21 Massachusetts
22 Michigan
23 Minnesota
24 Mississippi
25 Missouri
26 Montana
27 Nebraska
28 Nevada
29 New Hampshire
30 New Jersey
31 New Mexico
32 New York
33 North Carolina
34 North Dakota
35 Ohio
36 Oklahoma
37 Oregon
38 Pennsylvania
39 Rhode Island
40 South Carolina
41 South Dakota
42 Tennessee
43 Texas
44 Utah
45 Vermont
46 Virginia
47 Washington
48 West Virginia
49 Wisconsin
50 Wyoming

CANADA

51 Alberta
52 British Columbia
53 Manitoba
54 New Brunswick
55 North-west Territories
56 Nova Scotia
57 Newfoundland
58 Ontario
59 Prince Edward Island
60 Quebec
61 Saskatchewan
62 Yukon Territory

overlap the oceanic plate.) This type of overlap has caused the Ring of Fire, an arc of volcanoes around the Pacific Ocean and a prime earthquake zone.

Earthquakes also occur where plates scrape against one another, causing a split, or fault, in the earth's surface. The crust on either side of a fault moves in opposite directions.

Faulting is another process that can create mountains. Where plates move away from one another, the crust of the earth may split, causing a rift, the walls of which can form mountainous escarpments. Molten rock, called magma, seeps to the surface through the rift, cools and solidifies as lava, adding to the earth's crust.

Earthquakes, folding and faulting can occur away from plate boundaries, but usually result from the great forces that plate movements trigger within the earth.

The North American Plate

Some of the plates lie mostly or completely under the rock of the ocean floor, others mostly under continents. North America lies on a plate that extends from just off the west coast of the continent to the mid-Atlantic, where it is bounded by the Eurasian Plate. The western rim of the North American Plate confronts the edge of the Pacific Plate, which is entirely under the sea.

The North American and Pacific plates grind against one another as the former slides south-east and the latter north-west. The crack in the earth's surface that results is the famed San Andreas Fault. The conflicting movements of the plates put the rock along the fault under constant stress. Sometimes it breaks under pressure, relieving tension, and earthquakes occur – notably the San Francisco earthquakes of 1906 and 1989.

Why plates move

The rock that forms a plate is part of a continual process of movement: the undersea boundaries of plates coincide with a winding, worldwide system of mountainous ridges on the sea floor. This system of ridges is split by a series of great longitudinal rifts, where the plates are moving apart, weakening the crust of the earth. From within the mantle, molten rock, or magma, wells towards the earth's surface and pours out of the rifts on both sides. Above the surface the molten rock is called lava, which cools and solidifies, adding to the material of the plates. The North American Plate rises from the mid-Atlantic rift as lava continually adds to the plate, causing the sea floor to spread westward. Meanwhile, on the other side of the rift, lava is being added to the Eurasian Plate and the sea floor is spreading eastward.

While new material is constantly being added to a plate in this way in mid-ocean, on the opposite edge of a plate, where it meets a continental plate, the ocean floor dives under the continental plate. This is because the rock of the ocean floor, always relatively young, is denser than the older rock of continents. As this happens, a great trench is formed, through which the leading edge of the oceanic plate falls back into the earth's mantle. Therefore, the sea floor continually arises from the mantle at the rifts and re-enters the mantle at the trenches: reheated in the mantle, the rock eventually re-emerges and again cools, recycled as if on a conveyor belt.

Movements within the earth are evident in North America in ways both violent and beautiful. The geysers and hot springs of Yellowstone National Park are a wondrous manifestation of

LEFT: *Old Faithful, Yellowstone's most noted geyser, erupts almost on the hour. It shoots water and steam in a column that reaches 175 feet into the air. Yellowstone has many other geysers, but none as spectacular or as regular as Old Faithful.*

YELLOWSTONE NATIONAL PARK

THE presence of geysers and hot springs in Yellowstone National Park is evidence of concentrations of hot magma beneath the earth's surface. Scientists believe geysers occur when ground water seeps down and reaches an area where its temperature is raised to boiling point by heat from the surrounding molten rock. Pressure underground builds to such a point that the water gushes upward through an opening in the ground.

ABOVE: *Warm water heated deep within the earth wells up at the Glory Hole in Yellowstone and deposits minerals.*

what happens when water is heated by magma deep within the earth to be vented through the crust. Geysers spout from the ground where, far below, water has been heated sufficiently to steam. Hot springs bubble over where water has been warmed, but not enough to condense.

The eruption of Mount St. Helens, in the Cascade Mountains of Washington, in 1980 was a result of processes science is just beginning to understand. The eruption killed more than 60 people, levelled 44,000 acres of trees, and covered 6,000 miles of highways with ash. The top 1,200 feet of the peak was blasted away, sending up a mushroom cloud to a height of 63,000 feet.

Volcanism

A volcano is a vent in the earth's crust through which magma can be expelled above the surface as lava and can have a temperature of more than 2,000°F. Volcanoes become mountains when lava, ash, cinders and other materials build up around the opening. Some volcanoes produce mounded cones of cinders, rather than solid rock.

Violent volcanic eruptions occur when previously deposited materials seal up the opening of the volcano and hot gases build up to a tremendous pressure below. Eventually, the increasing gas pressure blows open the vent.

Small volcanoes sometimes arise from the slopes

The eruption of Mount St. Helens in 1980 levelled forests around the volcano. Volcanic peaks are typical of the geologically young Cascades Range. Geologically, the Pacific rim of the continent is more active than the Atlantic. This results largely from the movement of crustal plates.

OPPOSITE: *The stone monolith of Devil's Tower looms in the background of a ponderosa pine* (Pinus ponderosa) *at Devil's Tower National Monument in Wyoming. Devil's Tower is a neck of magma that solidified before reaching the surface of the earth, and was then worn away.*

ABOVE: *These painted dunes at Lassen Volcanic National Park in the Cascade Mountains of northern California are typical of the spectacular scenery of this area.*

INSET: *Lava that seeped from rifts in Craters of the Moon National Monument has taken on myriad rough forms. The park is covered in many areas by cinders and studded with volcanic cones.*

of large volcanic mountains. This is the case on Mount Lassen, in Lassen Volcanic National Park of the Cascade mountain range in California.

Volcanic pressures do not always cause an explosion. Sometimes the lava seeps out and flows across the landscape. An example of this is Craters of the Moon National Monument in southern Idaho. Occasionally magma forces its way upwards but does not break through the surface. Instead it cools and solidifies. This type of event created Devil's Tower in Wyoming.

Devil's Tower originated 60 million years ago when magma pushed upwards into layers of soft sedimentary rock. The magma cooled and turned into rock harder than that surrounding it. Over the ages the sedimentary rock eroded away, leaving the tapering neck of the Tower standing 867 feet above the surface, 300 feet long and 180 feet wide.

GLACIERS

The final changes to the present appearance of northern North America were made over four prolonged periods of global cooling in about the last million years, during the continental glaciations, or ice ages, of the Pleistocene epoch.

The continental glaciations had tremendous impact. Glaciers arise when more snow accumulates during the cold months than melts during the summer. Four times, vast glaciers covered the northern half of North America. These great sheets of ice, a mile or more thick in many places, stretched across the continent and out to sea for about 4,000 miles. The most extensive glaciation penetrated as far south as St. Louis, Missouri, and is known as the Wisconsin, or Würm, glaciation. The last glaciation, which began 100,000 years ago, started to retreat about 18,000 years ago and ended about 11,000 years ago, reached as far south as Wisconsin and New Jersey.

Meanwhile, mountain top, or alpine, glaciers, expanded, moving down the slopes. Continental glaciers and alpine glaciers move differently. Alpine glaciers flow downhill, propelled by the force of gravity, whereas scientists believe that continental glaciers expand at their fronts, which are pushed forward by the accumulation of ice and snow behind them.

The Pleistocene ice sheets buried mountains such as those of northern New England and pressed down with unimaginable weight on the earth's surface, picking up and carrying immense loads of rock, rubble and other debris. The pressure of the weight of ice, together with its cargo of boulders, sand, and gravel, eroded the land-

scape. Rock was scraped bare of soil and gouged and scoured. Mountain peaks, such as in the White Mountains of New Hampshire, were rounded off. Tongues of glacial ice sculpted U-shaped valleys (valleys cut by streams are V-shaped). Glacial gouging also created fjords, such as those of Kenai Fjords National Park in Alaska.

Glaciers bulldozed vast heaps of gravelly rubble ahead of them. This rubble formed ridges, called moraines, at the point where the ice stopped advancing. New York's Long Island, marking the extent of the last glaciation in that area, is formed of glacial moraine.

Many other traces of the Pleistocene glaciers can be seen in North America's landscape. Water melting off glaciers deposited loads of rubble that became hills. Here and there, chunks of ice fragmented from the glaciers and were covered by sand and gravel. These ice chunks were left behind when the glacier melted and the ice front retreated. Later, the chunks melted and the rubble that covered them fell in, forming circular basins called kettles. These are now ponds, common in the north-eastern United States, south-eastern Canada and on the western prairies, where they are called

BARRIER ISLANDS

Assateague Island, off Maryland and Virginia, is the site of a National Seashore.

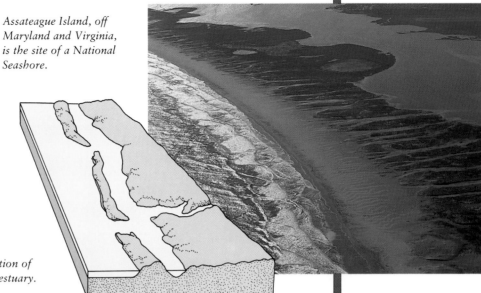

BARRIER islands are of tremendous ecological importance. They protect the coast and the aquatic ecosystems behind them from the ravages of wind, waves, tide and storms. Estuaries at river mouths, with extensive salt marshes, often lie behind barriers. The bulwark the barriers present against the ocean encourages the stable environment in which estuarine life thrives. Many barrier islands have been environmentally damaged by development, such as construction of seaside resorts.

The diagram to the right shows a cross section of typical barrier islands backed by bays and estuary.

axis of the Rockies, the divide lies very near the Pacific Ocean in Canada and Alaska, but runs further inland south of Canada.

Plateaux

Although rugged plateaux may have the physical aspects of mountains, they were formed not by folding but by erosion. In North America they include the Allegheny Plateau, just west of the Appalachians in Pennsylvania, West Virginia and Ohio; the Ozark Plateau of Missouri, Arkansas and Oklahoma; and the Colorado Plateau west of the Rockies in Colorado, Utah and Arizona.

The flat topography of these highlands was cut by rivers into hills, ravines and canyons. The Colorado Plateau, site of the Grand Canyon, has the most tortuous landscape on the continent.

The Canadian Shield

Another great but rolling plateau is the Laurentian of Canada. It stretches from the Northwest Territories and south around Hudson Bay, through Ontario and Quebec to Labrador. Much of this region coincides with the Canadian Shield, an area where some of the most ancient rock of the continent is exposed. (Most ancient rock lies thousands of feet below comparatively young rock.) Here scientists believe erosion by glaciers removed the softer rock that had accumulated over the ancient material. The Canadian Shield extends south of the Laurentian Plateau, to northern New York State, Minnesota and Wisconsin.

Forests

The Canadian Shield is in the heart of the northern coniferous, or boreal, forest, which is one of three major North American forest regions. The other two are the Eastern Mixed Forest, which is dominated by deciduous trees, and the Southeastern Forest, which is typically pine forest but also contains several deciduous species. Between these forests lie transitional areas of woodland, where dominant trees from each type of forest mix.

Grasslands and deserts

Between the Rockies and the Eastern Mixed Forest, south of the boreal forest, lie North America's grasslands, the Great Plains. Once a sea of grasses, the region has now been altered by agriculture and ranching. However, in places grasslands much like the original still remain.

West of the Rockies are North America's great deserts, which along many of their margins graduate into grasslands. The deserts differ in character, due to geography, geology and climate.

LEFT: *Forests of oaks (Quercus) and hickories (Carya) cover the rugged landscape of the Ozark Mountains, in Missouri, Arkansas and Oklahoma; these mountains are, in fact, the remains of an ancient eroded plateau.*

ENVIRONMENTS

Brant, or brent geese (Branta bernicla) fly over the marshes of Jamaica Bay Wildlife Refuge in New York City. The twin towers of the World Trade Center stand in the background. Even huge metropolises contain a wide variety of wildlife. The fact that brant nest as far north as northern Baffin Island in the Arctic links the wilderness and the city.

North America has a tremendous variety of environments. Conditions range from those of the barren Arctic Ocean ice pack to those in the lush woodlands and wetlands that verge on the tropical, and to real tropical in southern Florida.

The continent has a dazzling spectrum of animal life. In the far north of Canada and Alaska live shaggy musk oxen (*Ovibos moschatus*), large horned creatures that have changed little since the ice ages, when they roamed south of the advancing glaciers. Along the Mexican border, in the lower Rio Grande Valley and south-eastern Arizona, the green kingfisher (*Chloroceryle americana*) may occasionally be seen – a bird of the tropics.

Human activity has vastly altered North Ameri-

can wildlife habitats. Most of the former areas of true wilderness no longer exist, although in places such as the interior of Alaska and northern Canada, wild areas remain that are as primeval as any on earth. Proving nature's resilience, however, wildlife exists even in major urban areas. The park of a large city may harbor as many different species of birds as the surrounding countryside.

The shaping of the fauna

Fossils show that the fauna of North America once shared similarities with fauna in other parts of the world. During the Mesozoic era, from 220 million to 65 million years ago, North America was populated by dinosaurs and other great reptiles. Large numbers of their fossils have been found in Dinosaur National Monument, on the border of

Colorado and Utah. Here, in the Morrison beds, huge, plant eating dinosaurs such as *Diplodocus* and *Brachiosaurus* roamed. They were stalked by monstrous predators such as *Allosaurus*. Able to move quickly on long hind legs, *Allosaurus* had a massive head, long jaws and immense teeth. Fossilized dinosaur tracks abound in other areas, including the Connecticut River Valley in Connecticut and Massachusets.

After the Mesozoic, during the Cenozoic era (the Age of Mammals), prehistoric mammals left their fossils. Mammals' fossils can be seen in the Badlands of the Dakotas (*see Grasslands*). The fauna began to take its present shape in the Pleistocene. During the last ice age, the Wisconsin, the retreating sea exposed a great land bridge between Alaska and Siberia. Animal traffic passed over it in both directions, and humans are believed to have crossed from Asia through Siberia to colonize North America. True horses (*Equus*) traveled over the bridge from North America and repopulated Europe and Asia. Subsequently horses died out in North America. Camels, too, which originated in North America, spread to South America and Asia, then vanished from the land of their origins.

Meanwhile, many of the ancestors of modern North American ungulates arrived on the continent. They included the ancestors of the elk, or

FOSSILS

MANY areas of North America contain rich beds of fossils from the distant past. Those pictured here are of trilobites, from the Burgess Fossil Beds of Yoho National Park in British Columbia. Trilobites were sea creatures, distantly related to crustaceans.

Trilobites, most a few inches long, were once common but died out at the end of the Permean era, 280 million years ago.

wapiti (*Cervus elaphus*), the moose (*Alces alces*), the American bison (*Bison bison*) and the bighorn sheep (*Ovis canadensis*).

The pronghorn antelope (*Antilocapra americana*) of the western grasslands is an animal that is unique to North America. The species stems from an ancient North American family of ungulates called Antilocapridae, which was once composed of many more related species. The fossils of Antilocapridae have never been found in any other part of the world.

THE UNIQUE PRONGHORN

THE 'antelope' of the western plains is not a true antelope at all but the pronghorn antelope (*Antilocapra americana*), a species unique to North America. Pronghorn antelopes are the only living animals with branched horns and which shed sheaths over the horns annually. They can run at speeds of up to 40 miles an hour.

The pronghorn was greatly reduced in numbers by the beginning of this century. However, efficient wildlife management, including habitat preservation, has enabled the species to recover, so in many areas hunting is now permitted.

PRONGHORN
DISTRIBUTION MAP

NATIONAL PARKS

Some of the finest areas for wildlife and natural beauty in North America are within the national parks and preserves of Canada and the United States. Canada has 34 national parks, and many more provincial parks. The United States has 49 national parks, more than 100 national monuments, preserves and similar areas, plus 156 national forests and 300 national wildlife refuges. In addition, federal governments of both countries own many other tracts of land.

The oldest national park in the United States – and in the world – is Yellowstone, established in 1872. Canada's first national park was Banff, created in 1887. Additionally, conservation organizations such as the National Audubon Society, the Nature Conservancy and Ducks Unlimited have made it possible for critical wildlife areas to be protected for future generations.

The Angel Glacier on Mount Edith Cavell in Canada's Jasper National Park typifies the natural grandeur of national parks in Canada and the United States. The roots of the national park systems in both countries date back to the 19th century.

NATIONAL PARKS (CANADA): Purple

WESTERN REGION
British Columbia
1 South Moresby (R)
2 Pacific Rim (R)
3 Mount Revelstoke
4 Glacier
5 Yoho
6 Kootenay

Alberta
7 Jasper
8 Banff
9 Waterton Lakes
10 Elk Island

PRAIRIE AND NORTHERN REGION
North-west Territories
11 Wood Buffalo (NWT + Alta.)
12 Nahanni (R)
13 Auyuittuq (R)
14 Ellesmere Island

Yukon Territory
15 Northern Yukon
16 Kluane (R)

Saskatchewan
17 Grasslands
18 Prince Albert

Manitoba
19 Riding Mountain

ONTARIO REGION
20 Pukaskwa
21 Georgian Bay Islands
22 Bruce Peninsula
23 Point Pelee
24 St. Lawrence Islands

QUEBEC REGION
25 La Mauricie
26 Forillon
27 Mingan Archipelago (R)

ATLANTIC REGION
New Brunswick
28 Kouchibouguac
29 Fundy

Prince Edward Island
30 Prince Edward Island

Nova Scotia
31 Kejimkujik
32 Cape Breton Highlands

Newfoundland
33 Gros Morne
34 Terra Nova

(R) National Park Reserve

NATIONAL PARKS (USA): Green

The Pacific North-west
1 North Cascades
2 Olympic
3 Mount Rainier
4 Crater Lake

Rocky Mountain Region
5 Glacier
6 Theodore Roosevelt (North Unit)
7 Theodore Roosevelt (South Unit)
8 Yellowstone
9 Grand Teton
10 Wind Cave
11 Badlands
12 Rocky Mountain
13 Arches
14 Canyonlands
15 Capitol Reef
16 Bryce Canyon
17 Zion
18 Mesa Verde

The West
19 Redwood
20 Lassen Volcanic
21 Great Basin
22 Yosemite
23 Kings Canyon
24 Sequoia
25 Grand Canyon
26 Channel Islands
27 Petrified Forest

The South-west
28 Hot Springs
29 Carlsbad Caverns
30 Guadalupe Mountains
31 Big Bend

The Mid-west
32 Voyageurs
33 Isle Royale

The South-east
34 Mammoth Cave
35 Stones River
36 Great Smoky Mountains
37 Biscayne
38 Everglades

North Atlantic Region
39 Acadia

Mid-Atlantic Region
40 Prince William Forest Park
41 Shenandoah

Alaska
42 Gates of Arctic NP and Preserve
43 Kobuk Valley
44 Denali NP and Preserve
45 Wrangell St. Elias NP and Preserve
46 Lake Clark NP and Preserve
47 Kenai Fjords
48 Katmai NP and Preserve
49 Glacier Bay NP and Preserve

NATIONAL MONUMENTS (USA): Red

The Pacific North-west
1 John Day Fossil Beds
2 Oregon Caves
3 Craters of the Moon
4 Hagerman Fossil Beds

Rocky Mountain Region
5 Custer Battlefield
6 Devils Tower
7 Jewel Cave
8 Fossil Butte
9 Timpanogos Cave
10 Dinosaur
11 Colorado
12 Florrisant Fossil Beds
13 Black Canyon of the Gunnison
14 Great Sand Dunes
15 Yucca House
16 Hovenweep
17 Natural Bridges

NATIONAL PARKS, MONUMENTS AND PRESERVES

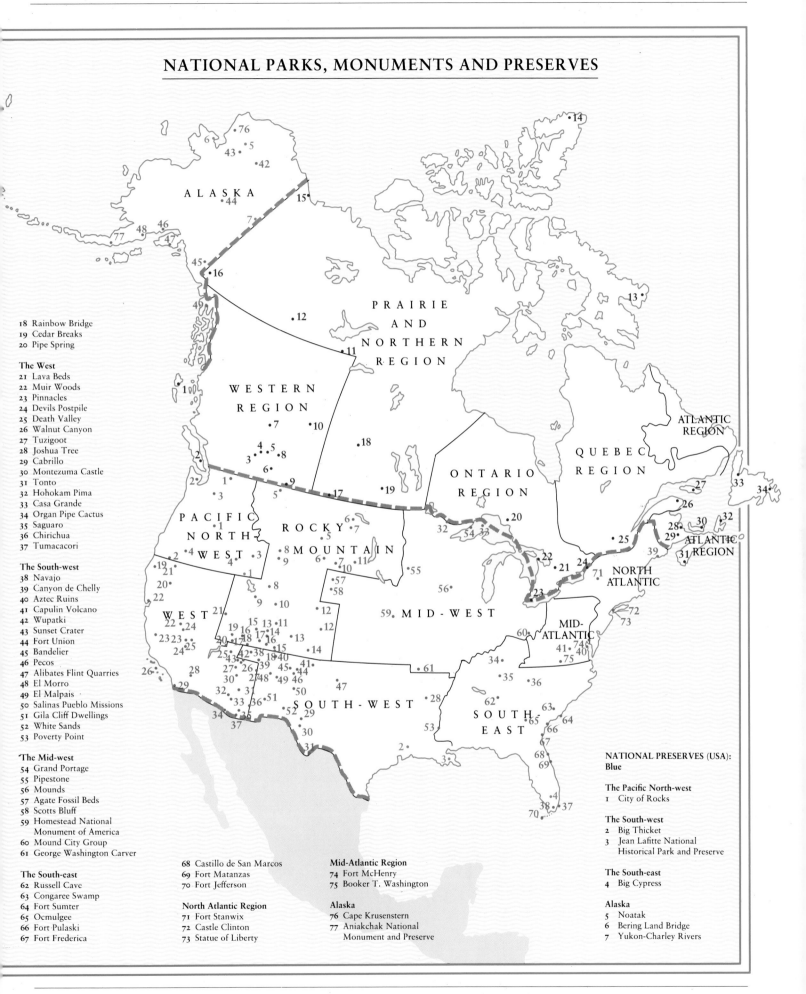

18 Rainbow Bridge
19 Cedar Breaks
20 Pipe Spring

The West
21 Lava Beds
22 Muir Woods
23 Pinnacles
24 Devils Postpile
25 Death Valley
26 Walnut Canyon
27 Tuzigoot
28 Joshua Tree
29 Cabrillo
30 Montezuma Castle
31 Tonto
32 Hohokam Pima
33 Casa Grande
34 Organ Pipe Cactus
35 Saguaro
36 Chirichua
37 Tumacacori

The South-west
38 Navajo
39 Canyon de Chelly
40 Aztec Ruins
41 Capulin Volcano
42 Wupatki
43 Sunset Crater
44 Fort Union
45 Bandelier
46 Pecos
47 Alibates Flint Quarries
48 El Morro
49 El Malpais
50 Salinas Pueblo Missions
51 Gila Cliff Dwellings
52 White Sands
53 Poverty Point

The Mid-west
54 Grand Portage
55 Pipestone
56 Mounds
57 Agate Fossil Beds
58 Scotts Bluff
59 Homestead National
   Monument of America
60 Mound City Group
61 George Washington Carver

The South-east
62 Russell Cave
63 Congaree Swamp
64 Fort Sumter
65 Ocmulgee
66 Fort Pulaski
67 Fort Frederica

68 Castillo de San Marcos
69 Fort Matanzas
70 Fort Jefferson

North Atlantic Region
71 Fort Stanwix
72 Castle Clinton
73 Statue of Liberty

Mid-Atlantic Region
74 Fort McHenry
75 Booker T. Washington

Alaska
76 Cape Krusenstern
77 Aniakchak National
   Monument and Preserve

NATIONAL PRESERVES (USA):
Blue

The Pacific North-west
1 City of Rocks

The South-west
2 Big Thicket
3 Jean Lafitte National
   Historical Park and Preserve

The South-east
4 Big Cypress

Alaska
5 Noatak
6 Bering Land Bridge
7 Yukon-Charley Rivers

The
HIGH ARCTIC
and
TUNDRA

The Arctic is a land of immense vistas, with towering mountain ranges and vast flatlands stretching as far as the eye can see. It is also a place of prodigious contrasts and paradoxes. Considered part of the continent, much of the Arctic is a frozen sea, surrounded on three sides by land. Some Arctic landscapes that are cloaked in ice and snow receive no more annual rain than North American deserts, yet can be as soggy as a swamp. This is because water is unable to drain through the permanently frozen soil of the Arctic when ice thaws in spring.

Arctic animals include some of the biggest land mammals on earth. Some of these are among the largest assemblages of mammalian life anywhere. Compared to the number of wildlife species in temperate and tropical regions, however, Arctic species are few, and, despite the immense concentrations of some, they are generally thinly dispersed.

A brown bear (Ursus arctos) *sits in the summer tundra of the Alaskan Peninsula. Brown bears inhabit coastal regions and nearby islands of south-western Alaska. The Arctic is home to many large mammals, some of which, like the caribou* (Rangifer tarandus), *live in herds.*

THE southern boundaries of the Arctic are difficult to delineate. The Arctic Circle, which is a creation of geographers, bounds a region north of which, during the course of a year, the sun does not rise for at least one day and set for another. Perhaps a better boundary marker is a line north of which the surface air temperature in the warmest month, July, does not exceed 50°F. Almost coincidental with this line, or isotherm, is the northern tree limit, which extends below the Arctic Circle, in what is usually called the Subarctic. The northernmost Arctic, stretching into islands beyond the continental mainland, is known as the High Arctic (*see* the map on page 93).

The Arctic region contains the greatest remaining wildernesses and wildlife concentrations on the continent. There are no game reserves in the Arctic, which continues to be a refreshingly hostile, often dangerous, wildlife domain.

Cold is the overriding fact of Arctic life. Winter rules the region. The sea ice of the Arctic Ocean is 5,105,700 square miles in area and can be thousands of feet deep. Here winter temperatures can plummet to more than 58°F below zero. Such temperatures are due partly to low sun elevation, which, coupled with long periods of darkness and daylight, gives the Arctic a net heat loss. In addition, snow and ice, which can cover the landscape for up to 10 months a year, reflect solar radiation back into space.

Surprisingly, the snow and ice cover of the high Arctic is not particularly deep – in many places it is only a few inches in depth. Some parts of the Arctic receive less than 5 inches of precipitation annually, and, given enough heat to evaporate the moisture, many such areas would easily qualify as desert. Because air temperatures are not consistently high, however, evaporation is drastically limited, which partly accounts for the persistence of snow cover. More importantly, permafrost prevents meltwater from percolating into the soil.

The frozen ocean

Gripped by bone-chilling cold throughout most of the year and characterized by months of either daylight or darkness, the heart of the Arctic is an expanse of sea ice, with open water exposed here and there. The region is barren of soil and plants, but, even in the ice pack, animals tied to the marine environment survive. Dependence upon the sea has not restricted animals thought of as truly marine, such as seals and polar bears. The polar bear (*Ursus maritimus*) is more at home in the water than most other four-footed mammals, and can swim for a distance of 50 or more miles without stopping. Most of the year it feeds on seals. The tapered head and body of this sea bear enable it to swim through water rather like a seal.

During the winter, sea ice expands to cap more than 5,000,000 square miles, melting to about half that in the summer. Some years, the winter ice extends as far as the southern shores of Hudson

AURORA BOREALIS, OR NORTHERN LIGHTS

THE aurora borealis, the great nocturnal light show which is a feature of the northern skies, is produced when charged solar particles cause an electrical discharge among rarified gasses high in the atmosphere. The aurora is linked to the earth's magnetism and is most pronounced over the magnetic poles. This spectacular electrical phenomenon has been compared to the production of light through the rarified gas in a neon tube. Most pronounced during periods when there is high sunspot activity, auroras can sometimes be seen as far south as the southernmost regions of the United States.

The aurora borealis was seen over Wisconsin in September and October 1989. No sound accompanies the aurora, making it even more eerie.

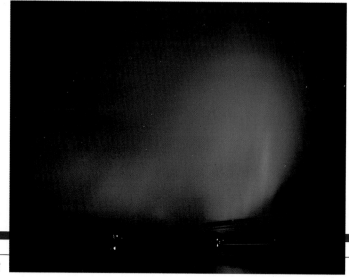

Bay and the northern coast of Newfoundland. The ice varies between a few feet and more than 100 feet in thickness, and, as on land, animals and people roam this white world.

The peripheral land

Arctic landforms cover an area from the towering folded mountain ranges which characterize north-western Canada and most of Alaska, to the great Laurentian Plateau, which covers most of Arctic and Subarctic Canada. Here the primal (original) underlying rock of the Canadian Shield is prominently revealed.

Fringing the Arctic Ocean, on the northern rim of the continent, an area of tundra stretches as far as the coniferous boreal forest to the south. Scientists have distinguished different varieties of tundra, including moist and dry, which vary according to soil drainage and not surface moisture. Alpine tundra exists at higher elevations – not just in the Arctic but on many mountain peaks farther south.

Like alpine tundra, tundra is dominated by cold, but temperatures can easily reach 70°F during the brief summer. More than 600 species of flowering plants, and myriad other plants, grow during the two or three months of warmth when ice and snow vanish from the tundra's face. Then tundra vegetation spreads a patchwork of color over land that was under a white blanket only a few weeks before,

*The antler of a caribou (*Rangifer tarandus), *shed on the tundra of Alaska's Denali National Park in early autumn. Although, like other deer, caribou shed their antlers, they are not typical in that antlers grow on both sexes.*

Cottongrass (Eriophorum vaginatum) flowers across tundra below Mount McKinley in Denali National Park. During the brief spring and summer, the tundra blossoms with a gorgeous array of vegetation.

and herbivorous animals such as caribou (*Rangifer tarandus*) gorge on the growing vegetation. In turn, carnivores, such as wolves (*Canis lupus*), feed on the caribou.

Climate and soil

The long and extreme Arctic winter creates permafrost – permanently frozen soil. It often lies just a foot or so below the surface, and can be 2,000 feet thick. The impermeability of rock-hard permafrost means that, even in arid regions, the surface of the tundra resembles a water-filled sponge during the spring thaw.

Plants which have adapted to the tundra root in the thin sheet of soil lying over the permafrost. This soil, however, wants for nutrients that promote plant growth, because low temperatures inhibit organic decomposition.

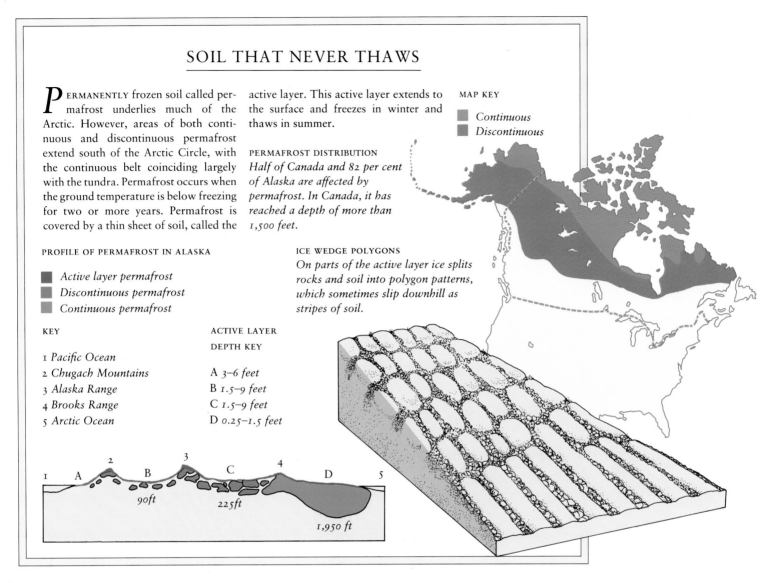

SOIL THAT NEVER THAWS

PERMANENTLY frozen soil called permafrost underlies much of the Arctic. However, areas of both continuous and discontinuous permafrost extend south of the Arctic Circle, with the continuous belt coinciding largely with the tundra. Permafrost occurs when the ground temperature is below freezing for two or more years. Permafrost is covered by a thin sheet of soil, called the active layer. This active layer extends to the surface and freezes in winter and thaws in summer.

PERMAFROST DISTRIBUTION
Half of Canada and 82 per cent of Alaska are affected by permafrost. In Canada, it has reached a depth of more than 1,500 feet.

MAP KEY

■ *Continuous*
■ *Discontinuous*

PROFILE OF PERMAFROST IN ALASKA

■ *Active layer permafrost*
■ *Discontinuous permafrost*
■ *Continuous permafrost*

ICE WEDGE POLYGONS
On parts of the active layer ice splits rocks and soil into polygon patterns, which sometimes slip downhill as stripes of soil.

KEY

1 *Pacific Ocean*
2 *Chugach Mountains*
3 *Alaska Range*
4 *Brooks Range*
5 *Arctic Ocean*

ACTIVE LAYER
DEPTH KEY

A *3–6 feet*
B *1.5–9 feet*
C *1.5–9 feet*
D *0.25–1.5 feet*

90ft   225ft   1,950 ft

Plant growth

Plant growth in the Arctic is restricted by unfavorable conditions. For much of the year the region is in darkness, and there are long periods of cold temperatures. With some exceptions, precipitation is scant. Soils are thin and poor.

These conditions make the tundra treeless. The plants that do grow there are low, some forming hardly more than a skin over soil or rock. Among them are lichens, pioneering plants that are composed of a fungus and an alga, which are thought to work in a symbiotic relationship (for their mutual benefit): the alga makes carbohydrates which are used by the fungus, and this in turn provides the alga with moisture and minerals.

Lack of moisture is particularly evident in the High Arctic, where gravel soils do not hold water. Here on the dry tundra most plants are lichens and mosses, which grow profusely only where water catches in basins. The short, cool growing season curbs the production of tissues that enable plants to reach any significant height. Were they able to grow taller, fierce winter winds would shear off their new growth and cut them down to size.

However, on the coast of south-western Alaska and the Aleutian Islands, well below the frigid Arctic climate, tundra exists at low altitudes. This wet tundra is not underlain by permafrost, nor, due to maritime influence, is it subject to extreme winter temperatures. However, summer temperatures, moderated by the sea, which remains cold, tend to be uniformly cool. Lack of warm weather, together with low light due to seemingly endless cloud cover, prevents the growth of trees. On higher elevations, which in the Aleutians can reach up to 9,000 feet, the tundra is dry, more like that to the north.

ADAPTATIONS

Apart from Antarctica, no environment on earth is as difficult for life as the Arctic. However, Antarctica has virtually no terrestrial organisms, except for along its extreme edge, while the Arctic has a full complement of terrestrial life forms. Their survival in this region is a testimony to the tenacity of living things.

Plant adaptations

Unusual, but logical, plant adaptations enable plants to survive the harsh tundra conditions of the Arctic. Arctic plants must be able to withstand prolonged low temperatures and flourish and reproduce during the brief, bright summer. In the winter, they are dormant, conserving energy needed for explosive growth in the flush of summer. Low growing, they are shielded from wind and bitter cold by the insulating blanket of snow. They are also frost hardy, functioning even when the temperature is below freezing; some are coated with hair, which serves as insulation.

Tundra vegetation, such as the alpine bearberry (*Arctostaphylos alpina*), often grows in low mats, or is globe-shaped, like the moss campion (*Silene acaulis*). These conformations expose more surface area to sunlight. Light absorption is also enhanced by broad leaves, such as those of the herb-like willow (*Salix herbacea*).

Evergreen leaves are ready to begin photosynthesizing as soon as winter ends, which gives them an advantage. Labrador tea (*Ledum groenlandicum*) and goldthread (*Coptis groenlandica*) are among the many evergreen Arctic plants, the former existing at the interface between tundra and boreal forest. Alpine bistort (*Polygonum viviparum*) has adapted very differently. It reproduces small bulbs that sprout leaves before leaving the mother plant. When they detach from the stem and take root, they are already photosynthesizing. Other Arctic plants have sprawling root systems to enable them to gather moisture and nutrients from as wide an area as possible.

By growing in low mats, tundra plants not only avoid wind damage. The air temperature is warmest at ground level, and the margins of a matted plant protect the interior and retain warmth from the ground surface. Such mats of plants create mini-environments (microhabitats).

A close-up look at the tundra in bloom within Denali National Park shows how lush the vegetation in this area can be in summer. Although precipitation on the tundra is not heavy and moisture is locked up as ice during the winter, the melt that occurs in spring creates very moist conditions, in which the tundra plants thrive. The animals that feed upon tundra plants range from polar bears (Ursus maritimus) to arctic ground squirrels (Spermophilus undulatus).

LOUSEWORT

*L*OUSEWORTS (*Pedicularis*) are among the plants that have adapted to the cold conditions of the tundra. The stems are covered with fine hairs that provide added protection for the plant by holding in warm air as insulation against cold. Some animals eat louseworts.

The buds of tundra louseworts are also covered with fine hairs to shield them against frost during the period in which they are growing and tender. Like many other tundra plants, louseworts are low growing.

Animal adaptations

The number of animal species inhabiting the Arctic is largely restricted by low temperature. Ectothermic reptiles and amphibians are absent, except for the wood frog (*Rana sylvatica*), whose range extends from the temperate forests to the tundra of northern Alaska. However, other amphibians occur very close to this region. They are the boreal toad (*Bufo boreas boreas*), boreal chorus frog (*Pseudacris triseriata maculata*), roughskin newt (*Taricha granulosa*) and northern leopard frog (*Rana pipiens*). Mammals and birds are better able to live in the Arctic, as metabolic processes in mammals and birds generate heat. Even so, only about two dozen species of mammals and half a dozen birds can survive the winter in true High Arctic. To survive, creatures that overwinter must be efficient at conserving energy.

Size contributes to energy conservation. In relation to their volume, large animals have proportionately less surface available for radiating heat than small ones. Many Arctic mammals, such as the moose (*Alces alces*), the Alaskan brown bear (*Ursus arctos*) and polar bear (*U. maritimus*) are the biggest members of their families.

Cold-weather animals generally have shorter extremities than their warm-weather counterparts, reducing body surface: the arctic fox (*Alopex lagopus*) has tiny ears, barely visible above the fur. Conversely the kit fox (*Vulpes macrotis*) of the hot south-western deserts has ears that look far too large for its head. The muzzle and legs are noticeably shorter in the Arctic animal than in the fox of the desert.

Insulation wards off cold. Arctic birds and mammals tend to have thick layers of fat below the skin and heavy coats, especially on parts of the body that are usually bare on non-Arctic creatures. The polar bear, like the seal, has a layer of insulating blubber beneath the skin for protection against cold water. Hair grows thickly on the muzzle of the caribou (*Rangifer tarandus*). The beak and feet of the snowy owl (*Nyctea scandiaca*), one of the few birds wintering on the tundra, are fringed with feathers, and the undersides of the feet of the polar bear, arctic fox and arctic hare (*Lepus timidus*) are hair covered. Caribou hairs thicken at the tips and so overlap to form a cold- and water-resistant outer coat, and for added insulation.

The caribou has a heat-exchange system in its

Shown here in winter, the white coat of the arctic fox (Alopex lagopus) turns dull brown or yellowish in the summer. Weighing up to 15 pounds, the arctic fox follows polar bears as they hunt seals on the ice pack during the winter. The foxes scavenge the remains of the great white bear's prey.

legs typical of many mammals of the Arctic. Arteries carrying warm blood from the heart to the feet lie close to veins returning cool blood to the heart. The venous blood picks up some of the heat from the nearby arteries, and thus carries warmth back to the body which would otherwise be lost in the legs. The legs and feet remain colder than the body, but still warm enough not to freeze – and due to the return of warm venous blood, the body as a whole does not lose much heat through the limbs.

As it does for plants, snow provides an insulating cover for some small mammals, such as the brown, or Norway, lemming (*Lemmus trimucronatus*) and arctic shrew (*Sorex arcticus*). They spend much of the winter in snow tunnels. The arctic ground squirrel (*Spermophilus undulatus*) and hoary marmot (*Marmota caligata*) avoid the worst of the cold by hibernating in burrows.

Locomotion in snow presents another challenge for animals. Hair or feathers on the bottom of the feet give traction on slippery surfaces. The willow ptarmigan, or willow grouse (*Lagopus lagopus*), grows winter feathers on its toes which act like snowshoes. The large, flat feet of the arctic hare and the wide, spreading hooves of the caribou serve a similar purpose.

GEOGRAPHY

The Arctic region ends beyond the tundra of the Labrador Peninsula and Quebec's Ungava Peninsula in the east, and the north-western coast of Alaska in the west. North and west of Ungava, in the Arctic Ocean, stretches the Arctic Archipelago.

This vast island group extends 1,400 miles from the southern end of Baffin Island, northwards to the tip of Ellesmere Island. Tundra covers this island kingdom, with mosses and lichens predominating. On Ellesmere Island, at higher elevations (up to about 9,000 feet), glaciers cover the rock.

Mainland tundra on the Ungava and Labrador peninsulas continues on the western side of Hudson Bay. There, the northern limit of the coniferous forest and southern boundary of the tundra converge at the Churchill River.

The tundra-forest interface
Forest and tundra gradually blend in the Manitoba community of Churchill. The unbroken cover of trees thins until the trees become just dots on the landscape. Tundra ponds appear with increasing

LEFT: *This male willow ptarmigan, or willow grouse (*Lagopus lagopus*), is changing from its brownish summer plumage to white winter coloring.*

TOP LEFT: *During the summer, the arctic ground squirrel (*Spermophilus undulatus*) gorges itself on vegetable matter and, if it can, meat.*

frequency as the tree height diminishes; the trees are finally replaced by small shrubs. At this point the land is virtually treeless, except where conifers hug certain river courses that flow northward into the bay.

The tree line arcs north-west from Hudson Bay across the heart of northern Canada – an area known as the Barren Ground. The tundra belt narrows until it is less than 100 miles wide north of the Brooks mountain range (on the northern slope of Alaska, bordering the Arctic Ocean). As previously described, expanses of interior Alaska and a sweep of the coast north of the Aleutians are also considered tundra. Here, tundra and great, rugged mountain ranges intermix in wilderness areas almost second to none.

Parks, preserves and refuges
In an area from the north-western coast of Alaska to Baffin Island, the Canadian and United States governments have established national parks and other protected regions in the Arctic wilderness. Areas of wilderness are increasingly threatened by society's need for resources such as oil.

One of Canada's newest parks, Auyuittuq National Park on Baffin Island, encompasses craggy stone peaks and rock-strewn tundra, traversed by icy streams. At the other end of Canada, on Alaska's north-eastern border, is Northern Yukon National Park, which is almost 2,432,000 acres in size. On the other side of the border, between the northern slope of the Brooks mountain range and the sea, lies the 19,000,000-acre Arctic National Wildlife Refuge. These two areas are vital to the existence of 180,000 caribou (*Rangifer tarandus*), known as the Porcupine herd.

The herd winters in the coniferous forest along the Porcupine River, south-west of the Brooks mountain range in the Yukon Territory. In early spring they head north, through Northern Yukon National Park and around the eastern flank of the Brooks mountain range, to the calving grounds in the Arctic National Wildlife Refuge. Females and young of the previous year arrive first, then the males. In less than a month, by early June, the calves are born.

The herd has for millennia provided food for native peoples and wild predators such as wolves. The modern world, however, has encroached on the herd. Conservationists wage an unceasing

A storm clears over the mountains of Denali National Park near a braided river. The term braided refers to the way in which the river is composed of many small interweaving channels. Rivers in the Arctic and Subarctic flow north to the Arctic Ocean.

battle to keep both oil and gas development from disrupting the natural environment on which the caribou depend.

On the north-western coast of Alaska, beside the Chukchi Sea, Cape Krusenstern National Monument protects 4,000-year-old Eskimo archaeological sites. The monument is also the seacoast habitat for many marine mammals, and the inland hills are inhabited by birds and mammals of both forest and tundra.

Between Cape Krusenstern and the Arctic National Wildlife Refuge, a great complex of parks, refuges and preserves protects wildernesses north of the Arctic Circle. The complex is almost unmatched in size by any other in the world. Within its bounds the boreal forest changes to Arctic tundra.

There are three major protected areas: Gates of the Arctic National Park and Preserve is one of the most remote wildernesses on the continent. It consists of nearly 8,000,000 acres, and straddles the central Brooks mountain range. These granite and limestone mountains rise to more than 7,000 feet; their north slope is covered by tundra that sweeps towards the ocean and the High Arctic. Abutting Gates of the Arctic on the west are the 6,574,481-acre Noatak National Preserve and the 1,750,421-acre Kobuk Valley National Park.

The arctic dunes of Kobuk

The Kobuk Valley begins about 100 miles from the point where its river enters Kotzebue Sound in the Chukchi Sea. About 25 miles wide, the sound is framed on the north side by the Baird Mountains, and on the south side by the lower Waring Mountains. In the valley, forest and tundra meet dramatically; Kobuk Valley marks the northernmost extension of the boreal forest.

During the last glaciation, the Wisconsin (or Würm), which ended about 11,000 years ago, the valley was part of an ice-free corridor which stretched from Siberia across the Bering Land Bridge through Alaska. Pleistocene game animals migrated through this corridor, followed by hunters. The land over which they traveled was semi-arid plain, known as arctic steppe.

Environmental traces of this steppe can be found only in a few places. Remains in the Kobuk Valley are most evident in an area of windswept sand, the Great Kobuk Sand Dunes. Up to 100 feet high, the dunes evoke the Sahara Desert and, under the 24-hour summer sun, can be extremely hot, even though the winter temperature often drops to 40°F below zero.

Although by no means a replica of the steppe that once supported ice age herds, the Kobuk dunes contain plants that probably grew on those ancient plains. These include the northern wormwood (*Artemisia borealis*) and a tough grass, *Bromus pumpellianus*.

Sand on the rim of the dunes has been colonized by several types of plants. The pioneer plants are grasses, such as red fescue (*Festuca rubra*). They stabilize the sand and, as they die and decay, enrich it, enabling trees to grow. Tundra plants, such as mountain avens (*Dryas integrifolia*) and various lichens, move in. The plants cover the sand in an endless battle between tundra and forest. As more and more of these plants cover the sand, small white spruces (*Picea glauca*) appear. Little by little, fingers of forest reach into the tundra.

The Kobuk Valley is a living laboratory for scientists studying the vegetation zones of the north. The tree line in Kobuk Valley is at 1,000 feet above sea level. Immediate conditions, such as local changes in climate, influence the boundary between tundra and trees. Over the centuries, depending on environmental changes, tundra and trees play an almost imperceptible game of give and take, which is measured in inches.

ARCTIC WILDLIFE

The wildlife that has adapted to the fierce Arctic cold is a select group. Most overwintering species are mammals. Over the entire year, however, the birds that can be found in the Arctic far outnumber mammals, in total as well as in number of species. During the warm months, the tundra and coastlines of the Arctic become a vast mating ground and nursery for millions upon millions of birds, some of which literally travel from the opposite ends of the earth to get there. As winter nears, the migrants depart, leaving the tundra to a few hardy avian species and the resident mammals.

MAMMALS The Arctic is the home of a number of large and impressive species of mammals which have adapted to the cold conditions. Even some of the mammals, however, such as the caribou, edge south of the tundra during the worst of the winter.

Hoofed mammals

The caribou (*Rangifer tarandus*), the same species as the Eurasian reindeer, roves the north from coast to coast and into the islands of the Arctic Archipelago. Scientists recognize several different subspecies, or races, of caribou, distinguished mainly by size and color, as well as by geography and habitat. For most purposes, however, these can be placed in three groups, the Barren Ground caribou, mountain caribou and woodland caribou. The form that ranges into the true Arctic is the Barren Ground caribou, with larger antlers and a less robust body than the southern, or woodland, type. Barren Ground bulls reach a maximum weight of about 400 pounds, which is a few hundred pounds less than the maximum weight of woodland caribou.

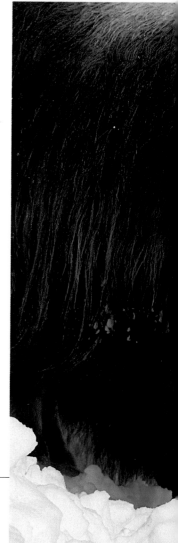

The only North American deer in which both sexes grow antlers, caribou subsist on tough northern vegetation, such as sedges and reindeer moss (*Cladonia rangiferina*) – the latter is actually a lichen. In the north, caribou live in herds that range in number from a few thousand to more than a hundred thousand animals. They frequent specific geographic regions and each herd has its own calving ground, not used by any other.

Powerful swimmers and excellent climbers, caribou cross rivers and mountains in migrations to and from the calving grounds. Their cross-country treks are not unlike those undertaken by the wildebeest of Africa's Serengeti Plain.

Caribou need extensive areas of wilderness and, especially, calving grounds where they will not be disturbed. Calving grounds are the center of a herd's life cycle and disruption of these areas threatens the herd's existence.

The other deer of the Arctic region is the moose (*Alces alces*). It is the largest member of the deer family, reaching up to 1,800 pounds in weight in Alaska, and is primarily a forest animal that, whenever possible, feeds heavily on aquatic vegetation (*see Coniferous Forests*). Summer brings the moose into wet tundra, especially along watercourses.

Musk oxen (*Ovibos moschatus*) could be termed the bison of the tundra, although they have never approached the numbers of bison on the North

Barren Ground caribou (Rangifer tarandus) winter in the northern coniferous forest. In the spring they migrate, sometimes in immense herds, back to the tundra, where the young, conceived during fall mating, are born. Wolves (Canis lupus) follow the caribou herds, killing the weak and aged. Caribou still provide an important source of protein for some native peoples.

A musk ox (Ovibos moschatus) is pictured near the edge of the Arctic ice pack. Musk oxen usually live in small herds and are true High Arctic animals, never coming south of the far northern tundra. The horns of the musk ox – which are found in both sexes – are 24–28 inches long, with a flat base covering the forehead and running down the sides of the head. These give them an effective defense against wolves and other predatory animals.

OPPOSITE: *Like the bighorn sheep (Ovis canadensis) to the south, Dall's sheep (O. dalli) of north-western Canada and Alaska is a mountain creature. The rams – one is pictured here – engage in head-butting for rights to the ewes. During the winter, the sheep descend from the heights to the shelter of lower slopes.*

American grasslands. Herds of musk oxen forage on the tundra for plants, which include willows, sedges and grasses, as well as non-flowering types such as lichens. During the winter, they use their massive horns and large front hooves to scrape away ice and snow and expose the low vegetation. Ironically, although the most northerly of all large herbivores, musk oxen cannot tolerate deep snow, which prevents them from digging out food plants. For this reason, they stick to the northern edge, which is the driest part of the tundra.

Large herds of musk oxen used to range across the entire tundra-clad lip of the Arctic Slope, to the northernmost points in the Arctic Archipelago. At the beginning of the last century, however, the number of musk oxen rapidly declined, largely due to the introduction of firearms among native hunting peoples. Since they form a circle around their young when threatened, horned heads facing outward, musk oxen are easily picked off by a firearm. Their defense works well against wolves, but not against modern weapons.

Protected under law, musk oxen recovered in Canada and have been reintroduced in Alaska, where previously the last herd of 13 animals was destroyed in the middle of the 19th century. All told, about 40,000 animals survive and herds are increasing.

Musk oxen are large animals, especially bulls, which weigh up to 900 pounds. Their shaggy coats serve as efficient insulation against the mid-winter Arctic cold. The outercoat is a drapery of long, coarse hair, hanging a yard long from the rump and undersides. Fine hairs, soft as cashmere, comprise the thick undercoat.

Virtually unchanged since the last Pleistocene ice age, the musk ox shares certain characteristics with cattle, goats and antelopes. It is a unique member of the Arctic fauna, and everything about it speaks of the frigid far north.

Hares and lemmings

Another true tundra mammal is the arctic hare (*Lepus timidus*), which on the tundra replaces the similar varying, or snowshoe, hare (*L. americanus*) of the boreal forest. Some scientists recognize two species, *Lepus othus* of Alaska and *L. arcticus* of Canada, but they are so similar in appearance they are often considered the same species. The arctic hare is the tallest on the continent, more than 2 feet long and almost a foot high from the shoulder to the ground. It can weigh up to 12 pounds.

The hare prefers to eat small willows but, like many other arctic creatures, makes the most of what is available, especially in winter. When need be, this usually herbivorous mammal will eat carrion. Long claws on its front feet help the hare dig out provisions from under ice and snow.

The arctic hare skims across the surface of the snow aided by large feet, more than 6 inches long and heavily furred. Sometimes it can leap as far as 10 feet, and can travel at speeds of more than 35 miles per hour. Colored brown in the summer and white in the winter, the hare relies on camouflage as well as speed to escape predators such as wolves (*Canis lupus*).

The little lemmings – brown (*Lemmus lemmus*) and collared (*Dicrostonyx*) – hide under the snow from enemies. Lemmings have 3- or 4-year reproductive cycles, during which their populations increase dramatically from previously small numbers. During population eruptions, occurring in the spring, brown and collared lemmings swarm en masse over the tundra, moving erratically. However, North American lemmings do not carry on the spectacular, direction-oriented mass migrations of their Eurasian counterparts, which often run pell-mell to their death in waterways or the sea.

The fluctuating numbers of lemmings dramatically affect their predators, such as the arctic fox (*Alopex lagopus*) and snowy owl (*Nyctea scandiaca*). When lemmings are plentiful, they promote the survival of young predators. However, large numbers of lemmings will outstrip the available food resources, and their numbers will then decline. As a result, predator numbers drop. Lemming scarcity in the Arctic can prove a boon for birders to the south, because snowy owls often stray as far south as New York city in search of food. Arctic and varying hares also undergo population cycles.

Cats and wild dogs

When varying hares are scarce in the forest, the lynx (*Felis lynx*) extends its hunting grounds from the trees to the tundra. Like its prey, the lynx has broad feet with long hair that act like snow shoes, preventing it from sinking into the snow.

The Arctic is the last major stronghold of the wolf (*Canis lupus*) in North America. This canine

BELOW: *This snowy owl (Nyctea scandiaca), a tundra resident, migrated to the New York city area during a winter when food became scarce in the north. These large white owls of the open tundra nest on the ground, and hunt by day during summer, as well as at night.*

A wolf *(Canis lupus) surveys the tundra. Wolves reach their largest size, more than 150 pounds, in the Arctic. Extremely intelligent, they hunt in packs and most of their large prey, such as caribou, consists of animals that are sick, weak or old. By killing the unfit, wolves help maintain healthy and vigorous populations of the animals on which they prey.*

predator – growing to more than 100 pounds in weight – has highly organized group behavior and is keenly intelligent. It is spread over the continent, through semi-tropical forest and desert to the far reaches of the north. A cooperative hunter of big game, it also feeds on small prey such as mice and birds' eggs.

This gray hunter (many Arctic individuals are white) needs plenty of space, however. The requirement stems not only from the nature of the species but also from misplaced human antipathy towards this largest of the wild dogs. Given some measure of protection, wolves can survive near cities, as they do in parts of Alaska. In such places, the cities are still bordered by vast wilderness into which the wolf packs can disappear.

Although the red fox (*Vulpes vulpes*) can be found on the tundra, the only other truly arctic dog other than the wolf is the arctic fox (*Alopex lagopus*). Indeed, the arctic fox roams far beyond land limits, following polar bears (*Ursus maritimus*) for many miles out onto the ice pack to scavenge their kills.

Bears

The polar bear is one of two Arctic bears which are the largest land-living carnivores on earth. Both bears can tower 2 or 3 feet above a tall man, and top 1,600 pounds in weight in autumn, after accumulating fat for the winter months. The other bear is the brown bear (*Ursus arctos*), which has at times been divided into several species by taxonomists. Scientists today generally agree that the brown bear of North America and Eurasia is a single species, with myriad subspecies. One of these subspecies in North America is the feared grizzly.

A loose distinction is made between brown bears and grizzlies. The largest brown bear is a subspecies found in the Kodiak Island area. Like the Kodiak subspecies, bears considered 'browns' tend to live in coastal areas, particularly in south-western Alaska. Grizzlies belong to the interior, including the open tundra; historically they ranged as far south as the Great Plains and the mountains of Mexico.

Both are omnivorous carnivores and they have largely the same diet, although the grizzly is more likely to stalk and kill large mammals. The Plains grizzly bear hunted bison, which it killed with swats of its enormous paw. Brown bears subsist on salmon when they are available, together with berries, mammals and, if necessary, carrion. Although brown and grizzly bears seldom deliberately stalk humans, these huge, aggressive creatures can be exceedingly dangerous if encountered in the wild.

Not even the grizzly has the predatory instincts of the polar bear, and no other bear is predominantly carnivorous. The great white bear, particularly the male of the species, spends the winter

incessantly roving in search of seals, its main prey. During the course of a year, individual bears have been known to travel many hundreds, even thousands, of miles over the ice. They have also been known to travel from North America to Siberia, over about 65 miles of ice.

Polar bears ambush seals at the seals' breathing holes in the ice, where they also enter and leave the water. When they stalk basking seals, the bears will leap out of the water to tear them from the ice edge. Humans are the only other animals on the ice of the same size and general shape as seals, and this may account for occasional unprovoked attacks on people by the bears.

As summer approaches, polar bears move on to the coastal tundra, sometimes coming more than 100 miles inland. As the tundra burgeons with plant life, the bears feed relentlessly on vegetation, adding birds' eggs and salmon to their diet as well. Summer's end sees the bears returning to the coast. In some places, such as on Cape Churchill, near Churchill, Manitoba, large numbers of bears concentrate near the shore while waiting for the sea ice to freeze.

A two-year-old grizzly bear (Ursus arctos) *stands among tundra flowers. The grizzly belongs to the same species as the brown bear, but is more aggressive. The name grizzly derives from the bear's grizzled (streaked with gray) coat.*

POLAR BEAR BREEDING AND LIFE CYCLE

FEMALE polar bears (*Ursus maritimus*) mate every other year, in April and May, when they are still on the ice pack. After a summer spent gorging herself ashore, the pregnant female digs a den in the snow in early winter, either near the coast or actually on the ice pack. Cubs, usually two, are born in the den during December and January. The heat of the mother's massive body helps keep the den warm, and the cubs seldom touch the snow because they snuggle into the warm fur of their mother. Polar bear milk is especially rich, being 10 per cent butter-fat. The cubs, which are 10 inches long and a pound and a half at birth, grow quickly. By the time they emerge from the den in the spring they already weigh 25 pounds. The cubs follow their mother and slowly learn from her how to hunt, remaining with her until their second spring. After this, she leaves to mate again. The cubs may remain with one another for a short while, but then split up and go their separate ways. Many of them do not manage to make the transition from dependency on their mother to self-sufficiency. A polar bear can, however, live to 30 years. They mature sexually between two and a half and four years. The males, except during the brief mating season, are loners, constantly wandering in search of food. For polar bears, ice, land, and water are all part of the environment that is home.

A female, or sow, bear leads her new cubs over the melting snow and ice. It is the start of their journey toward adulthood.

Seals, sea lions and walruses are known as pinnipeds, meaning fin-footed, in reference to their flippers. Nine species live in Arctic waters, coming ashore on rocky coasts of the mainland and islands to breed. The largest of the species is the walrus (*Odobenus rosmarus*), the bulls of which grow to 12 feet long and weigh almost a ton. The creature uses its long, ivory tusks in social communication, and as defensive weapons: a walrus can kill a polar bear with them.

BIRDS The hardy rock ptarmigan (*Lagopus mutus*), which changes plumage from brown to white when the snow falls, the snowy owl (*Nyctea scandiaca*) and common raven (*Corvus corax*) are birds most likely to be seen on the bleak tundra during the winter. Ptarmigan flocks head for whatever cover they can find in winter, staying out of the wind as much as possible. The adaptable predator and scavenger, the raven, manages to eke out a winter existence even on some of the Arctic islands; carrion furnishes it with much of its food supply.

King of the tundra is the snowy owl, which nests during the spring in a hollow scraped out of a ridge or rise on the tundra. These small elevations and frost heaves are used by the owl as perches, from which it is able to survey the landscape in search of lemmings, hares and other food. When food supply is scarce, especially in winter, this owl relies on finding carrion.

The migrants

Great irony exists in the view of the Arctic as lifeless, an opinion commonly held by those who

PREVIOUS PAGES: *Polar bears (*Ursus maritimus*) gather near Churchill, Manitoba. As the conifers in the background demonstrate, Churchill is within the zone where tundra and the northern coniferous forest meet.*

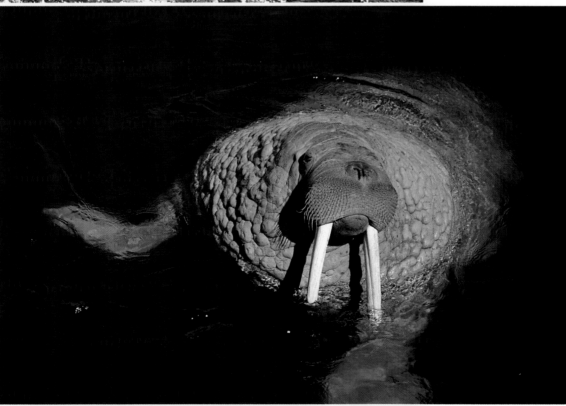

*Walruses (*Odobenus rosmarus*) live in herds among Arctic islands and ice floes, and like to haul out of the water to bask. The walrus feeds mostly on mollusks and other life from the sea bottom, which it may wrench from the seabed with its tusks. Sometimes, however, it kills and eats seals.*

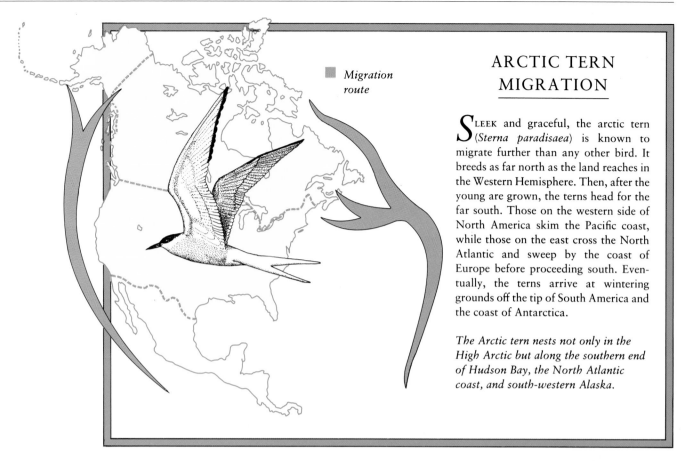

Migration
route

ARCTIC TERN MIGRATION

SLEEK and graceful, the arctic tern (*Sterna paradisaea*) is known to migrate further than any other bird. It breeds as far north as the land reaches in the Western Hemisphere. Then, after the young are grown, the terns head for the far south. Those on the western side of North America skim the Pacific coast, while those on the east cross the North Atlantic and sweep by the coast of Europe before proceeding south. Eventually, the terns arrive at wintering grounds off the tip of South America and the coast of Antarctica.

The Arctic tern nests not only in the High Arctic but along the southern end of Hudson Bay, the North Atlantic coast, and south-western Alaska.

A greater yellowlegs (Tringa melanoleuca) hunts for food in a tundra pond. This is one of the many shorebirds that winter far to the south and breed in the Arctic. During fall and spring migrations, it can be seen in wetlands and coastal areas throughout most of the United States and Canada.

live in temperate climes. The Arctic is the very source of a substantial portion of the birds that enliven the spring and summer of temperate zones. Millions upon millions of birds, especially waterfowl and other aquatic species, breed on the tundra of the Arctic mainland and islands.

When the Arctic is still in the grip of winter, but the land to the south is warming with the approaching spring, shorebirds such as Hudsonian godwits (*Limosa haemastica*), greater yellowlegs (*Tringa melanoleuca*), buff-breasted sandpipers (*Tryngites subruficollis*), long-billed dowitchers

(*Limnodromus scolopaceus*) and sanderlings (*Calidris alba*) wing north towards tundra nesting grounds. With perfect timing, they arrive in the north just as the winter ebbs and conditions become favorable for nesting. Sometimes, however, vagaries in the weather offset the birds' natural sense of timing and destroy almost an entire season's nestlings.

Many birds that nest on the tundra winter as far afield as the tropics – some even farther. The arctic tern (*Sterna paradisaea*) winters in the seas off Antarctica and nests in the High Arctic.

In the spring, brant (*Branta bernicla*), greater white-fronted geese (*Anser albifrons*) and snow geese (*Anser caerulescens*) flock to the tundra breeding areas. More than half a million snow geese winter in the coastal marshes of Louisiana and breed mainly on Baffin and Southampton Islands. The migratory snow geese do not leave the marshes until March. In the north, however, the tundra remains in winter's grasp. After resting in southern areas of Canada, the snow geese arrive on the breeding grounds in the first week of June and quickly begin nesting.

The tremendous importance of the Arctic as a nesting ground for birds is most clearly shown by a survey of 70,400,000 acres of land and water areas in Alaska. This territory is used for breeding, nesting, feeding and staging by 12 million ducks, a million geese, 50,000 sandhill cranes (*Grus canadensis*), 70,000 tundra swans (*Cygnus columbianus*), 3,500 trumpeter swans (*C. buccinator*) and millions upon millions of seabirds. Even whooper swans (*C. cygnus*) from Asia have been known to visit the region. According to some estimates, more than 10 million ducks – such as gadwall (*Anas strepera*) and American wigeon (*A. americana*) – are born annually in Alaska. Birds hatched there turn up in virtually every North American state and province, as well as in many other countries.

Seabirds

Most numerous of all Arctic birds – and, for some species, of birds anywhere – are seabirds, which spend most of the year offshore but come to rocky shores to breed. Among the most abundant seabirds are the auks (family Alcidae), often referred to as northern counterparts of penguins.

Unlike penguins, auks can fly, albeit clumsily. Otherwise the two unrelated avian groups share much in common: the auks – which include puffins (*Fratercula*), auklets (genuses vary), murres or guillemots (*Uria*) and their kin – also pursue fish and squid by 'flying' underwater. Both groups have heavy bodies with feet at the rear, both of which aid steering underwater but are inefficient for getting around on land. Both penguins and auks come ashore only to breed.

There are 22 living species of auks, some of which are circumpolar. The populations of some species number many millions, and individual breeding colonies can contain hordes of birds. Almost a million least auklets (*Aethia pusilla*), for instance, breed on Little Diomede Island in the Bering Sea.

Most familiar are the puffins. The western Arctic is the home of the horned puffin (*Fratercula corniculata*) and the tufted puffin (*F. cirrhata*), while the eastern Arctic is the realm of the Atlantic puffin (*F. arctica*). Puffins nest in burrows or rock crevices on cliffs walling the ocean. Once the young hatch, the parents both fish at sea and carry food back for the nestlings.

Here, horned puffins breed on a cliff in Alaska. Alcidaes (the family also includes guillemots and murrelets) nest often in vast colonies. Some species are among the most numerous of all birds, comprising millions of breeding pairs.

CLIFF BREEDERS

*P*UFFINS (*Fratercula*) are perhaps the best-known members of the auk family (Alcidae), seabirds that some people describe as northern counterparts of penguins. Unlike penguins, however, auks can fly, if clumsily. Like penguins, auks are streamlined for swimming underwater to catch fish and other marine prey. They have heavy bodies and small wings and their legs are set far back on the body. This is not a good arrangement for flight but is excellent for swimming, especially underwater. Under the surface, auks use their wings for swimming power and their feet as rudders. Like penguins, they spend most of their lives at sea and come ashore only during the annual breeding season. Most breed on rocky cliffs, in crevices or burrows. Depending on the species, they may nest on bare rock or in burrows. Puffins generally are burrow nesters. There are three species of puffins in North America, the tufted (*Fratercula cirrhata*), the Atlantic (*F. arctica*) and the horned (*F. corniculata*). The Atlantic puffin inhabits the coastal seas of the north-eastern part of the continent. The other two species are Pacific birds. The tufted puffin gets its name from yellow tufts which grow above the eyes in the breeding season, while the horned puffin is so called because of the fleshy tabs just above each eye. During the winter period, puffins disperse over the sea.

CONIFEROUS FORESTS

South of the tundra, stretching 4,000 miles from coast to coast across the continent, lies the second largest forest in the world. The boreal forest of North America covers Canada's heartland and the northern fringes of the United States, and is exceeded in size only by a similar taiga forest in northern Eurasia. Hardy deciduous trees, such as the quaking aspen (*Populus tremuloides*) and balsam poplar (*P. balsamifera*), grow in this northernmost of forests, but the forest is dominated by Subarctic conifers.

Red spruce (Picea rubens), *shown here in Maine, are a key transitional tree between the northern coniferous forest and the Eastern Mixed Forest to the south.*

ABOVE: *The quaking aspen (Populus tremuloides) is common in western North America. Its leaves are coppery-red in late summer, and brilliant gold in autumn.*

OPPOSITE: *Northern coniferous forest grows alongside the Bow River in Canada's sprawling Banff National Park, the nation's first national park.*

another coniferous region consists of the pine forests of the Atlantic and Gulf coastal plains (*see South-eastern Forests and Subtropical Wetlands*).

THE BOREAL FOREST

The boreal forest, in relative terms, is a lowland forest. Half a mile above sea level the boreal forests are replaced by mountain forests, such as those of the northern Rockies, which are coniferous but have a different community of trees. Before it gives way to tundra, near its northern extreme, the boreal forest gradually diminishes. There, in a band 100 to 200 miles wide, the trees are smaller and more widely spaced than in the heart of the forest, which in its virgin state is an unbroken sea of evergreen. The American Indian name given to the stunted forest on the northernmost limits of the boreal zone means 'land of little sticks.'

In Alberta and Saskatchewan, south of the boreal forest and in the western part of the continent, the forest peters out into the Great Plains. The transitional zone between the southern terminus of the boreal forest and the grasslands is dominated not by conifers but by the quaking aspen (*Populus tremuloides*), a poplar with leaves that tremble at the slightest breeze.

Temperatures in the boreal forest are similar to those of the tundra. Precipitation far exceeds that to the north, in some places amounting to more than 4 feet annually, mostly in the form of snow. The cool temperatures result in a low rate of

THE trees most typical of the forest are the black spruce (*Picea mariana*), which grows to 40 feet high, and the white spruce (*P. glauca*), which can reach 70 feet in height. South of the main boreal forest belt, similar cold-climate trees have been growing on top of mountain ranges since the last Pleistocene ice age (*see Mountains*).

The boreal forest is but one of several coniferous forest regions in North America. South of an approximate line that runs from Minnesota and Ontario to the Atlantic coast, the boreal forest is replaced by conifers that favor a temperate climate, then, farther south, with mixed deciduous forests (*see The Eastern Mixed Forest*). Other coniferous forests grow at middle and higher elevations in the Rockies and along the mountain ranges of the Pacific coast, in British Columbia, Washington, Oregon and California (*see Mountains*). Yet

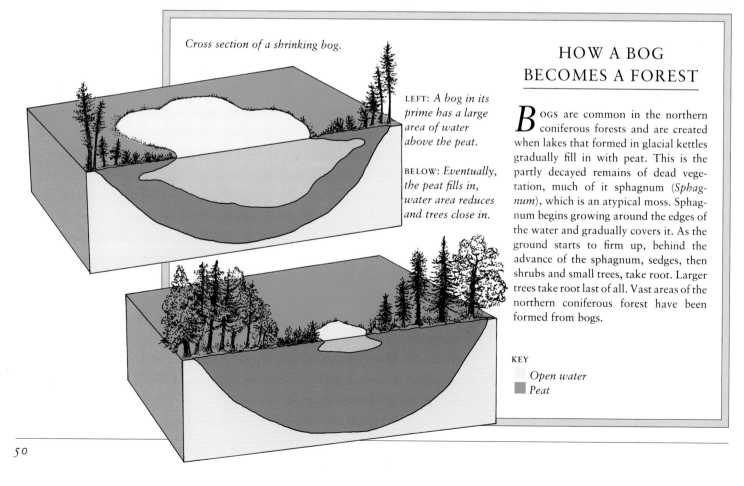

Cross section of a shrinking bog.

LEFT: *A bog in its prime has a large area of water above the peat.*

BELOW: *Eventually, the peat fills in, water area reduces and trees close in.*

HOW A BOG BECOMES A FOREST

BOGS are common in the northern coniferous forests and are created when lakes that formed in glacial kettles gradually fill in with peat. This is the partly decayed remains of dead vegetation, much of it sphagnum (*Sphagnum*), which is an atypical moss. Sphagnum begins growing around the edges of the water and gradually covers it. As the ground starts to firm up, behind the advance of the sphagnum, sedges, then shrubs and small trees, take root. Larger trees take root last of all. Vast areas of the northern coniferous forest have been formed from bogs.

KEY
☐ Open water
■ Peat

FORESTS

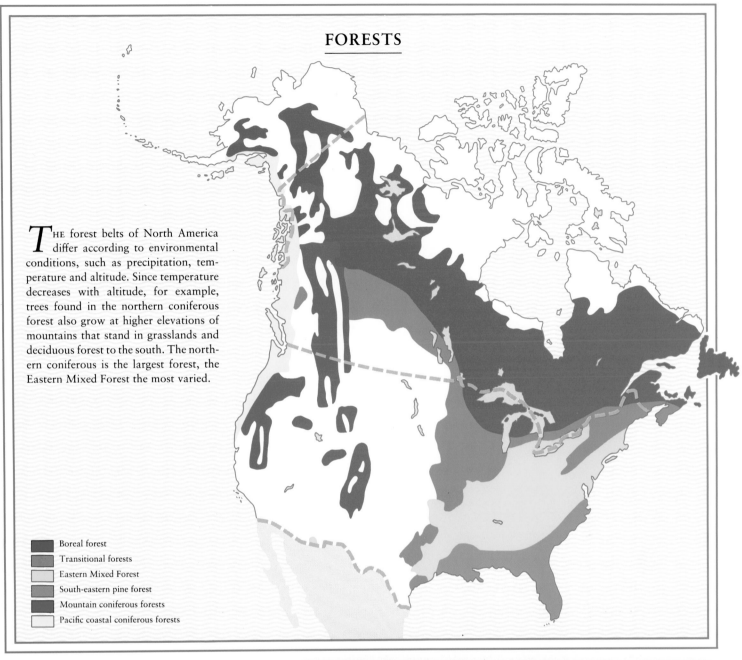

THE forest belts of North America differ according to environmental conditions, such as precipitation, temperature and altitude. Since temperature decreases with altitude, for example, trees found in the northern coniferous forest also grow at higher elevations of mountains that stand in grasslands and deciduous forest to the south. The northern coniferous is the largest forest, the Eastern Mixed Forest the most varied.

- Boreal forest
- Transitional forests
- Eastern Mixed Forest
- South-eastern pine forest
- Mountain coniferous forests
- Pacific coastal coniferous forests

evaporation, which enables the forest to retain moisture. Towards the northern limits of the forest the ground under the trees is swampy in places, creating a boggy soil called muskeg.

Muskeg is laden with peat that sometimes trembles underfoot. It develops when, after many centuries, forest soil becomes depleted. Cold temperatures and long periods of short diurnal light work against the decay of organic material and the resultant nutrient build-up in the soil. Eventually, hardpan develops in the soil, preventing water drainage; the water then saturates the surface layer. The presence of so much moisture further inhibits decay. The soil becomes acidic, rendering it less suitable for lush tree growth. Large trees cannot find secure anchorage for their roots and topple over. The result of these effects is a forest of widely spaced, smaller trees, or taiga.

This scene from Voyageurs National Park in Minnesota is typical of an area in which the northern coniferous forest begins to give way to the Eastern Mixed Forest. This region is dotted with thousands of lakes, the basins of which are largely the result of erosion by Pleistocene glaciers.

Boreal forest heartland

In far western Canada and Alaska, the jagged and high topography intercepts true boreal forest with high-altitude coniferous woodlands, but in the center of the continent the boreal forest continues without a break from horizon to horizon. The heart of the boreal forest coincides with 2,000,000 square miles of exposed rock of the Canadian Shield. This coniferous realm covers an area south of Hudson Bay to the Lake Superior region, just entering the United States in northern Minnesota, Wisconsin and Michigan.

Sizable tracts of boreal forest are preserved in parks along the borders of Minnesota, Michigan and Ontario. Pukaskwa National Park in Ontario supports rugged boreal forest fronting Lake Superior. South and east of Voyageurs National Park in Minnesota is the Superior National Forest, covering more than 2,000,000 acres. It includes the 150-mile-long Boundary Waters Canoe Area Wilderness. Across the border, to the east, is Quetico Provincial Park. Here, the great boreal wilderness lies within a few hours' drive of major population centers.

From its southernmost extension, the forest arcs north in two tines of a fork either side of Hudson Bay. In the North-west Territories, the limits of the forest sweep around two huge lakes, Great Slave (more than 10,000 square miles in area) and Great Bear (more than 11,000 square miles in area). Forest on the northern shores of these lakes is thin and stunted, while on the southern lakesides the forest is dense.

South of Great Slave Lake, overlapping the border of Alberta and the North-west Territories, Canada's largest national park straddles the transition between boreal forest and the Great Plains. The 11,072,000-acre Wood Buffalo National Park is only a few hundred miles from the tundra north of Great Slave Lake.

The park was established in 1922 to protect the last herd of wood bison, a darker, larger race of the plains bison (*Bison bison*). In 1922, some 500 wood bison remained in the area north of the Peace River and west of the Slave River. The park is a region of boreal forest, bogs and plains, where wood bison now number more than 15,000 animals, forming the largest wild herd anywhere. However, most of the bison are not a pure woodland race, although there is a small herd of pure wood bison in a remote part of the park. After the park was created plains bison were introduced to the area and the two groups interbred.

Established to preserve the bison, Wood Buffalo National Park coincidentally protects the breeding ground of a much rarer species, the whooping crane (*Grus americana*). The nesting area of this crane was discovered in 1954 in the remote wetlands of the park.

Trees of the boreal forest

The main trees of the boreal forest are the black spruce (*Picea mariana*) and the white spruce (*P. glauca*), which have both adapted to moist conditions, although the white is less amenable to moisture than its cousin.

The coniferous tamarack (*Larix laricina*), favors wet soils more than the spruces. Another typical conifer, except in the west, is the balsam fir (*Abies balsamea*), which grows mostly along streams and lakes. Jack pine (*Pinus banksiana*) grows throughout most of the region except in the far west, where it is replaced by lodgepole pine (*P. contorta*). Both of these latter species are found in dry soils and reach up to 70 to 80 feet in height. Paper birch (*Betula papyrifera*) and aspens (*Populus*) represent the deciduous community throughout the whole of the region.

Boreal forest species extend into the interior of Alaska, where they can be found at low altitudes. Higher up, the terrain is tundra. In Denali National Park, Alaska, sparse boreal forest grows in valleys and along watercourses and gives way to tundra above 2,700 feet.

Wildlife of the boreal forest

As an intermediate zone between Great Plains and Eastern Mixed Forest on one hand and tundra on the other, the boreal forest hosts a diversity of animal species. Some, such as the Barren Ground caribou (*Rangifer tarandus*), migrate southwards from the tundra in winter, to join their woodland kin that live in the forest throughout the year (*see The High Arctic and Tundra*). Others, such as the dark-eyed junco (*Junco hyemalis*) and white-throated sparrow (*Zonotrichia albicollis*), head north to the forest to breed in spring, migrating into the United States during winter.

MAMMALS The most typical predator of the boreal forest is probably the lynx (*Felis lynx*). The distribution of this cat almost perfectly coincides with the limits of the northern forest. The main prey of the lynx is another creature that is primarily a boreal forest species, the varying hare (*Lepus americanus*).

*The Canadian lynx (*Felis lynx*) ranges throughout the northern coniferous forest, as well as mountain coniferous forests in the west. Its broad, heavily furred feet act like snowshoes, enabling it to travel through deep snow without becoming bogged down. The lynx lives mainly on small mammals. It is replaced in the Eastern Mixed Forest by its cousin the bobcat (*F. rufus*).*

COLOR CHANGE IN VARYING HARES

The varying, or snowshoe, hare (*Lepus americanus*) undergoes a seasonal color change from white in winter to brown in summer. This characteristic is shared by some other animals of the far north, including the arctic hare (*L. timidus*), and birds such as the ptarmigan (*Lagopus*).

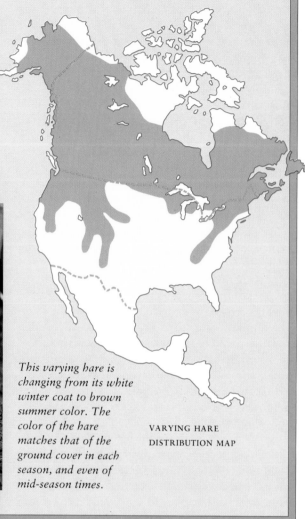

This varying hare is changing from its white winter coat to brown summer color. The color of the hare matches that of the ground cover in each season, and even of mid-season times.

VARYING HARE
DISTRIBUTION MAP

OPPOSITE: *This is an exceptionally large black bear (*Ursus americanus*). Three hundred pounds is a more than respectable weight for a black bear, but some individuals far surpass that, approaching 500 pounds. Of all North American bears, this is most common and widespread. It is typical of coniferous forests but also dwells in deciduous forests and large swamps.*

Known also as the varying hare, this hare, like the lynx, has wide, padded feet that facilitate locomotion in deep snow. The hind feet of the hare are more than 6 inches in length (its overall length including tail is about 24 inches), and provide it with leverage for split-second turns when pursued by predators. Although only about 5 pounds in weight, the hare is a powerful animal for its size, and can run at up to 30 miles an hour. Varying hare populations peak and fall over periods of several years. Lynx numbers follow suit, a year behind.

The black bear (*Ursus americanus*) also inhabits the boreal forest, but is also found in myriad habitats to the south. Virtually all habitat types in North America apart from the tundra suit the black bear, although it thrives best in heavily forested and mountainous areas.

Black bears, not as large as their brown bear cousins, can occasionally reach a weight of more than 300 pounds, although most are smaller. Not all black bears are black: this species also has some cinnamon- and brown-colored bears.

The home range of the black bear varies (males need a greater range than females) from about 5 to 100 square miles. Females have a gestation period of about 7 months and give birth in mid-winter, usually to two young. The young weigh no more than 10 ounces.

Wolves and coyotes

Boreal forest and tundra both provide a suitable habitat for wolves (*Canis lupus*). When Europeans first arrived in North America, wolves ranged throughout most of the United States and Canada apart from pure desert regions. As human populations have encroached on the wolf south of Canada, the tundra and boreal forest have become its retreat, with substantial numbers of wolves in Ontario's Quetico Provincial Park and Algonquin Provincial Park.

The largest wolf population in the 48 North American states exists in the boreal woods of northern Minnesota, Michigan and Wisconsin. In this area, about 1,000 wolves rove Voyageurs National Park, Grand Portage National Monument, Saint Croix National Scenic Riverway, and Isle Royale National Park.

The moose (Alces alces) lives exclusively in, or on the margins of, coniferous forest. It is chiefly an animal of the northern forest, but its range extends further south along the Rocky Mountains. Moose feed heavily on aquatic plants and are excellent swimmers.

Isle Royale lies close to the Sibley Peninsula of Ontario but is part of Michigan, separated from the rest of the state by 73 miles of water. 134,400 acres of coniferous wilderness covers the heart of the national park, which is on Isle Royale. Since the late 1950s, Isle Royale has been the site of a long-term study of wolves and their predation upon moose (*Alces alces*). The study revealed that a healthy moose in its prime is almost invulnerable to wolf attack. A full-grown moose's sharp hooves can deal deadly damage to attacking wolves. Wolves therefore tend to select old, or otherwise weakened, moose as victims. By eliminating the unfit, the wolves help keep the moose herd healthy.

Moose first crossed to the island by swimming from Canada in the early 1900s. They quickly established themselves there, and were followed by wolves in the winter of 1948 to 1949, when the water between Isle Royale and the peninsula froze. Since the wolves arrived, their population has averaged 23 animals, whereas there are about 1,000 moose. The number of wolves began to drop in 1984; scientists are investigating whether inbreeding or diseases such as canine heartworm have caused the decline.

Small numbers of wolves also remain around other protected areas south of the Canadian border – Glacier National Park, Montana, and, perhaps,

Chiricahua National Monument, Arizona. Conservationists are now seeking to reintroduce the wolf into Yellowstone National Park, in Wyoming, Montana and Idaho (*see Conservation*).

Wolves live in packs, usually of about 2 to 12 animals. A dominant male and female head the pack, which is generally made up of their offspring, and often adult siblings of the dominant pair as well. Occasionally outsiders are permitted to join the group.

Wolves have one of the most complex family lives of any wild animal. In packs, strong bonds exist between siblings, young and adults and between the adults themselves. Young are cared for solicitously: when a female has a new litter of pups, her older offspring and male partner will hunt and then regurgitate or carry back food for the mother and young. The young engage in endless rounds of play fights, which prepare them physically and mentally for predation and survival. Adult wolves readily take small animals, including mice, but large mammals, especially those of the deer family, are essential to the pack's existence.

The wolf cub has to learn the order of dominance within the family; the power structure descends from the male, who rules the pack. His rule, as far as the young are concerned, is benign. When they beg for food, he readily gives it to them. This sharing of bounty is critical to cooperative hunters such as wolves, which must work together to bring down large prey. Bonds established among the young and between the young and their elders evolve as the cubs mature, and enable the pack to hunt as a group.

At the age of about two months cubs begin accompanying the pack on hunts. They learn the hunting tactics of their elders, which include methods as sophisticated as running after prey in relays and ambushing. By the time they are a year old, the young wolves are full members of the hunting organization.

During a night's hunting, a wolf pack may cover a distance of up to about 40 miles, running at speeds of up to 35 miles per hour for several miles at a stretch.

Wolves communicate with one another over long distances by howling. The howling of a pack, which has long been a symbol of the wilderness, can be a means of marking territory. Canadian scientists have pioneered the use of wolf howls to map the location of packs within the dense boreal forest, where observation of these creatures is more difficult than on the open tundra. Studies in the 1,920,000-acre Algonquin Provincial Park indicated that pack members may identify one another over long distances by the unique sound of each individual's howl.

Among the other wild canids inhabiting the boreal forest are coyotes (*Canis latrans*). They tend to live on the edges of the boreal forest, where it meets grasslands and mixed forest. The red fox (*Vulpes vulpes*), on the other hand, occupies virtually all boreal forest areas. Smaller than many people believe, it seldom exceeds 12 pounds in weight. It is active and intelligent, and hunts a variety of small creatures such as rodents, rabbits and nestlings. Especially in deep snow, the fox itself is prey to the Canadian lynx (*Felis lynx*): foxes do not have the wide furred feet of animals adapted for heavy snow cover, and lose much of their agility and quickness in snow.

Weasels

One of the most opportunistic predators of the forest – and of the tundra – is the wolverine (*Gulo gulo*), the largest terrestrial member of the weasel family in the Americas. It is said to be an insatiable eater, resulting in its European name of 'glutton'. (The species is circumpolar.) It is shaggy, walks with a humpbacked gait, and looks like a small bear, although it only weighs from 35 to 60 pounds; it has a reputation for being as tough as a grizzly.

Stories abound of wolverines killing bears in combat, routing cougars and wolves and bringing down prey as large as caribou. They have killed deer, but usually only those that are old or weakened. More usually they prey on rodents and rabbits, and eat vegetable matter as well. Wolverines will also rob cabins of food and destroy what cannot be eaten on the spot or carried away.

RIGHT: *An extremely adaptable species, the red fox* (Vulpes vulpes) *inhabits coniferous forest as well as many other environments. This one is in Denali National Park, Alaska, where northern coniferous forest is mixed with tundra.*

BELOW: *An American, or pine, marten (Martes americana) has caught a squirrel. This member of the weasel family is almost exclusively a species of coniferous woodlands and ranges across the whole continent.*

BOTTOM: *The preference of the red squirrel (Tamiasciurus hudsonicus) for coniferous forests is demonstrated by its other name of 'spruce squirrel.' Although it does range into deciduous forest, it is not as common there.*

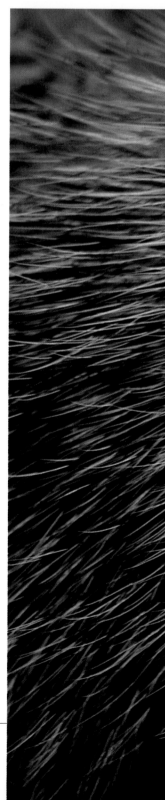

LEFT: *Large, tough and tenacious, the wolverine (Gulo gulo) is a member of the weasel family. Like other weasels, the wolverine has powerful anal scent glands. It is primarily an animal of the northern coniferous forest, as well as tundra, but also inhabits some western mountains.*

However, although some wolverine lore is true, they are not quite such ravening beasts that many people believe them to be.

Wolverines are fiercely tenacious, strong beyond their size and tremendously resourceful. Once a wolverine finds a productive trap line, it will follow from trap to trap, removing bait set out for lynxes or other valuable furbearers. Alaskan trappers frequently anchor their traps to spruce logs four or five inches in diameter. Wolverines have been known to chew through such logs with their crushing jaws, freeing the traps and carrying them off. The same jaw power enables these scavengers to bite through the leg bones of dead moose.

If a hungry wolverine scents food inside an unoccupied cabin, it will inevitably find a way to enter. After rummaging for its meal, the cabin can be left a shambles and smelling strongly from the foul secretions of the wolverine's musk glands with which it marks the food site. (Musk glands are typical of weasels, reaching highest development in the skunk.)

Several other members of the weasel family inhabit the boreal forest. The American marten (*Martes americana*) is a true boreal creature, ranging the continent from Labrador to the coast of Alaska and southwards along mountain ranges where boreal-type forest grows at higher altitudes. Martens den in rocks and hollow logs. They are nimble and adept at moving through the trees, where they are a major predator of the red squirrel (*Tamiasciurus hudsonicus*).

The least weasel (*Mustela rixosa*), which barely weighs more than 2 ounces, is the world's smallest living carnivore, but none-the-less a deadly predator. It lives almost exclusively upon mice, which it kills with a single bite through the base of the skull. Like the ermine, or stoat (*M. erminea*), which weighs up to 6 ounces, the least weasel changes color in winter. The ermine turns white during winter, except for its black tail tip. The tip of the least weasel's tail turns white in winter.

A weasel of moderate size, the fisher (*Martes pennanti*), which weighs up to 20 pounds, is among the few animals that occasionally prey on porcupines (*Erethizon dorsatum*); most predators shun porcupines because of their sharp quills.

Rodents

Porcupines are common in the boreal forest. Its quills are modified hairs topped with barbs, which can be raised at will. If attacked, the porcupine lowers its head and lashes its tail. Once embedded, the quills detach, and can work their way through flesh, causing harmful wounds. The belly of the porcupine, however, is unprotected. Fishers try to kill porcupines by getting underneath them and biting into the exposed underparts.

The nocturnal porcupine is good at climbing but moves slowly on the ground. It eats buds, twigs and

LEFT: *An ermine, or stoat* (Mustela erminea), *in its winter coat is as white as snow. It inhabits all coniferous forest areas of the continent except for the south-eastern United States and also ranges on to the tundra of the High Arctic, Eastern Mixed Forest and desert scrub lands of the west.*

BELOW: *Clumsy and slow on the ground, the porcupine* (Erethizon dorsatum) *is an able climber and often rests high in trees. Young porcupines are born with their eyes open, can climb and eat solid foods when only a few hours old. Their quills harden an hour after birth.*

bark. Weighing up to 30 pounds, it is the second largest rodent in North America after the beaver (*Castor canadensis*), which inhabits aquatic environments throughout the boreal forest, as well as in forests to the south.

Small rodents of the boreal forest include the least chipmunk (*Eutamias minimus*), which weighs 1 or 2 ounces; various voles (*Microtus*); the arctic ground squirrel (*Spermophilus undulatus*); and the deer mouse (*Peromyscus maniculatus*).

BIRDS Several species of owls hunt at night through the conifer boughs of the boreal forest. The great horned owl (*Bubo virginianus*), 2 feet long, is one of the major avian predators of the boreal zone, and can be found in forests all the way to the southern tip of South America. Powerful and aggressive, it attacks a wide variety of prey, including varieties of waterfowl, raccoons and even skunks.

Larger than the great horned owl, and, in fact, largest of all North American owls, the great gray owl (*Strix nebulosa*) inhabits only boreal forest. Its body is almost 3 feet long. The northern hawk owl (*Surnia ulula*) is a swift-flying species that looks for prey from high perches, then swoops down for the capture. It hunts during the day.

Birds are the main prey of the northern goshawk (*Accipiter gentilis*), which in boreal areas also feeds on gray and red squirrels. The red-tailed hawk (*Buteo jamaicensis*) lives in the boreal habitat across North America.

OPPOSITE: *A few inches longer than the snowy owl* (Nyctea scandiaca) *but weighing less, the great gray owl* (Strix nebulosa) *haunts the coniferous forests of the north and the western mountains, such as the Rockies and Sierra Nevada. It is abundant, however, only in the northern coniferous forest, where it is found to the margins of the tundra.*

LEFT: *An immature northern goshawk* (Accipiter gentilis) *feeds on a gray squirrel* (Sciurus carolinensis). *This bird lives mostly in the northern and mountain coniferous forests, but during the winter migrates south well into the United States. It frequently preys on rodents, snowshoe, or varying, hares* (Lepus americanus), *ruffed grouse* (Bonasa umbellus), *and ducks. It is a swift, powerful hunter.*

ABOVE: *The great horned owl* (Bubo virginianus) *is more widely distributed than any other owl in the Western Hemisphere. It ranges from coast to coast, and from the northern limits of the coniferous forest as far south as Tierra del Fuego. A paler form inhabits the forests at the tundra's edge.*

The orange-crowned warbler (Vermivora celata) includes coniferous forest among its breeding habitats. It is most abundant in the mountainous west and in the north.

ABOVE: *A common loon, or great northern diver (Gavia immer), sits on its nest. This is a true bird of the northern forests and tundra, although it migrates far south along both coasts in winter. Its yodeling call is often described as the song of the wilderness. Loons are diving birds that must run over the surface of the water to become airborne. Once in the air, however, they fly powerfully. They spend most of their time on the water and are ungainly on land.*

At the edges of lakes and streams, the common loon (*Gavia immer*) builds its nests. The long, quavering call of the loon is a typical sound of the wilderness.

Birds that dwell primarily on the ground include the spruce grouse (*Canachites canadensis*), which is a true boreal forest bird. Feeding mostly on conifer buds and needles (especially those of spruces), this grouse retreats from habitats encroached upon by civilization.

Many birds that winter in the Eastern Mixed Forest, or even as far south as the tropics, start their lives in the boreal forest and return in spring each year. Several are sparrows, such as the white-throated (*Zonotrichia albicollis*) and the American tree sparrow (*Spizella arborea*).

The boreal forest is an extremely important nesting ground for warblers. Some, such as the Tennessee warbler (*Vermivora peregrina*), Cape May warbler (*Dendroica tigrina*), bay-breasted warbler (*D. castanea*), blackpoll warbler (*D. striata*) and palm warbler (*D. palmarum*) nest nowhere else. The breeding range of the orange-crowned warbler (*V. celata*), however, is not confined to the boreal forest but is widespread in a variety of wood and brush habitats in the West.

The flutelike call of the hermit thrush (*Catharus guttatus*) permeates the boreal forest. Among the woodpeckers, the three-toed (*Picoides tridactylus*) and black-backed (*P. arcticus*) are almost exclusively boreal forest birds. The noisy and active black-capped chickadee (*Parus atricapillus*) and the similar boreal chickadee (*P. hudsonicus*) thrive

AVIAN IRRUPTIONS

Sᴏᴍᴇ pine siskins (*Carduelis pinus*) regularly migrate south of the northern coniferous forest in winter. The majority, however, remain there unless food supplies dwindle, when they, too, swarm south. In 1987, vast numbers of pine siskins headed south, apparently because of a poor crop of birch and alder seeds in the northern forest. These deciduous trees, which mix with the conifers, are the prime source of the siskin's food. This invasion was an excellent example of an irruption of northern birds in the south.

The pine siskin is a finch that breeds across the northern coniferous forest and down along the western mountains. It is a hardy bird, able to handle the cold of the boreal winter, so long as it has an abundant food supply.

in the boreal woods. The black-capped chickadee is also found as far south as California, Pennsylvania and New Jersey, and in the northern United States is frequently a back-yard bird. The boreal species, as its name implies, lives strictly in the northern woods.

Boreal birds such as warblers and sparrows migrate south regularly every year. Other species winter in the south irregularly, in great numbers in some years and in others very few at all. Among these birds are the Bohemian waxwing (*Bombycilla garrulus*) and pine siskin (*Carduelis pinus*). An irruption of great numbers of such birds in southern areas is believed to be caused by a failure of seed and berry crops in the northern forests.

THE EASTERN TRANSITION

From Minnesota eastwards through the Canadian Maritime Provinces and northern New England, the boreal forest merges with the Eastern Mixed Forest (*see also The Eastern Mixed Forest*). The belt in which they merge still has typical boreal forest trees. Black and white spruces and balsam fir grow there, although they are at the southern end of their range.

The true boreal trees mix with other conifers. In the east of the transitional belt, red spruce (*Picea rubens*) appears, along with eastern white pine (*Pinus strobus*), red pine (*P. resinosa*) and eastern hemlock (*Tsuga canadensis*). The last three trees extend west to the Upper Great Lakes region.

Deciduous trees such as red maple (*Acer rubrum*), northern red oak (*Quercus rubra*) and black oak (*Q. velutina*) are also found in the mixed forest just to the south. The ground is often covered with wildflowers and ferns.

Where the forest meets the sea

Along the coast of Maine and the Maritime Provinces, the transitional coniferous forest grows right to the edge of the rocky, rugged coastline, which was shaped by glaciers. The weight of Pleistocene glaciers, in this area between 3,000 and 9,000 feet thick, pressed down heavily upon the land, tilting it towards the sea and breaking it up into narrow, steep-walled valleys. In some places, geologists believe, the landscape was depressed more than 1,000 feet, although it regained some elevation after the glaciers melted. With the disappearance of the glaciers and rising sea level, the ocean advanced far up the valleys. Ground that remained above the water became the headlands and islands characteristic of the Maine coast, which eventually were covered with forest.

The forest meets the sea amidst a typical welter of craggy headlands and islands in the 35,000-acre Acadia National Park, on the central Maine coast. The park lies on Mount Desert Island and several adjacent islets, plus the nearby Schoodic Peninsula. Its terrain is rugged and studded with low mountains, the highest of them being Cadillac Mountain at 1,530 feet.

Before glaciation, the highland that was to become Mount Desert Island was a ridge of granite

Vegetation on the floor of the coniferous forest. In contrast to the trees of the deciduous forest, those of the coniferous forest do not become bare from fall to spring, so vegetation must be extremely shade tolerant. Even so a variety of low plants grow there, including oak ferns, mosses, lichens, and fungi.

THE MAINE COAST

*I*T is called the 'rockbound coast of Maine', appropriately so. The shoreline of Maine is rimmed by stark, rugged, and seemingly indestructible rock. In fact, it is not. Even the granite bulwarks that fringe the Maine coast suffer erosion from the pounding of the Atlantic surf. Nothing in nature is immutable.

On Pemaquid Point on the coast of Maine, ancient rock, millions of years old, has been exposed by the scouring of the Pleistocene glaciers.

PREVIOUS PAGES: *Highbush blueberries (*Vaccinium corymbosum*) blaze red in fall on Champlain Mountain in Maine's Acadia National Park. Wild blueberries grow vigorously in clearings throughout the region.*

bedrock, running on an east to west axis and cut by valleys in the same direction. The last glaciation, which wore away evidence of earlier ice sheets, had the most profound impact upon the region. The leading edge of the ice sheet expanded from Canada, and when it reached the Mount Desert highland, ice surged through the valleys, eventually covering the high ground and flowing seaward for 300 miles across the exposed continental shelf.

As great tongues of ice forced their way into the valleys, sometimes at the rate of only a few inches or feet a day, the granite eroded and the valleys deepened. The grinding of the glacier smoothed out the northern slopes of the highland and gouged rock from the southern slopes, creating steep, jagged cliffs.

When the ice finally retreated, the sea flooded the valleys, creating the shoreline described. Two of the valleys inland of the sea filled with fresh water and became lakes.

The valleys flooded by the ocean were narrow, so estuaries of the region, such as those on Mount Desert Island, are correspondingly narrow. The glaciers stripped the rock bare of soil and wore away its surface, thus preventing the formation of the great, sandy barrier islands (*see The Evolution of a Continent*) that are typical of the coastline below the southern termination of the ice sheets in the East, at New York's Long Island.

Forest eventually returned to the land and grew down to the edge of the sea. Spruces (*Picea*) are especially suited to rocky shorelands because they have shallow roots that can anchor to rock with only minimal soil cover.

Wildlife of Acadia National Park

Much of the forest has been cut from the seacoast, but in places such as Acadia National Park, where the forest continues to the coast, wildlife typical of the interior big woods roams right down to the ocean. In this region the boreal forest meets the mixed deciduous zone.

MAMMALS Although now eradicated, the lynx (*Felis lynx*) once lived in the park; its cousin, the bobcat (*F. rufus*), still belongs to habitats south of the boreal realm. The whitetail deer (*Odocoileus virginianus*), another southern species, thrives in the park. Occasionally, moose visit the area, too.

BIRDS The mourning dove (*Zenaida macroura*) nears the northern end of its range in northern New England, yet is common in Acadia throughout the year, as is the boreal chickadee (*Parus hudsonicus*). The great blue heron (*Ardea herodias*) comes from the south in summer, while during the winter period the snowy owl may sometimes visit from the northern tundra.

The spruce grouse (*Dendragapus canadensis*), which favors open coniferous forest with dense undergrowth, inhabits the park, but is uncommon. Its relative the ruffed grouse (*Bonasa umbellus*), however, flourishes there. The name ruffed grouse is derived from the ruff of feathers around its neck. This grouse is not a purely coniferous forest bird, but prefers a mix of coniferous and deciduous trees for its habitat.

Surrounded by the sea, Acadia National Park is the home of many seabirds, such as ring-billed gulls (*Larus delawarensis*), herring gulls (*L. argentatus*) and black-legged kittiwakes (*Rissa tridactyla*). Sea ducks such as the common eider (*Somateria mollissima*), white-winged scoter (*Melanitta fusca*) and surf scoter (*M. perspicillata*), which visit southern New England only in winter, can be seen in waters off Acadia throughout the year.

Winter brings the spectacular king eider (*Somateria spectabilis*), which is rare south of Canada, to the Park. The king eider is about the size of a goose, and the male has a massive bill and bluish head.

MATING DISPLAY AND HABITATS
OF RUFFED AND SPRUCE GROUSE

THE spruce grouse (*Dendragapus canadensis*) and ruffed grouse (*Bonasa umbellus*) share much of their range throughout the northern coniferous forest. The latter, however, extends southward into deciduous forest and thrives in the transitional woodland between the two forest belts. During the spring mating season, the males of both these species engage in most spectacular courtship displays which are designed to attract mates. Each of these displays is unique to the species. Elaborate mating displays are typical of the grouse and their relatives, including prairie-chickens (*Tympanuchus*).

RUFFED GROUSE DISTRIBUTION MAP

In spring, the male ruffed grouse produces a powerful drumming sound by slapping its wings, as shown here. This is usually done while perching on a fallen log. To court the female, the male spreads its fan-like tail and fluffs out the ruff of feathers around its neck.

SPRUCE GROUSE DISTRIBUTION MAP

When displaying, a male spruce grouse struts, tail spread, and makes wild flights in the air.

PACIFIC COASTAL FORESTS

On the western margin of the continent, other coastal coniferous forests contain some of the most magnificent trees in North America, if not in the world. The coastal forests are not as extensive as the boreal woodlands to the north, and in some areas grow no more than 50 miles inland. Amidst the glaciers and coastal tundra of Kenai Fjords National Park in south-western Alaska, coastal forests exist only in narrow bands along fjords and in some valleys, below 500 to 1,000 feet.

Trees of the coastal forests

Along the southern coast of Alaska, trees such as the towering Sitka spruce (*Picea sitchensis*), western hemlock (*Tsuga heterophylla*) and Alaska cedar (*Chamaecyparis nootkatensis*) begin to dominate in the place of boreal trees. Sitka spruces can live for more than 700 years, have a trunk diameter of up to 10 feet and a height of more than 200 feet. Western hemlock at its maximum height is almost as tall, with a trunk diameter which seldom exceeds 5 feet. Its western limits are on the Kenai Peninsula, where, in the Kenai Fjords National Park (famed for its coastal glaciers) it grows in pure stands. The Alaska cedar grows to 100 feet tall.

The coastal forests of Alaska are the northern extension of the lush coniferous forests that grow along the Pacific coast and south to northern California. From British Columbia to Oregon in drier areas, increasing numbers of Douglas fir (*Pseudotsuga menziesii*) can be seen in the coniferous forest. The Douglas fir also grows in the Sierra Nevada and Rockies. Along the Pacific coast, the Douglas fir reaches its maximum size, at 250 feet high and with a trunk of 8 feet in diameter.

The coastal forest reaches its peak of luxuriance on Washington's Olympic Peninsula, a rugged, 4,000,000-acre wilderness which was still largely unexplored until the early years of this century. On the Olympic Peninsula grows one of the rarest forest types in the world – temperate rain forest.

The temperate rain forest

Temperate rain forest grows in only three parts of the world: in New Zealand, southern Chile and on the Olympic Peninsula, in the valleys of the Hoh, Quinault and Queets rivers. The Olympic temperate rain forest has developed due to the mild climate, low elevation, summer fogs and heavy annual rains. Parts of the Olympic Peninsula receive 12 feet of precipitation a year – more than many tropical rain forests receive. On the Olympic Peninsula, the rain forest is found along the coast and in west-facing valleys.

The chief reason for the evolution of the Olympic rain forest is the presence of the Olympic Mountains. Jagged and forbidding, they rise from

RIGHT: *The bases of Sitka spruce (*Picea sitchensis*) are covered with mosses in the lush Hoh Rain Forest of Olympic National Park on Washington's Olympic Peninsula.*

the edge of the sea up to heights of no more than 8,000 feet. The mountains intercept moisture-laden air masses which move inland from the Pacific Ocean. Forced over the mountains, the air cools and releases its load of moisture. This moisture is released as rain on lower elevations during the warm months, and as snow at high elevations and during the winter. Some areas on the eastern slopes receive only about a twentieth of the precipitation that falls a few miles away on the peaks facing the Pacific Ocean.

The mountains also shield the valleys support-ing rain forest from winds and cold weather. Temperatures in the valleys rarely drop below freezing in winter, and seldom rise above 80°F in summer, although the peaks are shrouded by glaciers. (The cold temperatures at high altitude coupled with heavy precipitation cause glaciers.)

The rain forest of the Olympic Peninsula is like a temperate jungle. Mosses and lichens blanket the ground and beard the trunks and branches of trees. Ferns such as bracken (*Pteridium aquilinum*) and sword fern (*Polystichum munitum*) grow thickly on the forest floor and even on trees.

The tree most closely associated with the temperate rain forest is the Sitka spruce (*Picea sitchensis*). Western red cedar (*Thuja plicata*) and western hemlock are also common. The western hemlock reaches record size in the park, with one tree at 164 feet in height, with a trunk circumfer-ence of more than 27 feet. The park also has a 120-foot-tall western red cedar with a circumference of slightly more than 66 feet. Deciduous trees include the bigleaf maple (*Acer macrophyllum*) and the vine maple (*A. circinatum*), both of which are virtually confined to the coastal forests of the Pacific North-west.

The big trees, especially the Sitka spruce, actually promote the growth of the rain forest. The ground is so heavily matted with vegetation that tree seedlings find it difficult to gain a foothold in the soil. Many seedlings root on fallen spruce logs, multitudes of which are strewn over the forest floor. Several seedlings may grow on a single log. When they mature, they form a colonnade of trees, looking almost as if they had been deliberately planted in a row. Some of the trees that grow on fallen logs have stilt-like roots showing above the ground. Such roots become apparent when a log that has served as a base for the tree decays, leaving its roots exposed.

Above the temperate rain forest, another type of woodland takes over, as Douglas fir (*Pseudotsuga menziesii*) appears and Sitka spruce vanishes. Western hemlock (*Tsuga heterophylla*) is the most abundant tree in this zone, where western red cedar also grows. Higher up the slopes, western red cedar is no longer seen, but Pacific silver fir (*Abies amibalis*) becomes common. As altitude continues to increase, subalpine fir (*A. lasiocarpa*), mountain

hemlock (*Tsuga mertensiana*) and Alaska cedar (*Chamaecyparis nootkatensis*) appear.

Within the park a number of trees of record dimensions grow, including the largest Douglas fir, at 221 feet high, with a trunk 45½ feet in circumfer-ence; the tallest subalpine fir, at 129 feet high and with a trunk just over 21 feet in circumference; the largest recorded Alaska cedar, which is 120 feet high and has a trunk of almost 38 feet in circumference; and a huge Pacific silver fir that is 206 feet tall and has a trunk circumference of more than 21 feet.

Wildlife of the Olympic Peninsula

The temperate rain forest and other woodlands of the Olympic Peninsula have a rich fauna, including several creatures unique to this isolated area.

MAMMALS Mammals peculiar to the region are the Olympic marmot (*Marmota olympus*) and Olym-pic chipmunk (*Eutamias townsendi*). The best known mammal of the region is the Olympic, or Roosevelt, elk, a large race of the elk (*Cervus canadensis*) that, unlike other elk, lives in herds.

BIRDS The pileated woodpecker (*Dryocopus pile-atus*) favors the deep forests, drilling its oblong holes into tree trunks of the rain forest and other Olympic woods. The winter wren (*Troglodytes troglodytes*), gray jay (*Perisoreus canadensis*), varied thrush (*Ixoreus naevius*) and white-crowned sparrow (*Zonotrichia leucophrys*) also inhabit the region.

AMPHIBIANS Of all creatures, none are more suited to the temperate rain forest and its margins than amphibians. It is the haunt of the Pacific giant salamander (*Dicamptodon ensatus*), with its remarkably large head. Some specimens of this salamander's aquatic larvae do not metamorphose into adults, but remain gilled, water-living forms. The larvae can grow to a foot long.

THE GIANT TREES OF CALIFORNIA

Two closely related trees growing along the Pacific margins of the United States are natural wonders. They are the coast redwood (*Sequoia sempervirens*) and giant sequoia (*Sequoiadendron giganteum*), immensely old trees and the largest in the world. Some giant sequoias standing today began life before the birth of Christ. Threatened by the timber industry and other forms of habitat destruction, giant sequoias and coast redwoods are now protected within national parks and preserves.

Coast redwoods – the only other redwood is the dawn redwood (*Metasequoia glyptostroboides*) of central China – grow within 30 miles of the misty, fog-shrouded coast, and can be found growing northwards from central California to the southern border of Oregon. They grow at elevations up to 3,000 feet above sea level. Within this strip are two sanctuaries where the trees remain untouched, Redwood National Park (which covers more than 57,600 acres) and, to the south, the 553-acre Muir Woods National Monument. The giant sequoia is found farther inland on the western slope of the Sierra Nevada, growing between 4,000 and 8,000 feet above sea level, in a 16,000,000-acre area. The trees are preserved within Sequoia National Park, Kings Canyon National Park and, to a lesser degree, Yosemite National Park.

LEFT: *Coast redwoods* (Sequoia sempervirens) *rise from the moist soil of Redwood National Park in California. Redwoods are related to trees that were much more widespread more than 65 million years ago.*

LEFT BELOW: *The white-crowned sparrow* (Zonotrichia leucophrys), *breeds across the northern coniferous forest in Alaska and Canada, and also nests throughout much of the west. It is sometimes a bird of residential areas as well as woodlands.*

Other salamanders include the Olympic salamander (*Rhyacotriton olympicus*), the northwestern salamander (*Ambystoma gracile*), long-toed salamander (*A. macrodactylum*), Van Dyke's salamander (*Plethodon vandykei*), western redback salamander (*P. vehiculum*), Oregon quasatina salamander (*Ensatina eschscholtzii*) and roughskin (Pacific) newt (*Taricha granulosa*).

A most unusual amphibian living in the region is the tailed frog (*Ascaphus truei*), so-called because the male bears a tail-like copulatory organ, an adaptation to mating in fast-flowing water, which would otherwise sweep away the sperm before it could fertilize the eggs. The red-legged frog (*Rana aurora*) also inhabits the area, breeding in ponds and quiet streams on the peninsula. At 5 inches long, it is the largest native western frog.

PACIFIC GIANT SALAMANDER

MOIST mountain forest, like that of the Great Smokies and the Olympics, provides prime habitat for salamanders, especially forms that are terrestrial as adults. Abundant moisture is a boon to salamanders, which occur under logs in such conditions, and probably lay their eggs in similar situations.

*Salamanders, isolated by rugged terrain, tend to evolve into highly specialized forms. The Pacific giant salamander (*Dicamptodon ensatus) *lives along the northwestern coast and a few areas in the northern Rockies. These areas may once have been linked.*

More than 60 million years ago, during the Age of Reptiles, more than 40 species of sequoias and redwoods grew over much of the Northern Hemisphere. They flourished for millions of years in North America and Eurasia. The coast redwood and giant sequoia remain, although their natural range has been drastically reduced by the cold temperatures of past glacial periods.

Giant sequoias

The giant sequoia is between 250 and 300 feet high, with a trunk diameter of between 20 and 30 feet. Scientists believe that this magnificent species can live for more than 3,000 years. The General Sherman Tree, in Sequoia National Park, is thought to be between 2,300 and 2,700 years old.

The General Sherman Tree is 274 feet 9 inches high and has a trunk diameter of 36 feet 5 inches. Its first large branch is 130 feet above ground level, and the diameter of its largest branch is almost 7 feet. According to some estimates, the tree weighs 1,385 tons. It is as tall as a 26-story building and its base exceeds the width of many city streets. The tree was discovered on August 7 1879 by James Wolverton. He named it after the General under whom he had served as a First Lieutenant in the Ninth Indiana Cavalry.

The giant sequoia reproduces only by seeds. The Douglas squirrel (*Tamiasciurus douglasi*), a relative of the red squirrel (*T. hudsonicus*) of the boreal forest, gorges on green giant sequoia cones. Driven by a metabolic rate almost twice that of most mammals, the squirrel also cuts and stores cones for the winter. Through cone storage and droppings, the rodent disperses the seeds of the tree, but few seedlings ever develop from cones buried by rodents. Beetle larvae also bore into cones, cutting the veins of the cones and causing them to dry out, so that the seeds drop to the soil.

The giant sequoia is a seed factory. A mature tree produces more than 2,000 cones annually, containing half a million seeds. This is three times the seed-per-cone ratio of the coast redwood. Cones may stay green and closed on the giant sequoia for up to 20 years. Forest fires, however,

The moist conditions of the redwood forests favor the growth of fungi, such as this beautiful fly agaric (Amanita muscaria), which is especially common among conifers. However, fly agaric is considered deadly poisonous.

can dry the cones, so that they open and the seeds explode, falling like a shower to the ground.

Fire can help the giant sequoia by eliminating trees that would compete with the growing sequoia, such as Douglas fir (*Pseudotsuga menziesii*). The parent tree itself is virtually immune to fire. Even at the comparatively young age of a few hundred years, the giant sequoia is armored in porous bark up to 6 inches thick. Mature trees can have bark almost a yard deep. The spongy bark contains little resin, unlike spruces and firs, so it does not fuel the flames.

Coast redwoods

The coast redwood grows taller than the giant sequoia, usually from 300 to 350 feet, and is thought to live for up to 2,000 years. However, based on estimates derived from its trunk circumference, there is one fallen giant sequoia that is thought to have stood 400 feet high. The redwood's trunk diameter is much smaller than the giant sequoia's, and is on average between 8 and 13 feet. The largest coast redwood, Redwood National Park's Tall Tree, is 367 feet 8 inches high, with a trunk diameter of 14 feet. It is estimated to be 700 years old, which is about an average lifespan for the species. Despite the size of the redwood, its seed is only about three times the size of a pinhead.

Young coast redwoods do not bear cones until they are 20 years old. The cones mature in a year, ripening in August and September. Only one out of ten seeds released by a cone germinates.

The redwood seed, which is $\frac{1}{8}$ inch long with small lateral wings, is carried by the air and usually falls within 200 to 400 feet of the parent tree. If conditions are sufficiently moist – which they commonly are because of the humid climate – the seed may germinate in a month, and may grow 2 to 3 inches in its first year.

Coast redwoods also reproduce by sprouting at the stump of the parent tree. Dormant buds grow around the base of the parent tree and, if the tree is severely damaged, the buds sprout, and feed off the roots of the parent. This gives the redwood a major advantage over trees that reproduce by seeds alone. The roots of the mature tree penetrate up to 13 feet into the soil and have been known to spread out 80 feet from the tree.

Redwoods grow tallest on flood plains of streams and under cool, moist conditions. The coastal climate of northern California, where the ocean moderates the climate, provides these conditions. Annual rainfall is from 25 to 122 inches and in summer, warm, moist marine air passing over the cold sea creates fog that often lasts until the afternoon. More fog may be created at the end of the day. In fog, the redwood's water loss through evaporation and transpiration decreases and the soil is moistened, both of which also promote the redwood's growth.

GIANT SEQUOIA AND COAST REDWOOD

THESE are the kings of trees, and indeed of the plant world. The giant sequoia (*Sequoiadendron giganteum*) and coast redwood (*Sequoia sempervirens*) are remnants of a group of trees that grew around the world when dinosaurs ruled the earth. Now, they grow only in a few areas in the mountains along the western rim of the United States. They are, in girth and height, the biggest trees in the world. One redwood, 367 feet 8 inches tall, is the world's highest known tree, although it is possible that, given time, redwoods could grow much taller than this.

Redwoods live for about 2,000 years. Their relatives, the giant sequoias, live twice that long. Not as tall as the redwoods, the sequoias are bigger in terms of bulk. The biggest known giant sequoia stands 274 feet 10 inches above the base, not as tall as the mightiest redwoods, admittedly, but its trunk circumference at its base is 102 feet. It is the largest living thing known to man. So massive is the giant sequoia that its outer bark can be almost a yard thick. Imagine if a member of the dinosaur family were discovered living today; the world would be agog with excitement. We forget that in the plant world, we have giant life forms of the past, as ancient as the dinosaurs and much larger, living today in the coniferous forests of the western rim of North America.

The giant sequoia and coast redwood survive in western mountains of the United States.

| GIANT SEQUOIA | COAST REDWOOD |

SEQUOIA AND REDWOOD DISTRIBUTION MAP

Like the bark of the giant sequoia, coast redwood bark acts as a protective barrier against fire. Stringy and tough, it shields the interior of the tree from all but very hot, repeated fires.

Preservation of the trees

The size of coast redwoods and giant sequoias, their straight trunks and the lasting quality of the wood made them invaluable to the timber industry. Both types of trees were felled in the middle of the last century, with devastating effect. By 1890, however, the 402,482-acre Sequoia National Park (after Yellowstone National Park, the second to be established in the United States) was created. Days later, Yosemite (761,170 acres) followed. Early in this century, lands were added to the protected area, with Kings Canyon National Park (461,901 acres) linked to Sequoia in 1940. Yet more land has been added since.

Conservationists had a more difficult task saving the redwoods, although in 1902 a small state park was created to preserve some redwood habitat. Mature redwoods, however, continued to be felled apace. The Save-the-Redwoods League was organized in 1918 and campaigned long and hard. It added private monies to state park funding to protect groves of redwoods from the ax and chain saw. Finally, in 1968, Congress created Redwood National Park, in order that the trees which had survived when dinosaurs roamed the earth would still grace the landscape.

Wildlife among the trees

The parks that protect the big trees are also a haven for myriad species of wildlife, including many that are imperiled. In Redwood and Sequoia national parks, the endangered peregrine falcon (*Falco peregrinus*) can be seen. The mature forests in the parks provide much-needed habitat for the rare spotted owl (*Strix occidentalis*), which is threatened in many places because its nesting grounds are lost when trees are felled. The wolverine (*Gulo gulo*), extending its range southward via mountain ranges, roves the Sequoia area.

Redwood National Park is the home of a herd of Roosevelt elk, which are the most commonly seen mammals in the park. Redwood and Sequoia national parks are both inhabited by mule deer (*Odocoileus hemionus*) and cougars (*Felis concolor*). Marine animals such as California sea lions (*Zalophus californianus*) and migrating gray whales (*Eschrichtius robustus*) can also be seen from Redwood National Park, which faces the Pacific Ocean.

The
EASTERN
MIXED FOREST

From the Upper Great Lakes region through northern New England and the southern Maritime Provinces, the coniferous forest of the north merges with the fringes of temperate deciduous forest. Sometimes called the Eastern Mixed Forest, this wooded region contains almost 150 species of trees, with maples, oaks and hickories among the dominant types. Since Europeans first arrived on the continent, the original forest has been almost entirely cleared and replaced by new generations of woodlands. Today, however, this forest zone still contains more species of trees than all of Europe.

Red maples (Acer rubrum) *blaze with fall colors in the Great Smoky Mountains National Park. The Great Smokies contain some of the finest deciduous forest in eastern North America.*

THE Eastern Mixed Forest extends west to the Mississippi River and into the Ozark plateau region of southern Missouri, northern Arkansas and eastern Oklahoma. It stretches south to Tennessee and over the lower slopes of the Appalachians to northern Georgia. The mixture of trees in the forest is not uniform. Oaks and hickories dominate in the west and maples in the north, where northern conifers also intrude. In the south, pines characteristic of sandy soils invade the deciduous zone.

Although the expanse covered by the Eastern Mixed Forest includes some of the nation's most urbanized areas and has been intensively exploited for nearly three centuries, this realm still contains deep wildernesses. Moreover, even in highly populated areas, a rich variety of plants and wildlife is evident, including some of the most adaptable species on the continent.

The northern transition

The boreal forest changes to deciduous forest over less than 200 miles. The deciduous tree that most characterizes this transitional zone is the sugar maple (*Acer saccharum*), which grows up to 100 feet tall and is the source of New England's famed maple syrup. In autumn, the brilliant reds and yellows of the sugar maple, and yellow of the American beech (*Fagus grandifolia*), lend a beauty to these woodlands unparalleled by any other fall foliage display in the States. Alongside sugar maples and beeches grow trees typical of the boreal forest, such as eastern white pines (*Pinus strobus*),

red spruce (*Picea rubra*), as well as trees characteristic of the mixed forest, such as northern red oak (*Quercus rubra*) and red maple (*A. rubrum*).

The Great Smoky Mountains

South of the transitional zone, the Eastern Mixed Forest comes into its own, despite the fact that over the years many of its trees have fallen before the ax, and later the chain saw and bulldozer. It is still possible, however, to see the forest almost as it appeared to the early pioneers and to the native Americans before them. The Great Smoky Mountains of eastern Tennessee and western North Carolina contain the largest remaining tract of essentially unaltered forest east of the Mississippi.

More than 95 per cent of the 512,000 acres of Great Smoky Mountains National Park is dominated by forests, almost half of them near virgin. More than 1,300 kinds of flowering plants, 350 mosses and liverworts, 230 lichens and 2,000 fungi have been recorded in the park. The region has more than 100 species of native trees, some of which reach record proportions there. The lushness and profusion of plant life in the Smokies and, for that matter, in almost all the southern Appalachians, are due to abundant rainfall and the richness of the soil. The great Pleistocene ice sheets never extended that far south and thus did not scour the landscape as in the north.

Cove, hemlock and hardwood forest

The most primeval of Great Smokies' forest grows in sheltered areas below 4,500 feet, much of it in

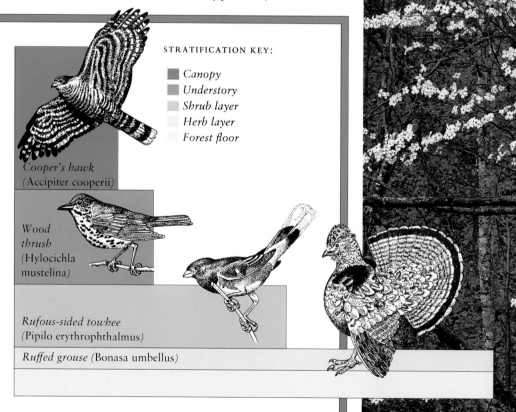

DECIDUOUS FOREST STRATIFICATION

ANY forest, whatever its type, is layered into zones from the treetops to the ground. The boundaries between the different layers, however, are not always distinct. The crowns of the tall trees in the deciduous forest form the canopy layer. Below that, where smaller trees reach their peak, is the understory. Shrubs form the next layer down, while the small plants that grow on the forest floor make up the herb layer. Lowest of the layers is the forest floor itself. Some animals range through all or most layers, while others stay in just one.

Ruffed grouse nest on the forest floor, while the towhee frequently nests just above the floor. Wood thrushes commonly nest in the understory and Cooper's hawks in the canopy.

STRATIFICATION KEY:

■ Canopy
■ Understory
▨ Shrub layer
□ Herb layer
□ Forest floor

Cooper's hawk (Accipiter cooperii)

Wood thrush (Hylocichla mustelina)

Rufous-sided towhee (Pipilo erythrophthalmus)

Ruffed grouse (Bonasa umbellus)

The flowering dogwood (Cornus florida) *and* *eastern redbud* (Cercis canadensis) *pictured in the Great Smoky Mountains National Park. Their blooms rival those of wildflowers.*

great ravines called coves. Common cove forest trees include yellow buckeye (*Aesculus octandra*), white basswood (*Tilia heterophylla*), sugar maple, red oak, white ash (*Fraxinus americana*) and yellow poplar (*Liriodendron tulipifera*). The last-mentioned, which has tulip-like flowers and a magnificently straight trunk, can reach 200 feet in height. Slightly lower in altitude, on slopes and along streams, eastern hemlocks (*Tsuga canadensis*) grow thickly together with deciduous species. Of all the conifers hemlocks are among the most adapted to growing in the shade, which enables them to secure footholds among mature deciduous trees. Between the cove and hemlock forests and the coniferous woods of the summits lies a narrow band of hardwood forest, somewhat similar to that of the transition zone to the north.

Oak-hickory forest

West of the Appalachians the forest contains a greater variety and abundance of oaks and hickories, such as the shagbark hickory (*Carya ovata*) and bitternut hickory (*C. cordiformis*). For example, out of almost 70 species of trees in the 52,480-acre Mammoth Cave National Park of western Kentucky (probably the world's longest cave system), four are hickories and 11 are oaks. No other group of trees in the park has as many species as either of these two. Through most parts of Ohio, Indiana and Illinois, however, there is little forest to be seen, since much of the land has been put to agricultural use. In primeval times, parts of Ohio, Indiana and Illinois had no forest at all, but were covered in eastern extensions of the tallgrass prairie that is the dominant vegetation type west of the Mississippi River.

West of the Mississippi, before the trees give way to prairie, the oak-hickory forest reaches its zenith on the rugged terrain of the Ozarks, an area of 55,000 square miles of upland that looks mountainous. However, the upland is actually on a plateau which has been eroded and carved over eons into rugged ridges and valleys.

The floral carpet

The moist, rich forest floor and sunlit clearings of the Eastern Mixed Forest can be a natural garden of many-colored wildflowers, ferns, mushrooms, lichens, mosses and other low-growing plants. Wildflowers abound, especially in spring, before leaf growth on the trees intercepts the sunlight. Many woodland wildflowers, such as the fragile yellow lady's slipper (*Cypripedium parviflorum*), are becoming increasingly rare.

The colors and types of woodland flowers are endless. They include the bright red cardinal flower (*Lobelia cardinalis*), the purple gay wings (*Polyga paucifolia*) and the yellow woodland sunflower (*Helianthus divaricatus*). The Turk's cap lily (*Lilium superbum*) is an edge species which grows in the geographical area encompassed by the Eastern Mixed Forest, and can be seen along roadsides or stream edges where there is sun. It has nodding flowers of darkly speckled orange-red. The rose pogonia (*Pogonia ophioglossoides*), which favors bogs and swamps, has small, fragrant flowers of rosy pink. Dutchman's breeches (*Dicentra cucullaria*) are creamy white. The flower of the Indian pipe (*Monotropa uniflora*) is white or pink. Looking as if it were made of white wax, this plant obtains nutrients from living trees with the aid of fungus: the fungus provides a connection between the roots of the Indian pipe and the roots of the surrounding trees.

OPPOSITE: *Water tupelo* (Nyssa aquatica), *trees of the south-eastern United States, intrude into the Eastern Mixed Forest along its southern and western margins, such as here in Missouri's Mark Twain National Forest.*

ABOVE: *The yellow lady's slipper* (Cypripedium parviflorum), *an orchid, is one of the rare and beautiful wildflowers that grow in the deciduous forest from Nova Scotia to Alabama. This orchid prefers moist areas.*

LEFT: *This jack-in-the-pulpit* (Arisaema atrorubens) *is one of several members of its genus found from Nova Scotia to Florida. Many species of songbirds feed on its red fruit, which appears in the fall.*

WILDLIFE

Approximately halfway between Boston and New York, in the populous North-east Corridor, lies Killingworth, Connecticut. The state of Connecticut as a whole is one of the most urbanized in the nation. However, many small town communities near public forest land, park, or protected watershed remain somewhat rural, and typify the Eastern Mixed Forest region.

Killingworth is a typical microcosm of the Eastern Mixed Forest region. It is by no means urban, but neither is it wilderness. Some of the creatures there would not be able to thrive without at least the moderate areas of woodland that exist in the vicinity. Many others, however, can survive around and even in cities as well as in the hinterlands.

In Killingworth, wildlife often encroaches on human territory, entering gardens from the woodlands of brush, oaks and maples behind the town. Common raccoons (*Procyon lotor*) and Virginia opossums (*Didelphis virginiana*) will sometimes poach food set out for a cat, while whitetail deer (*Odocoileus virginianus*) will browse on low brush at the edge of the trees. Such creatures represent three groups of mammals, and all of these creatures have readily adapted to substantial human presence in their forest environment.

Adaptable species

Of all wild animals the raccoon is probably the best adapted to a human environment. This ring-tailed, black-masked creature, which can be found from southernmost Canada to Central America, derives its name from the Algonquin Indian word 'arakun', meaning 'he who scratches with his hands'. The reference is to the raccoon's extremely dexterous, hand-like front paws with flexible digits used to manipulate food items.

The raccoon weighs between about 10 and 40 pounds. A carnivore, but essentially omnivorous, it eats an incredible variety of foods, from crayfish to corn. Leftovers from the human dinner table provide a bounty for raccoons, which regularly raid trash cans in backyards and campsites. Animals killed on roads also create a food supply that raccoons lacked in an earlier era. Although the spread of human settlements has caused many of the large trees in which they like to den to be felled, it has not meant a shortage of accommodation, as racoons will readily hole-up in empty buildings, culverts and other man-made structures.

This ability to adapt has helped raccoons survive even in the midst of large cities. They flourish in several New York City parks, for example, including Manhattan's Central Park. In experiments in Cincinnati, biologists observed that raccoons quickly learned to use an underpass in order to cross a newly constructed highway safely.

A raccoon (Procyon lotor) peers from its den tree. Raccoons have proven to be one of the most adaptable mammals in North America, living in myriad habitats. Raccoons do not hibernate, but accumulate fat reserves during summer and the fall to see them through the winter.

Another mammalian survival expert that manages at least as well in populated areas as in the wilderness is the eastern gray squirrel (*Sciurus carolinensis*), for which the hardwood forest, with its nuts and acorns, is an optimum habitat. When Europeans arrived in North America, perhaps a billion gray squirrels inhabited the Eastern Mixed Forest. Squirrels formed part of the staple diet of pioneer American woodsmen and their families, who shot them with muskets and Kentucky long rifles; these weapons came to be known as squirrel guns. Many of the woodsmen who defeated the Black Watch regiment at the Battle of New Orleans had honed their marksmanship while subsistence hunting for squirrels. Introduced into Europe, the gray squirrel quickly adapted and now far outnumbers native squirrels.

The squirrel of the woods behaves very differently from the half-tame creature that begs for peanuts in urban parks and raids bird feeders in suburban backyards. The former is a wary woodland will-o'-the-wisp with lightning moves, that feeds most heavily around dawn.

Gray squirrels habitually store acorns and nuts an inch or two deep in the forest floor. Since forgotten caches often sprout into seedlings, the gray squirrel is a prime agent of tree distribution.

In the north-east much agricultural land has reverted to forest, and this has encouraged the population growth of the whitetail deer. The best whitetail habitat is the point at which open country and deep woods meet, such as where forest edges old pasture, golf courses or highway. There the deer browse on leaves, buds and twigs in addition to eating mast (including hickory nuts, beech nuts and the fallen acorn crop), agricultural legumes such as alfalfa, and other crops.

Improved habitat, coupled with the disappearance of major predators – a situation which may be reversed by the relatively recent appearance of the coyote (*Canis latrans*) in the east – has expanded whitetail numbers so significantly this century that in certain areas deer are considered a nuisance. Suburban householders complain about whitetail plundering in backyards, and collisions between deer and motor vehicles are common.

Whitetails in the vicinity of human settlements tend to be more nocturnal than their wilderness counterparts, feeding from late afternoon into the night, and resuming in the early morning hours. They bed down in brush, swamps and, sometimes, in out-of-the-way fields. They have dun coats which blend with the trees and brush, and are wary animals. Such qualities help them to thrive even on the edges of major cities – which is unusual for animals of their size (they often surpass 200 pounds in weight) and when you consider that they are hunted by man.

In some areas whitetails have reached numbers that threaten to surpass the carrying capacity of the habitat, prompting state wildlife agencies to increase the hunting limit on the species. Control of the number of deer hunted remains a key wildlife management tool for maintaining healthy populations of flourishing game species such as the whitetail.

Changes in wildlife patterns

Sound wildlife management by state and federal agencies coupled with a resultant change in habitat have brought the return of important species to parts of the Eastern Mixed Forest, from which they vanished long ago.

Reclamation of agricultural land for forest has permitted wildlife departments of many states to reintroduce wild turkeys (*Meleagris gallopavo*) over much of their former range. Slim and swift – over short distances they can fly fast as a hawk and outrun a person – wild turkeys are one of North America's largest game birds, sometimes surpassing 20 pounds in weight.

Millions of these magnificent birds once inhabited the deciduous forests of the east as well as mixed pine and oak forests in the south-east. Hardwoods provide essential mast and seeds for wild turkeys, as well as perches for roosting at night. As forests were felled, turkeys vanished from areas where they had previously thrived. Those few that remained, however, provided a reservoir from which birds were relocated and re-established. Today there are wild turkeys in more than 40 states. A quarter of a century ago, Connecticut had no wild turkeys, but now they can occasionally be seen on the fringes of towns.

Some animals have naturally re-emerged. The black bear (*Ursus americanus*) no longer existed in southern New England 50 years ago. Gradually, however, bears from northern New England and New York State spread into Massachusetts, where

ABOVE: *Whitetail deer (Odocoileus virginianus) range throughout the Eastern Mixed Forest. They happily survive amidst large numbers of people.*

ABOVE RIGHT: *The aggressive northern mockingbird (Mimus polyglottos), a southern native, colonized New England during the middle of this century.*

LEFT: *This opossum (Didelphis virginiana), only three months old, belongs to a species that is highly adaptable.*

a breeding population developed. During the 1980s, bears appeared in Connecticut with increasing frequency and there are now a few that have become breeding residents.

Like the whitetail, the black bear can be surprisingly elusive for such a large animal. The bear is omnivorous, so if one food is unavailable it readily turns to another. Black bears, however, need a home range of at least 5 square miles. Their need for space suggests they will never be abundant in areas with large human populations. They should prosper, however, in regions such as northern New England, upstate New York, the Pennsylvania mountains and the southern Appalachians.

Invading species

Since the beginning of the century, the northern marshes of the Eastern Mixed Forest have been invaded by species which have not previously been seen in these areas. The cardinal (*Cardinalis cardinalis*) and mockingbird (*Mimus polyglottos*) gradually spread from the south-east and now are familiar birds as far north as southern Canada. The same is true of the Virginia opossum (*Didelphis virginiana*), the only native marsupial north of the Mexican border. During severe northern winters, the frostbitten tips of the opossum's naked tail and ears testify to its southern origins.

Few invading species have created more of a sensation than the coyote (*Canis latrans*), which rivals the raccoon for its ability to adapt. The coyote's traditional range covered the western half of North America from the fringes of the tropics to the Arctic. By the middle of this century, however, coyotes were spreading east through the upper Mid-west and southern Canada. Today, the coyote is established as a member of the Eastern Mixed Forest fauna and has spread as well into the south-east.

New York and New England woodlands now echo to the howl of the coyote. This wild dog – which preys on creatures ranging in size from mice to deer – also resides in suburban and even urbanized areas in the east and west, and an estimated several thousand coyotes live within the city limits of Los Angeles.

Eastern coyotes are considered a separate race from their western brethren. The eastern coyote is about a third larger than its western counterpart, weighing up to 40 pounds. Some scientists believe the size increase resulted from interbreeding with wolves as coyotes migrated across Canada.

MAMMALS Myriad small mammals find good hunting amidst the rich humus of the forest floor. These include one of the smallest known living mammals, the pygmy shrew (*Sorex hoyi*), which weighs as little as a ninth of an ounce. Typical of shrews, it is a fierce hunter, consuming vast numbers of earthworms, insects and other small creatures. This variety of prey also constitutes the diet of the moles which tunnel vigorously under the surface of the forest floor.

Rodents are the most common forest mammals. The woodchuck (*Marmota monax*) is another of those creatures that have benefited from human activity, since it is an edge species (a species that lives at the interface of two different habitats). A 10-pound member of the squirrel family (Sciuridae), the woodchuck digs burrows for itself in the soil. Abandoned burrows offer ready-made homes for red foxes (*Vulpes vulpes*), striped skunks (*Mephitis mephitis*), cottontail rabbits (*Sylvilagus*) and several other mammals.

At night in the forest the flying squirrels (*Glaucomys*) emerge. The southern species (*G. volans*) is most common in the mixed forest while the northern (*G. sabrinus*) prefers the northern coniferous forests. Broad flaps of skin spread between their front and rear limbs enable these large-eyed rodents to glide between trees. Steering with the skin flaps and tail, flying squirrels are regularly airborne for 20 or 30 feet, and sometimes manage flights of more than 50 yards. Many other small nocturnal rodents, typically the deer mouse (*Peromyscus maniculatus*) and white-footed mouse (*P. leucopus*), forage for nuts, seeds or insects on the forest floor.

Small rodents are the targets of carnivores such as the ermine (*Mustela erminea*) and longtail weasel (*M. frenata*). During winter in northern areas their brown coats turn white as snow, except for a black tail tip. One of the largest felines of the deciduous forest is the bobcat (*Felis rufus*), which weighs about 25 pounds, and is about 55 inches

*Nocturnal, solitary and secretive, the bobcat (*Felis rufus*) closely resembles the lynx (*Lynx canadensis*) of the boreal forest, which it replaces in the deciduous forest. This wild cat is so elusive that it is seldom seen, even where it is not uncommon. During the spring mating season, however, its nocturnal yowling can reveal its presence.*

THE LIFE CYCLE OF THE MONARCH

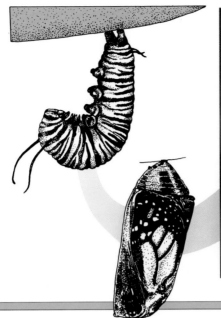

*T*HE monarch butterfly (*Danaus plexippus*) lays its eggs only on the undersides of milkweed (*Asclepias*) leaves. The caterpillar goes through five stages and then becomes a pupa. The caterpillar skin is discarded and a hard shell, the chrysalis, forms. The butterfly develops within the chrysalis.

The caterpillar hangs by silk in a J-shape as the pupa develops. The skin splits and the chrysalis forms, then the pupa develops into the adult butterfly.

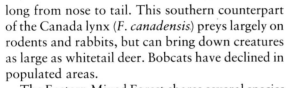

long from nose to tail. This southern counterpart of the Canada lynx (*F. canadensis*) preys largely on rodents and rabbits, but can bring down creatures as large as whitetail deer. Bobcats have declined in populated areas.

The Eastern Mixed Forest shares several species of bats with other regions of the continent. The little brown bat (*Myotis lucifugus*), the eastern pipistrel (*Pipistrellus subflavus*) and the big brown bat (*Eptesicus fuscus*) are among the most common species to be seen.

BIRDS The mixed forest of the east hosts four different groups of birds. Some birds, such as the ubiquitous blue jay (*Cyanocitta cristata*), inhabit the region year round. Others winter in the far

A surprising variety of wildlife exists even within large metropolitan areas. Central Park in New York City, for example, is a major birding spot. Even rare creatures, such as this barn owl (Tyto alba) being chased by a common crow (Corvus brachyrhynchos) across the sky of New York City's Staten Island, sometimes inhabit cities.

One of the most spectacular forest birds of eastern North America is the pileated woodpecker (Dryocopus pileatus), *which drills large, oblong holes in trees.*

south and breed in the mixed forest during spring and summer. The vociferous ovenbird (*Seiurus aurocapillus*), a wood warbler that makes an oven-shaped nest on the ground, is one of the latter. During spring and fall, birds such as these, including the bay-breasted warbler (*Dendroica castanea*), pass through the mixed forest on migration. Conversely, the American tree sparrow (*Spizella arborea*) nests in the northern woodlands and winters in mixed forest.

There is an ever-changing and great variety of birds in the mixed forest and cities of the eastern region. Out of approximately 700 bird species north of the Mexican border, more than half appear in New York City at one time of year or another.

Neighboring rural areas display a further variety of bird life. In Killingworth woodpeckers thrive among trees. These include the pileated wood-pecker (*Dryocopus pileatus*), the largest wood-pecker commonly found in North America. A big woods bird the size of a crow, this has a flaming red capped head. Others to be found include the red-bellied (*Melanerpes carolinus*), the hairy (*Picoides villosus*) and downy (*P. pubescens*) woodpeckers. Mourning doves (*Zenaida macroura*) can be seen daily. In common with pigeons (of the same family, Columbidae), mourning doves have an unusual method of feeding their young. The lining of the adult dove's crop secretes a nutritious liquid known as pigeon's milk, which chemically resembles the milk of a rabbit. For most of their two-week duration in the nest, the young doves live on this secretion.

Several other species often share year-round residence with the woodpeckers and doves. In Killingworth, the piercing song of the Carolina wren (*Thryothorus ludovicianus*) can be heard at any time of the year, and so can the hooting of a barred owl (*Strix varia*) or great horned owl (*Bubo virginianus*) at night. Black-capped chickadees (*Parus atricapillus*) and tufted titmice (*P. bicolor*) can also be seen in any season.

During the winter, the resident chickadees and titmice are joined by flocks of slate-colored juncos (*Junco hyemalis*) and white-throated sparrows (*Zonotrichia albicollis*) from the north. Pine siskins (*Carduelis pinus*) are abundant some years and rare other years, depending on the availability of seeds in the northern coniferous forest. In years when the northern crop fails, the siskins head south into the mixed forest.

BACKYARD FEEDER BIRDS

PROVIDING seeds for birds at backyard and window feeders has become a popular hobby, especially in winter, when species resident year round and migrants from the north are hard put to find enough food. Typical resident birds in the Killingworth area are black-capped chickadees (*Parus atricapillus*) and white-breasted nuthatches (*Sitta carolinensis*). Migrants such as white-throated sparrows (*Zonotrichia albicollis*) often winter near feeders. Unusual northern birds sometimes show up during population irruptions.

When food is in short supply in the boreal forest during the winter, large flocks of evening grosbeaks (Coccothraustes vespertinus) will visit backyard feeders.

Mid-winter may be highlighted by the sight of a bald eagle (*Haliaeetus leucocephalus*) soaring overhead. Scores of eagles now winter on the lower Connecticut River, although as yet none have remained to breed.

Early spring brings the first breeders from the southern United States northward: red-winged blackbirds (*Agelaius phoenicus*), common grackles (*Quiscalus quiscula*) and American robins (*Turdus migratorius*), arriving in that order. Later, ruby-throated hummingbirds (*Archilochus colubris*) and great crested flycatchers (*Myiarchus crinitus*), breeding species that winter in the tropics, arrive. Before summer red-shouldered hawks (*Buteo lineatus*) return to their large stick nests which they make in oaks and red-tailed hawks (*B. jamaicensis*) wheel overhead in mating flights. The broad-winged hawk (*B. platypterus*) winters in the tropics, leaving the mixed forest as the days grow short in autumn. The red-tailed hawk often remains in the mixed forest for winter.

During the spring, and less so in autumn, thickets buzz with the twittering of warblers, resting after a night's journey through the region in flights of mixed species. The early days of autumn may be marked by the appearance of a solitary migrating green-backed heron (*Butorides striatus*) or great blue heron (*Ardea herodias*), which will sometimes stop to feed in garden ponds.

By October, sharp-shinned hawks (*Accipiter striatus*) migrating south fly overhead on air currents over ridges. These hawks will sometimes remain until winter, preying on songbirds feeding in backyards.

HAWK MIGRATIONS

DURING migrations, hawks and other birds of prey save energy by riding thermals. These are updrafts of warm air that rise as the air is forced upwards as it encounters ridges and mountains. The long, north-east–south-west trending ridges of the Appalachians are a key aerial highway for hawks, which in late summer and fall travel south along the mountain chain in vast numbers. Hawk Mountain, on Pennsylvania's Kittatinny Ridge in the Blue Mountains of the Appalachians, causes strong thermals that sometimes draw thousands of hawks on a single day. Among the species that pass overhead are red-tailed hawks (*Buteo jamaicensis*), red-shouldered hawks (*B. lineatus*), broad-winged hawks (*B. platypterus*), sharp-shinned hawks (*Accipiter striatus*), Cooper's hawks (*A. cooperii*), northern goshawks (*A. gentilis*), northern, or hen, harriers (*Circus cyaneus*), ospreys (*Pandion haliaetus*) and turkey vultures (*Cathartes aura*). Some species peak in numbers over Hawk Mountain at specific periods between August and November. One study showed that the majority of the broad-winged hawks travel past in September, while the largest numbers of red-tailed hawks are seen in mid-October through early November. Sharp-shinned hawk numbers begin increasing in late September, peak at the beginning of October and then level off, ending in November.

The red-shouldered hawk (Buteo lineatus) flies with several quick wingbeats, then a glide.

*Recognizable by the vivid gold, yellow or cream collar around its neck, the slender northern ringneck snake (*Diadophis punctatus*) feeds on small amphibians and reptiles, as well as on earthworms and insects.*

REPTILES AND AMPHIBIANS These creatures also appear seasonally as they do in wet habitats throughout the deciduous forests of eastern North America. In autumn, when the air becomes crisp, they go into hibernation in the forest floor, on pond bottoms or in any number of other hidden places, only emerging in spring.

By late February or early March, when ice thaws, the male wood frogs (*Rana sylvatica*) begin to call from murky water beneath red maples in seasonal woody swamps. This is a finger-length species of frog, bronze in color with a black mask somewhat reminiscent of the raccoon's. This cold-weather amphibian is able to live as far north as the tundra.

A chorus of wood frogs so much resembles the quacking of ducks that the noise is often mistaken for the sound of waterfowl. Wood frogs mate in a frenzy, with males frantically swimming after and trying to clamber on to females. By April, the frogs have dispersed throughout the woodlands and are replaced by spring peepers (*Hyla crucifer*).

Throughout the spring and summer, the sounds of night herald new arrivals to breeding ponds. The flute-like call of the American toad (*Bufo americanus*) trills through the air soon after the peepers arrive. The toad's call is followed by the pickerel frog (*Rana palustris*) giving forth its low-pitched

snore, and then the twanging 'plunk' of the green frog (*R. clamitans*) and the basso profundo 'jug-o-rum' of the bullfrog (*R. catesbeiana*). The bullfrog, at 6 inches long, is the largest frog to be found north of Mexico.

Painted turtles (*Chrysemys picta*) and spotted turtles (*Clemmys guttata*) frequent the ponds during the warm months. Occasionally, an eastern box turtle (*Terrapene carolina*) or a wood turtle (*Clemmys insculpta*), a land-dwelling species, can be seen.

Killingworth backyards with ponds may also be visited by the common garter snake (*Thamnophis sirtalis*), the most widely distributed snake in North America. It prefers to live near water, where it finds the amphibians that constitute a major portion of its diet. Occasionally, the brown snake (*Storeria dekayi*) may be seen in a backyard, or a small ringneck snake (*Diadophis punctatus*) may emerge from under logs or rocks. Astonishingly the brown snake has also been found in vacant lots in the heart of Manhattan.

Two venomous snakes typical of the Eastern Mixed Forest are the copperhead (*Agkistrodon contortrix*), an unaggressive, venomous pit viper patterned like the leaves of the forest floor, and the more dangerous timber rattlesnake (*Crotalus horridus*), which is rare in Connecticut. In the

Many species of salamanders inhabit Killingworth. The first warm spring rains send spotted salamanders (*Ambystoma maculatum*) to mate in swamps where the wood frogs breed. Eastern newts (*Notophthalmus viridescens*) inhabit ponds. The newts hatch as gill-bearing larvae and transform into terrestrial forms, red efts, which in turn become air-breathing but aquatic adults.

No area of North America provides a better habitat for salamanders than the moist forests of the southern Appalachians. The Great Smoky Mountains National Park alone has more than 27 kinds of salamanders.

Several southern Appalachian salamanders are restricted to only a few sites. The so-called imitator salamander (*Desmognathus ochrophaeus*) inhabits a tiny portion of the Great Smokies. The Shenandoah salamander (*Plethodon shenandoah*) lives only in Shenandoah National Park in Virginia's Blue Ridge Mountains. The West Virginia spring salamander (*Gyrinophilus subterraneus*) is known to inhabit only one stream in the General Davis Cave, West Virginia.

DESTRUCTION OF THE FOREST

Uniquely rare creatures remain in the Eastern Mixed Forest and others have returned to it, and this region has more wildlife and wild places than it did at the beginning of the century. Ironically, however, forest conservation is in the balance. Environmental hazards such as acid rain threaten the trees, and rapid industrial and agricultural development imperil both woodland and wildlife. At the same time, a growing public awareness of endangered habitats has encouraged conservation efforts; but in spite of these the future of the forest is as yet by no means certain.

suburban town of Glastonbury, however, lies a hilly area where this species dens (denning occurs communally) in the winter. Twenty years ago, this area was rural but is now surrounded by housing developments, and residents have little appreciation of the snakes, even though the state has declared them an endangered species.

SPRING PEEPER

THE spring peeper (*Hyla crucifer*) is a tiny tree frog about 1 inch long — almost small enough to sit on your thumbnail. It lives in much of the eastern half of the country, its habitat being moist woodlands, and breeds in just about any water it can find during the spring. The calling of peepers, which when several are in chorus sounds not altogether unlike distant sleigh bells, is in many areas an early sign of spring. Individually, however, the call is a note that is high and clear – a kind of 'peereep, peereep'. Only the males call, to attract mates.

Approximate size

A spring peeper prepares to call (above). When it calls, it fills its throat sac with air (right), and, with nostrils and mouth sealed, pumps the air over the inflated skin pouch.

MOUNTAINS

The major Eurasian mountain systems such as the Alps and Himalayas lie on an east to west axis. Those of North America tend north to south, crossing latitudes ranging from Arctic to tropical. Because temperature decreases with altitude, on their heights the North American mountain systems extend northern environments hundreds, even thousands, of miles to the south into temperate regions, while the lower slopes support the same types of plants and animals that inhabit surrounding lowlands.

The majestic Grand Tetons in Grand Teton National Park, Wyoming, rise more than a mile above the landscape around them. These jagged peaks stand in a wilderness area where many forms of wildlife, including North America's largest herd of elk, or wapiti (Cervus elaphus), roam.

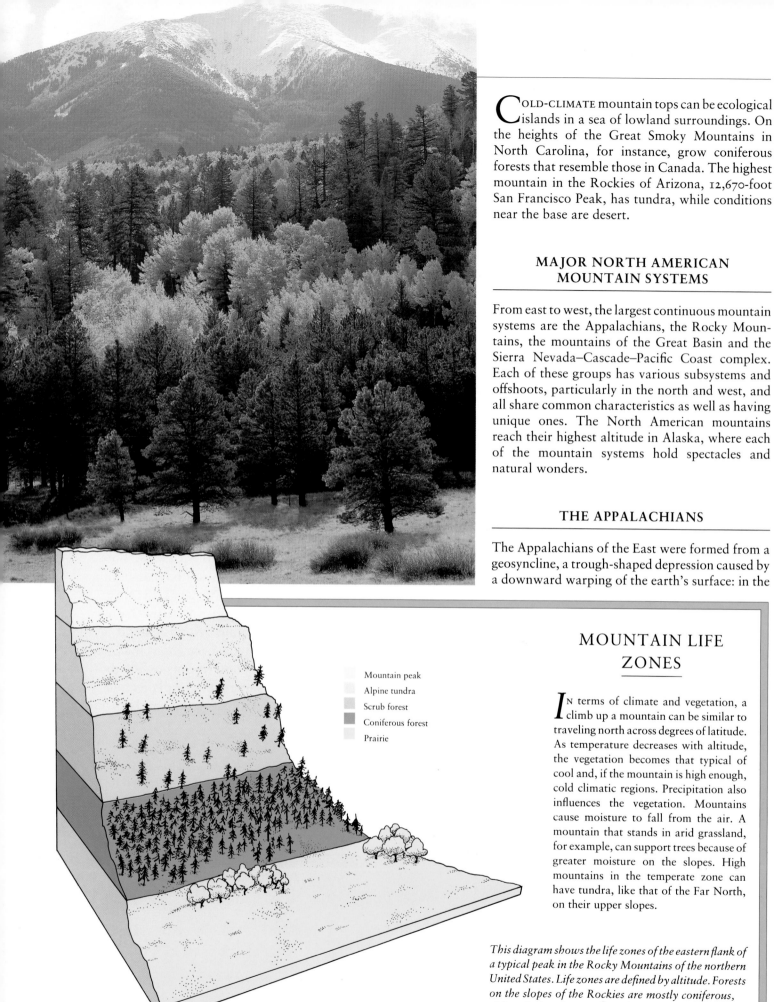

COLD-CLIMATE mountain tops can be ecological islands in a sea of lowland surroundings. On the heights of the Great Smoky Mountains in North Carolina, for instance, grow coniferous forests that resemble those in Canada. The highest mountain in the Rockies of Arizona, 12,670-foot San Francisco Peak, has tundra, while conditions near the base are desert.

MAJOR NORTH AMERICAN MOUNTAIN SYSTEMS

From east to west, the largest continuous mountain systems are the Appalachians, the Rocky Mountains, the mountains of the Great Basin and the Sierra Nevada–Cascade–Pacific Coast complex. Each of these groups has various subsystems and offshoots, particularly in the north and west, and all share common characteristics as well as having unique ones. The North American mountains reach their highest altitude in Alaska, where each of the mountain systems hold spectacles and natural wonders.

THE APPALACHIANS

The Appalachians of the East were formed from a geosyncline, a trough-shaped depression caused by a downward warping of the earth's surface: in the

Mountain peak
Alpine tundra
Scrub forest
Coniferous forest
Prairie

MOUNTAIN LIFE ZONES

IN terms of climate and vegetation, a climb up a mountain can be similar to traveling north across degrees of latitude. As temperature decreases with altitude, the vegetation becomes that typical of cool and, if the mountain is high enough, cold climatic regions. Precipitation also influences the vegetation. Mountains cause moisture to fall from the air. A mountain that stands in arid grassland, for example, can support trees because of greater moisture on the slopes. High mountains in the temperate zone can have tundra, like that of the Far North, on their upper slopes.

This diagram shows the life zones of the eastern flank of a typical peak in the Rocky Mountains of the northern United States. Life zones are defined by altitude. Forests on the slopes of the Rockies are mostly coniferous, although they do support a few deciduous trees.

MOUNTAINS AND TUNDRA

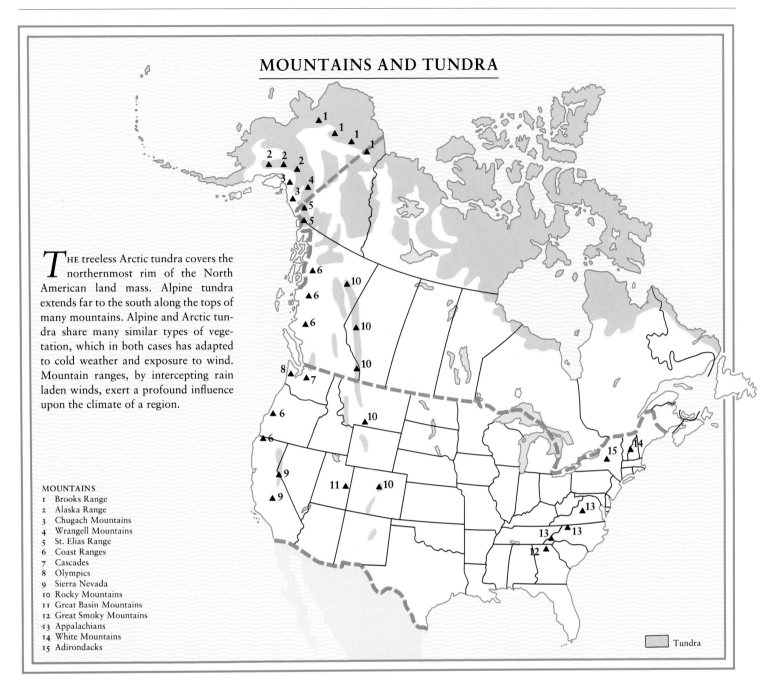

*T*HE treeless Arctic tundra covers the northernmost rim of the North American land mass. Alpine tundra extends far to the south along the tops of many mountains. Alpine and Arctic tundra share many similar types of vegetation, which in both cases has adapted to cold weather and exposure to wind. Mountain ranges, by intercepting rain laden winds, exert a profound influence upon the climate of a region.

MOUNTAINS
1   Brooks Range
2   Alaska Range
3   Chugach Mountains
4   Wrangell Mountains
5   St. Elias Range
6   Coast Ranges
7   Cascades
8   Olympics
9   Sierra Nevada
10   Rocky Mountains
11   Great Basin Mountains
12   Great Smoky Mountains
13   Appalachians
14   White Mountains
15   Adirondacks

    Tundra

area where the mountains now stand, sediments gradually accumulated up to 40,000 feet thick. The earth's surface sank under all that weight, warping, then folded up, while in some areas volcanism sent molten rock out of the earth's crust. The risen earth gradually eroded into a broad plain. Geological processes in the earth raised the landscape. Eventually, the present Appalachian landscape emerged, with parallel chains of ancient mountains (such as the White Mountains of New Hampshire and the Green Mountains of Vermont) separated by long, verdant valleys (such as the Connecticut River Valley). While it is difficult to say when any mountain range really began, because mountains are formed on top of older mountains, the Appalachians are thought to have arisen about 500 million years ago.

The Appalachians extend over almost 2,000

miles, from the Long Range Mountains of Newfoundland to the foothills in Alabama. They peak in North Carolina, where Mount Mitchell, rising to 6,684 feet above sea level, makes the highest point east of the Mississippi River. However, they are most rugged in northern New England, where Mount Washington, at 6,288 feet above sea level in the Presidential Range of New Hampshire's White Mountains, is a bare-topped, granite peak that experiences some of the most severe winter weather on earth.

Ice age glaciers never reached the southern Appalachians, but in the north they gouged grooves in the granite, left behind huge boulders and carved out round valleys, called cirques, all of which are prominent features today. The best known cirque is the White Mountains' Tuckerman's Ravine, where snow lasts until July; here a

OPPOSITE: *Quaking aspen* (Populus tremuloides) *and ponderosa pines* (Pinus ponderosa), *typical of cool climates, grow in the high country of Arizona's San Francisco peaks, which rise from warm desert grassland and scrub.*

MOUNT WASHINGTON

Mount Washington, in the Presidential Range of New Hampshire's White Mountains, has what many experts believe is the worst weather in North America. Although you can reach the summit in summer by automobile or a cog railroad, more than 30 hikers have died on this mountain. Winds above 100 miles an hour rake the summit every month of the year. The highest wind ever recorded outside a tornado, at 231 miles an hour, swept the peak in April 1934. January temperatures at the peak average 5.8°F. Summer temperatures average in the mid-forties. The mean annual temperature is 26.9°F. Especially dangerous to hikers is that the weather can change instantaneously. A warm summer sun can disappear behind chill fog and wind can create a wind chill factor near zero even in midsummer. The mountain can be draped in fog and clouds for days at a time. These meteorological conditions make the climate atop Mount Washington similar to that of the Arctic.

The bleak summit of Mount Washington is mostly barren rock, encrusted with mosses and lichens, and tundra. Timberline in the Presidential Range varies between 4,800 feet and 5,200 feet, depending on exposure to the wind. Timberline runs in an unbroken stretch along the tops of the Presidentials for more than 8 miles.

During the fall, the forest on the lower slopes of New Hampshire's Presidential Range blazes with the gorgeous reds and oranges that make New England a mecca for foliage viewers. Above the forest towers rugged Mount Adams. The peaks of the Presidentials undergo some of the fiercest weather on the continent. Though hardly more than a mile high, many of the peaks are above the timberline.

slight drop in average annual temperature could give rise to a small glacier – although given the present worldwide climatic conditions, which give rise to theories that global warming is on the increase, this is unlikely to happen.

Different life zones belt a mountain according to altitude. In the White Mountains these zones are clearly marked by the distribution of vegetation. At the foot of the White Mountains grow trees of the transitional belt between the boreal and Eastern Mixed Forests, such as sugar maples (*Acer saccharum*). Higher up are boreal trees such as the black spruce (*Picea mariana*). At the timberline, which is as low as 4,800 feet above sea level, trees including the black spruce, which grow to 50 feet or more on the lower slopes, are only a few inches high, forming mats of gnarled dwarf trees, known as krummholz. Above the timberline is tundra, where temperatures can drop to below freezing at any time of year.

The warmer southern Appalachians, though higher in altitude, do not rise above the timberline. Although untouched by glaciers, the southern Appalachians were probably capped with snow during the ice ages. Northern plants began to spread into these southern mountains ahead of the advancing glaciers, but retreated north or remained only on mountain tops as glaciers melted. The red spruce (*Picea rubens*), found in northern New England and south-eastern Canada, also grows on the upper slopes of these mountains.

ABOVE: *A view from the top of 5,267 foot Mount Katadhin in Maine. Near the summit is a narrow ridge, a mile long, which is the knife edge that forms the rim of a great basin, carved in the rock by the Ice Age glaciers. Mount Katadhin stands in Baxter State Park, which preserves 200,000 acres of Maine wilderness.*

LEFT: *The Hudson River rises in the Adirondack High Peaks of New York State. The wilderness at the Hudson's source is in stark contrast to the megalopolis at its mouth, between New York City and New Jersey.*

A unique tree of the southern Appalachians in the Great Smoky Mountains area, is the Fraser fir (*Abies fraseri*), which is closely related to the balsam fir (*A. balsamea*) of the boreal forest.

Wildlife in the Appalachians

Since the Appalachians are not especially high, the animals which live on upper slopes are mostly the same as those that live in the lower regions (*see The Eastern Mixed Forest*).

MAMMALS Moose (*Alces alces*) are common in the northern Appalachians, spotted skunks (*Spilogale putorius*) in the south and whitetail deer (*Odocoileus virginianus*) throughout the range. Some northern animals extend along Appalachian heights far south of their range. The varying hare (*Lepus americanus*), northern pygmy shrew (*Microsorex hoyi*) and northern water shrew (*Sorex palustris*) can be found on mountain tops of western North Carolina and eastern Tennessee.

BIRDS Some birds can also be found south of their usual range in the Appalachians. The gray-cheeked thrush (*Catharus minimus*) summers in the Arctic and also on the alpine tundra of the White Mountains, where its haunting call can be heard echoing throughout the crags until July. The Canada warbler (*Wilsonia canadensis*), which usually nests in the north, also nests well into the southern Appalachians. Ruffed grouse (*Bonasa umbellus*) nest there and, together with the Guadelupe Mountains of western Texas, the southern Appalachians mark the southernmost breeding range of the dark-eyed junco (*Junco hyemalis*).

LEFT: *The Great Smoky Mountains of North Carolina are the heart of the southern Appalachians, and contain some of the finest deciduous forests on the continent. Although some of the peaks are higher than those of New England, none is above the timberline, due to their southern latitude.*

INSET: *The red-backed salamander (*Plethodon cinereus*) is one of at least 27 species and subspecies of salamander found in the Great Smoky Mountains. The moist forest floor provides them with excellent habitat.*

THE ROCKY MOUNTAINS

Far higher than the Appalachians of the East, the Rocky Mountains, which include more than 60 ranges, form the backbone of the continent; the continental divide runs along their crest (*see The Evolution of a Continent*). Geographically, the Rockies begin in the north at the Brooks mountain range in Alaska, and continue through western Texas and Arizona into New Mexico.

The highest peaks of the Rockies are in Colorado, where more than 50 summits rise over 14,000 feet above sea level. Mount Elbert is the highest, at 14,433 feet. Mount Robson is the tallest peak of the Canadian Rockies at 12,792 feet above sea level, situated in the 2,688,000-acre Jasper National Park of Alberta and British Columbia.

The central Rockies rise from the Great Plains on the east and from desert on the west, while in the north they emerge from plains and lowlands of boreal forest and tundra.

The geology of the Rockies is extremely complex. In Colorado, Rocky Mountain National Park is in the Front Range of the Rockies, which is 200 miles long and 40 miles wide. The park crosses the continental divide. About 100 million years ago, before the range was formed, the region was covered by a great sea that divided the continent from north to south. Sand, silt and mud sediments on the bottom of the sea gradually hardened into shale, some of which is now exposed in the foothills east of the park.

BELOW: *Hallet Peak and Bear Lake are in the heart of Rocky Mountain National Park, Colorado. The park contains several peaks above 14,000 feet.*

Geological upheavals within the earth forced up the sea bottom, and as it rose, it buckled, forming a long ridge. Layers of rocks from the ridge fractured and slipped, while other rocks were thrust up from the bottom of the sea. Lava oozed out of some of the fractures.

The core of the mountains was crystalline rock, which had lain below the sea bed and was more ancient than the sedimentary rock of the old sea floor, which now capped the mountains. As time passed, the sedimentary layer wore away, exposing the core as a rolling upland. Then, about 60 million years ago, and continuing for 20 million years, the ancient rocks uplifted again, forming the peaks we know today.

Different processes formed the Rockies elsewhere. The Grand Tetons, on the Wyoming–Idaho border, were formed within the last 10 million years. They arose along a 40-mile fault. On the eastern edge of the fault, a great block of rock sank,

while on the western side, a huge area of ancient rock, three billion years old, was forced upwards by movements beneath the earth's surface. So steep was the rock's eastern face that the Tetons have no eastern foothills but descend precipitously to their base. During the ice ages, glaciers sculpted horn-shaped peaks and gouged out long valleys orientated east to west.

The northern Rockies in Glacier National Park, Montana, and north across the Canadian border, were also sculpted by glaciers, but they originated differently. From the west, a slab of rock doubled back over itself towards the east, and finally cracked. The rock west of the crack continued to move eastward, sliding over the rock beneath it, so that the resulting eastern face of the mountains is precipitous. Further north, the Canadian Rockies are largely the result of great blocks of rock, moving in an easterly direction, thrust upwards along a fault, one over the other. Hence here, too,

the western sides of the Rockies are sloping, and the eastern faces precipitous.

Yellowstone National Park, straddling the Rockies in Wyoming, Idaho and Montana, was the first national park to be established in the United States. Yellowstone is a plateau formed of lava that flowed from the earth during the processes that created the Grand Tetons. The plateau lies between 7,000 and 8,500 feet above sea level (above the highest peaks east of the Mississippi) with some summits reaching more than 11,000 feet. Geysers and hot springs in the park are relics of the ancient volcanic activity that created the present landscape of the area.

A string of great national parks straddles the Rockies, including, in Canada, Banff (the country's first national park) and Jasper, and Glacier and Yellowstone in the United States. Much of the mountains' original plant and animal life is preserved in these parks.

VEGETATION The western slopes of the Rockies intercept rain clouds moving east and are relatively high in annual precipitation. The eastern slopes, however, tend to be drier. Plant species on the Rockies change with local conditions, although many of the lower slopes on both sides have forests of Douglas fir (*Pseudotsuga menziesii*), lodgepole pine (*Pinus contorta*) and western larch (*Larix occidentalis*). In valleys on the moist western slopes western red cedar (*Thuja plicata*) and western hemlock (*Tsuga heterophylla*) may grow. Engelmann spruce (*Picea engelmanni*) and subalpine fir (*Abies lasiocarpa*) are especially common on the dry eastern slopes. The latter two trees and whitebark pine (*Pinus albicaulis*) grow here and there on upper slopes as far as the timberline, where they become weathered and twisted krummholz, with only a few living branches.

Above the timberline plants similar to those of Arctic tundra grow in meadows and on tundra. They include moss campion (*Silene acaulis*), avens (*Geum*), cinquefoils (*Potentilla*) and lichens such as *Rhizocarpon geographicum*. Sedges (*Carex*) and tough grasses such as tundra bluegrass (*Poa rupicola*) grow in the sparse soil, while bladder ferns (*Cystopteris fragilis*) grace cracks and crevices in the rocks.

DALL'S SHEEP

THE Dall's sheep (*Ovis dalli*), a close northern relative of the bighorn (*O. canadensis*), is an excellent example of a species that has adapted to its habitat – in this case, living on the stony heights of mountains. Like the bighorn, the Dall's sheep summers at higher elevations than it frequents during the winter.

DALL'S SHEEP
DISTRIBUTION MAP

The hoof of Dall's sheep is adapted for mountain life. It has a hard, narrow outer rim, curved inward, that helps it gain purchase on rocks. The bulging pads on the bottom of the hoof are elastic and treaded, aiding traction on hard, steep surfaces.

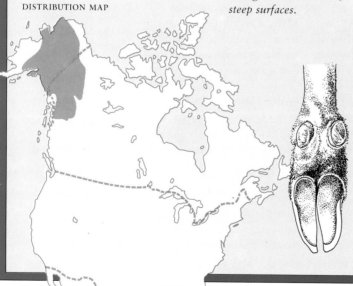

The Dall's sheep inhabits mountains from northern Alaska as far south as British Columbia.

Wildlife of the Rockies

The Rocky Mountains embrace creatures of forest and prairie, temperate and arctic conditions. The creatures include a number of mammals of impressive size and appearance.

MAMMALS The northern Rockies are the home of the (alpine) mountain goat (*Oreamnos americanus*), and Dall's sheep (*Ovis dalli*) of the northwestern Canadian and Alaskan mountains. The animal most typical of much of the Rockies, however, is probably the bighorn sheep (*O. canadensis*). (Some scientists consider Dall's sheep to be the same species.) The male reaches a weight of almost 300 pounds, with horns sometimes spanning almost 3 feet.

The bighorn is the largest mammal of the high peaks throughout much of its range. The male and female adult bighorns stay in separate flocks except in the fall mating season, when the males battle for control of female harems. In combat, the males lower their heads and run at one another, meeting with crashing impact. The thunder of their collisions echoes through the mountains, although injuries seldom occur from such fights.

Moose (*Alces alces*) follow the Rockies from the boreal forest into the heart of the United States, living near waterways and lakes in valleys. Bison (*Bison bison*), primarily grassland beasts, also inhabit valleys between the mountains (about 2,000 bison live in Yellowstone National Park). Occasionally pronghorn antelopes (*Antilocapra americana*), true grassland creatures, move across the lower valleys of some ranges.

Mule deer (*Odocoileus hemionus*) are widespread in the Rockies, which are also the stronghold of the elk, or wapiti (*Cervus elaphus*); they migrate up and down mountains according to season. Elk populations are now scattered, and numerous only in a few places, such as in the National Elk Refuge, which covers 24,700 acres of mountain valley in the Grand Tetons at Jackson Hole, Wyoming. During the winter, thousands of elk gather in this beautiful valley, feeding on grasses and other plants. Unlike the whitetail deer (*Odocoileus virginianus*), which browses, the elk grazes, but it will eat bark and leaves in winter when other food is scarce.

The refuge was established early in this century because forage critical to the winter survival of elk was being diverted to cattle. The elk come to the refuge from several different areas, mostly north of the valley, having spent summer higher on the slopes. The refuge lies approximately between

OPPOSITE: *Purple mountain saxifrage (*Saxifraga oppositifolia*) is among the plants hardy enough to grow in high mountains. Certain species are thought to have medicinal properties, breaking kidney stones.*

BELOW: *Elk, or wapiti (*Cervus elaphus*), cross the Madison River in Wyoming's Yellowstone National Park. The park shelters not only elk but the American bison (*Bison bison*).*

6,000 and 7,000 feet above sea level, and is surrounded by high mountains, Two major waters, the Gros Ventre River and Flat Creek, run through the refuge. The climate is typical of the high valleys of the Rockies, with up to 4 feet of snow during the long winter, and with extreme annual temperatures ranging from over 90°F during the summer to 35 to 40°F below zero in the winter. Average temperatures are 14°F in January and 62°F in July.

Elk in the Jackson Hole area number about 11,000. About 7,000 of them use the valley annually from November to May. Half of these come from Grand Teton National Park, a quarter from Yellowstone National Park and the remainder from nearby national forest lands. They follow traditional migration routes from the high country into the valley.

During the winter the elk paw their way through the snow to forage. In the heart of winter they are also fed pelleted alfalfa hay by federal authorities. By late April and early May, the elk follow the receding snowline back to higher mountain meadows, where, soon afterwards, the calves are born.

The hoofed mammals of the Rockies are hunted by several large predators, including gray wolves (*Canis lupus*), mainly in Canada, and cougars (*Felis concolor*). Coyotes (*Canis latrans*) are common, as are black bears (*Ursus americanus*). The northern Rockies of the United States are virtually the last North American stronghold of the grizzly bear (*U. arctos*), although the creature still ranges the Canadian Rockies into the Arctic.

BIRDS One of the most spectacular nesting birds of the Rockies is the trumpeter swan (*Cygnus buccinator*), the largest of North American swans which can have a wingspan of as much as 98 inches. It nests on marshes and ponds, and was once common throughout the western half of North America, but by the early 1900s market hunting and habitat destruction had reduced its numbers to just a handful of birds south of Alaska in the Wyoming area and Alberta. Since then, protection and habitat preservation have rescued this bird from extinction.

OPPOSITE: *An adult cougar (*Felis concolor*) prowls along a stream.*

INSET: *Cougar cubs begin life with spots, which are lost before maturity. Cougars, also known as mountain lions, are the second largest cats in the Americas – only the jaguar (*Panthera tigris*) is larger. The cougar has been exterminated in many areas but still holds out in wildernesses, especially in the western mountains.*

RIGHT: *A yellow-bellied marmot (*Marmota flaviventris*) stands watch outside its den in Rocky Mountain National Park.*

Mount McKinley and Mount Brooks tower above the Alaskan tundra. McKinley is higher in relation to its surrounding countryside than any other mountain peak in the world. The mountains of North America are at their most rugged and spectacular in Alaska, where in many areas they range to the edge of the sea.

MOUNTAINS OF THE PACIFIC COAST

The Sierra Nevada–Cascades–Pacific Coast complex of mountains extends approximately from the mountains in south-western Alaska along the western edge of the continent into Mexico's Baja California.

Northern mountain ranges of the Pacific Coast

The mountains of Alaska are stark and spectacular, especially towards the coast. Some were formed in a similar way as the Rockies, others like ranges that continue south along the Pacific Coast. Most of the mountains in the Alaska mountain range are between 6,000 and 9,000 feet above sea level, but the range includes the highest point in North America, Mount McKinley, at 20,320 feet above sea level. Mount McKinley is situated in Denali National Park and Preserve; 'Denali' is taken from the Athabascan Indian name for the mountain, and means 'the high one'. The Alaska mountain range curves from the south-central part of the state towards the Aleutian Peninsula, where it meets the peaks of the volcanic Aleutian mountain range, which extends from the peninsula to the Aleutian Islands.

Other Alaskan mountains include, in the south-eastern part of the state, the Wrangells, inland, and the Chugach, on the coast. The St. Elias Mountains rise from the Gulf of Alaska and continue into Canada. No other coastal mountains in the world are higher than the St. Elias, several of which surpass 15,000 feet above sea level. The highest is Mount St. Elias, at 18,008 feet.

The coastal ranges of Alaska are largely the result of continual pressure caused as the Pacific crustal plate slides under the North American plate (*see The Evolution of a Continent*). Faulting, uplift, volcanism and myriad other mountain building processes are spawned by this sliding of the plates. That such movements within the earth are continuing apace today is evidenced by the earthquakes and volcanic eruptions that periodically rock the coast between Alaska and California. Some geologists think that parts of the Alaskan mountain range may be gigantic chunks of landscape carried to the Alaskan shores by the Pacific plate from as far away as the tropics. (*See The High Arctic and Tundra* and *Coniferous Forests* for wildlife and plants of the Alaskan mountains.)

The Coast Ranges

The westernmost mountain range south of Canada is the Olympic of Washington's Olympic Peninsula (*see Coniferous Forests*), followed by the Coast Ranges. These rise out of the Pacific Ocean from northern British Columbia, just south of the St. Elias Mountains, and decrease in height as they enter central and southern California. In northern California the Coast Ranges harbor the last natural habitat of the coast redwood (*Sequoia sempervirens*) – see *Coniferous Forests*. The mountains include the western Siskiyous, Trinity Alps, Santa Cruz Mountains, and the Santa Lucia Mountains of California's central coast, where the bristlecone fir *Abies bracteata*, which grows nowhere else, can be found.

The heavy rains and generally moist conditions that encourage the growth of the redwood and the bristlecone fir in northern Coast Ranges gradually diminish with southern latitude, until the mountains become arid and covered with dwarf forest, growing to about 20 feet high, called chaparral.

Chaparral is the most extensive type of ground cover in southern California. It also grows further east, where it can be found on the mid slopes of mountains in Arizona, New Mexico and other parts of the south-west. It is similar to what in Australia is called bush, and in southern Europe is called *maquis*.

Trees and shrubs that characterize the chaparral include the California scrub oak (*Quercus dumosa*), greasewood (*Adenostoma fasciculatum*), poison oak (*Rhus diversiloba*), mountain mahogany (*Cercocarpus betuloides*) and manzanitas (*Arctostaphylos*). Yuccas (*Yucca*) also grow in this desert-like environment.

MAMMALS Living in the chaparral are forest, grassland and desert mammals, some of which can be found in all three environments. They include the western gray squirrel (*Sciurus griseus*), a woodland creature, and the spotted skunk (*Spilogale putorius*), which inhabits broken woodland or open country. Merriam's kangaroo rat (*Dipodomys merriami*) is of a desert race. The coyote (*Canis latrans*) and cougar (*Felis concolor*) are highly adaptable to habitat, and coyotes will even live within city limits. Both cougars and, more usually, coyotes sometimes venture into the brush canyons within the Los Angeles area.

BIRDS The chaparral-covered mountains of southern California were once the home of the legendary California condor (*Gymnogyps californianus*), a giant among birds. The few remaining wild condors have been caught and are subject to a captive breeding program in hopes of reintroducing them into the wild (*see Conservation*). Until a few years ago, however, it was still possible, with luck, to see a condor, its 10-foot-long wings held out, as it soared on the updrafts of a ridge in the low, rugged mountains of the Los Padres National Forest (north of Los Angeles).

The Cascades

The Cascade Mountains are the interior range of the north-western coast, running from British Columbia's Frazer River to Lassen Peak in northeastern California. Their high, ice-covered peaks flow with the cascading waters that give them their name, and tower above timbered lower slopes. The Cascades are marked by a series of large, isolated volcanoes that stud the landscape from Lassen Peak to Mount Garibaldi in British Columbia. The explosion of Mount Baker in 1975, and of Mount St. Helens in the 1980s, graphically demonstrated that the Cascades are part of an area where volcanism is still a fact of life.

The Cascades rest upon an ancient plateau that rose as the crust of the earth folded (bent upwards) and buckled along a north to south axis. Millions of years later volcanic explosions sent molten rock, magma, to the surface, erupting as lava. About a million years ago more, larger, volcanoes rose on the plateau, including Mount Shasta, Mount Hood, and Mount Rainier.

Heavy winter snow on the western slopes of the Cascades produces myriad streams, which encourage the growth of rich forests, not unlike those on the Olympic Peninsula. As in the Rockies, the eastern slopes are comparatively dry.

The Cascades are at their most formidable in the North Cascades, which divide the state of Washington. The northern section of the Cascades lies in North Cascades National Park of the United States and Manning Provincial Park of British Columbia. This rugged interior region ends at the Straits of Juan De Fuca.

The Cascades have many glaciers – there are 318 alone in North Cascades National Park. Many of the peaks rise above 8,000 feet and their jagged terrain makes them virtually inaccessible. They are not as high as the volcanoes, however, many of which have sloping peaks that hikers can ascend with reasonable ease. The sheer peaks of the North Cascades are covered with ice fields, presenting climbers with some of the most difficult conditions in North America.

VEGETATION A cross section of vegetation on the Cascades shows how prevailing winds and altitude affect vegetation. Rainfall on the western sides can be as much as 80 inches per year, because the

Pelton Peak, seen from the timberline at Cascades Pass, is one of the many impressive mountains in Washington's North Cascades National Park. The mountains of the North Cascades are extremely rugged and their terrain is often described as tortuous. Some of the peaks were not climbed until the 1970s.

mountains squeeze out moisture from winds off the Pacific. The lowest western slopes are covered by forests of western hemlock (*Tsuga heterophylla*), Douglas fir (*Pseudotsuga menziesii*) and western red cedar (*Thuja plicata*), like the western slopes of the moist Olympic Mountains. Pacific silver fir (*Abies amabilis*) grows above these trees, then mountain hemlock (*Tsuga mertensiana*) and subalpine fir (*Abies lasiocarpa*), which culminates at the timberline.

Rainfall on the eastern slopes can be less than half that of the western sides. Starting in the foothills, the landscape is scattered with ponderosa pines (*Pinus ponderosa*) with hardly any understory of vegetation beneath them. Above the level of the ponderosa pines are lodgepole pines (*Pinus contorta*) and yet higher, thinly dispersed whitebark pine (*Pinus albicaulis*), subalpine larch (*Larix lyallii*) and some subalpine firs.

Volcanic peaks

As Mount St. Helens testifies, the Cascades contain active as well as dormant volcanoes, whose snow clad cones include the highest peaks of the range. Among them is Mount Baker, in the Mount Baker–Snoqualmie National forest, at 10,775 feet above sea level. One of the most spectacular volcanoes is Mount Mazama in Oregon, which is more than 8,000 feet high. About half a million years ago the cone of Mount Mazama began to build up as magma was forced up towards the surface. Tremendous eruptions occurred and recurred. Ash, pumice and cinders from the eruptions also built up, forming a mountain 12,000 feet high. Smaller cones appeared on the main mountain and vents opened, weakening the mountain.

Finally, about 6,850 years ago, a massive explosion blew so much rock out of the cone it collapsed. The top half of the mountain fell in, creating a 4,000-foot-deep caldera, a bowl-shaped depression formed by the collapse of a volcano.

Inside the bowl-shaped cone, the ground seethed with heat. Lesser volcanism caused a small cone to build up within the caldera, which later became today's rugged Wizard Island. Finally, about 1,000 years ago, all volcanic activity ceased and water collected in the caldera. It now holds the deepest lake in the United States, which is the second deepest lake in the Western Hemisphere. The lake was erroneously named Crater Lake, for a crater is a vent from which active volcanoes erupt.

Crater Lake averages 1,500 feet deep, is 1,932 feet at its greatest depth, and is almost 10 miles wide. Precipitation on the lake averages 69 inches per annum. The great lake stores so much of the sun's heat in the summer that it hardly ever freezes; the last time it froze was in 1949. The lake exists in a state of equilibrium, with no outlet streams. Precipitation falling into the lake equals water lost through seepage into the ground and evaporation.

The explosions of Mount Mazama were 42 times more powerful than those of Mount St. Helens. They scattered half a foot of ash over 13,000 square miles, and must have had a horrendous impact upon flora, fauna and humans.

Mount Rainier

Many of the volcanoes of the Cascade Mountains are isolated and stand well above surrounding land. The glaciated summit of Mount Rainier, in Washington, for example, towers 9,000 feet over the surrounding highlands. Mount Rainier's glacier system, which is the largest in the lower 48 states, covers 22,400 acres, and can be seen for more than 100 miles on a clear day.

Mount Rainier formed between a million and half a million years ago, along with several other large Cascades' volcanoes such as Mount Hood, Mount Baker, and Glacier Peak. Magma (molten rock) flowed to the surface and broke through as lava, which built up through the ages, creating the main cone of the mountain. The peak may have stood 1,000 feet higher in the past, but diminished with explosions and landslides. The last major eruption occurred in the 1850s.

Wildlife of Mount Rainier

The wildlife of the 241,920-acre Mount Rainier National Park reflects the rich faunal diversity of the Cascades. Many species range between different altitudinal life zones, although they are generally adapted to just one or two life zones.

MAMMALS Only one large mammal is typical of the highest zone, well above the timberline. It is the mountain goat (*Oreamnos americanus*) which inhabits the zone in the summer. It is white and has hooves with flexible, treaded soles and sharp edges that help it cling to rocks.

The mountain goat is restricted to the mountains of the Pacific North-west and the western

BELOW: *Seen from Reflection Lake, Mount Rainier, in the Cascades, glows in the pink of a sunrise. More than 2,500 people climb to the 14,410 feet high summit each year. Two craters at the summit testify to the fact that Mount Rainier is a volcano.*

Rockies from south-western Alaska to Washington and northern Oregon, eastwards to Alberta, western Montana and Idaho. It has been introduced, however, to the Black Hills of South Dakota. Weighing up to 300 pounds, the mountain goat comes down from the crags to feed on the vegetation of alpine meadows during the morning and evening. It also consumes the tough plants that grow amidst the rocks. The goats can also be seen in Glacier, Olympic and North Cascades national parks in the United States, and Banff and Jasper national parks in Canada.

Both elk (*Cervus elaphus*) and the black-tailed race of mule deer (*Odocoileus hemionus*) can be found in high meadows and subalpine forests during the summer, and retreat to lower slopes when the snows come.

Rodents include the beaver (*Castor canadensis*), the hoary marmot (*Marmota caligata*) and the yellow pine chipmunk (*Eutamias amoenus*). The rodent-like pika (*Ochotona princeps*), the size of a guinea pig and a relative of hares and rabbits, can be seen on the rock-strewn slopes. Pikas do not hibernate like some other rodents such as marmots and chipmunks, but remain active throughout the winter, eating from a store of dried leaves, flowers and fruit of alpine plants. They gather the vegetation from the edges of meadows during the summer and stack it in small piles like haystacks to dry in the sun. They hide the dried plants under rocks and in crevices to eat when food is scarce.

Small animals living in colonies in the open, pikas must continually be on the alert for predators. If imperiled while gathering food, a pika will freeze in place and attempt to blend into the vegetation. If threatened while among the rocks, a pika will let out a sharp squeak and then dart to the nearest hole or crevice.

The so-called mountain beaver (*Aplodontia rufa*), a primitive rodent, gets its name 'beaver' because it tunnels extensively near small streams. It is not closely related to the beaver but is the single species of the Aplodontidae family, and is confined to mountains from southern British Columbia to central California.

Mammalian predators in Mount Rainier National Park include the bobcat (*Felis rufus*), cougar (*Felis concolor*), coyote (*Canis latrans*), red fox (*Vulpes vulpes*) and black bear (*Ursus americanus*). Especially dangerous to pikas are the American marten (*Martes americana*), long-tailed weasel (*M. frenata*) and ermine (*M. ermineae*).

BIRDS Pikas also have to fear predatory birds such as the northern goshawk (*Accipiter gentilis*), which breeds in the High Arctic but is also common in the park at high altitudes during the warm months, and the magnificent golden eagle (*Aquila chrysaetos*). The golden eagle frequents high mountains, tundra, remote deserts and grasslands.

LEFT: *A pika (*Ochotona princeps*) gathers hay to store for the winter in the Rockies of Colorado. Grayish or brown, pikas have short, wide, rounded ears and short tails. They grow to approximately 8 inches long and weigh up to 6 oz.*

RIGHT: *Mountains are among the habitats preferred by the majestic golden eagle (*Aquila chrysaetos*). The legs of this predatory bird are covered with feathers all the way to its toes. The golden eagle feeds mostly on mammals, such as rodents. It has also been reported to prey on the young of mountain goats (*Oreamnos americanus*) and bighorn sheep (*Ovis canadensis*).*

As in other western mountains, common ravens (*Corvus corax*) are abundant throughout the year. So are the mountain chickadee (*Parus gambeli*), the black-capped chickadee (*P. atricapillus*) and the chestnut-backed chickadee (*P. rufescens*). Another western mountain bird frequently seen in the park is the gray crowned form of the rosy finch (*Leucosticte arctoa*), which can be seen as far north as the High Arctic.

In northern California, the Cascade Mountains merge on the west with the Coast Ranges and on the east with the lofty Sierra Nevada, which is the youngest large mountain system in the United States, and the highest of all the mountain ranges south of Canada.

The High Sierras
South of the Cascades, the Sierra Nevada range continues the mountain wall which separates the west coast from the interior desert. The Sierras run from the Feather River for 450 miles, ending near the Coast Ranges north of Los Angeles. The range is 60 to 80 miles wide. Cupped between the Sierras and the Coast Ranges are the lush Sacramento Valley to the north and San Joaquin Valley to the south. Known as the Central Valley of California, this area between the mountains was once a great grassland, with soils enriched by the remains of an ancient sea and where elk, grizzly bears and wolves roamed. Now the same soils make it fertile farming country, but the areas of wilderness that remain are on the slopes of the Sierra.

These mountains are formed from a great granite batholith that is still rising and is topped by the remains of more ancient rocks. The eastern side is a steep escarpment, and the western side a gradual slope.

The southern part of the range is known as the High Sierras, comprising the highest mountains in the contiguous United States, with eleven peaks rising more than 14,000 feet above sea level. The highest of these is Mount Whitney, at 14,495 feet.

Four hundred million years ago the site of the Sierras was covered by a shallow inland sea. To the west rose a great range of mountains that extended into the Pacific Ocean. Streams flowing from these mountains carried sediment into the sea. Limestone formed from the remains of shells was also deposited on the sea bed. These deposits built up to tens of thousands of feet, until the sea floor sank under their weight.

Eventually, overriding (a sliding over) of the earth's crustal plates (*see The Evolution of a Continent*) caused high pressure that heated rock deep in the earth to melting point. Above this liquid rock, pressure changed the limestone into marble, which can still be seen in outcroppings of rock. Finally, pressures decreased and the liquified rock slowly cooled, to form a large block of granite.

Crustal plate movement began again, and inner pressures bowed the granite block into mountains. The mountains had a granite base capped by the sedimentary rock from the sea bed. Over the passage of time, the sedimentary cap was eroded,

Highest level of glaciation
Pre-glacial profile

GLACIAL VALLEYS

Mountains throughout North America contain U-shaped valleys, with gently sloping sides and a concave floor. These valleys were scoured out of older, stream-eroded V-shaped valleys by glaciers. As the ice, laden with rocks, flowed down the valley, it eroded the walls and floor, deepening and widening them in the process. As the glaciers melted, sediment from run-off water refilled part of the floor.

Yosemite Valley in the Sierra Nevada is probably the best known U-shaped valley, but this geological feature is found from coast to coast.

The diagram on the left shows the evolution of a typical mountain U-shaped valley. As the ice melted, the valley floor was filled with sediment. Even so, the U-shaped valley is deeper than before it was scoured by glacial ice.

SIERRA NEVADA ECOLOGICAL ZONES AND VEGETATIONAL COMMUNITIES

Below is a chart of the location of
Sierran vegetational communities

WEST SLOPE

9,500–13,600	*Alpine*
8,400–10,400	*Subalpine forest*
7,000–10,200	*Lodgepole pine forest*
6,400–8,400	*Red fir forest*
5,000–10,400	*Alpine meadow*
5,000–9,500	*Montane chaparral*
4,000–7,400	*White fir forest*
1,750–6,000	*Ponderosa pine forest*
400–5,000	*Chaparral*
Below 1,000	*Grassland*

EAST SLOPE

10,000–13,500	*Alpine*
9,000–11,000	*Subalpine meadow*
8,000–11,000	*Montane meadow*
8,000–10,500	*Lodgepole pine forest*
8,000–9,000	*Red fir forest*
7,000–8,000	*Sierran mixed coniferous forest*
6,000–8,000	*Pinyon pine woodland*
Below 6,000	*Sagebrush community*

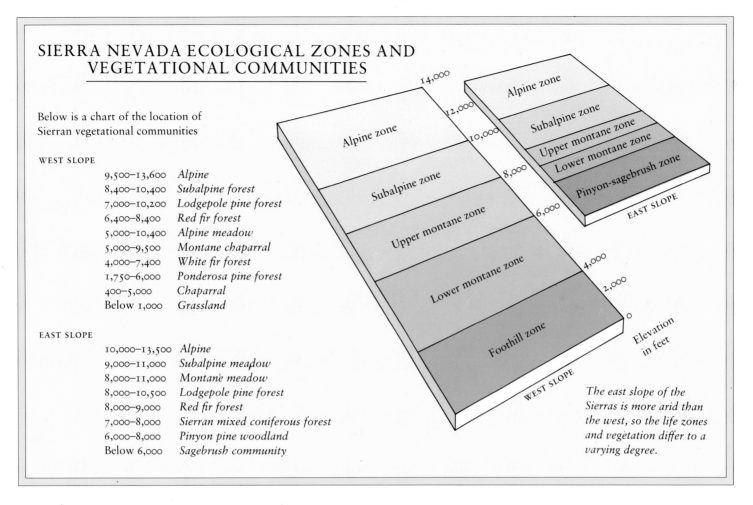

*The east slope of the
Sierras is more arid than
the west, so the life zones
and vegetation differ to a
varying degree.*

and its deposits carried into a sea that covered the Sacramento and San Joaquin valleys. Erosion continued for about 60 million years, and stopped 10 million years ago, when the cap was worn almost level.

Crustal pressures again caused movement in the earth, and the great granite block began to tilt to the west, then cracked along what is now the Sierras' eastern escarpment. Movement continued, forming what is now a precipitous eastern face. Tilting occurred in four major episodes, separated by long stationary periods. The last movement raised the peak of the range to almost 15,000 feet above sea level, to its approximate position today. By 3 million years ago the Sierra Nevada range was formed in its present state.

Glacial activity after the birth of the Sierras helped shape their modern appearance. Mountain glaciers carrying rocks moved through river canyons, carving them into the wide U-shaped cross section that is typical of canyons in the High Sierra. Yosemite Valley in Yosemite National Park is the most spectacular of these valleys carved by the glaciers. Today glaciers still lie in cirques on the high peaks.

The Sierra Nevada is noted for its heavy winter snowfall as its Spanish name, meaning snowy mountains, implies. In all of Canada and the United States, only the northern Coast Ranges receive more snow. Parts of the Sierra Nevada have been covered by more than 70 feet of snow. In many areas on the western slopes snow can be 10 or even 15 feet deep during an average winter (the eastern slopes are drier). Summers are virtually rainless, giving the mountains a precipitation pattern like that of lowland California.

VEGETATION The western slopes of the Sierra Nevada stand in the grasslands of the Central Valley, and the eastern in the sagebrush desert of the Great Basin and the Mohave Desert (*see Deserts*). Above the grassland on the western side lies chaparral; higher still coniferous forests grow, dominated by the ponderosa pine (*Pinus ponderosa*), white fir (*Abies concolor*), then the California red fir (*A. magnifica*) – restricted to the Sierra region – and lodgepole pine (*Pinus contorta*). The following zone is subalpine forest, in which whitebark pine (*P. albicaulis*) is prominent, growing in this region mainly as a shrub to about 50 feet tall at most.

The eastern slope has similar coniferous forests at higher elevations (above 7,000 feet) although they are sparse due to lack of precipitation. Some desert plants such as Great Basin sagebrush (*Artemisia tridentata*) climb from the desert below 7,000 feet all the way to the timberline. The impact of the desert is felt even above the timberline,

where much of the vegetation of the meadows and tundra of this alpine zone is remarkably unlike that of other alpine tundra or the Arctic. For example, there are far more annual plants here than in other alpine or Arctic tundra areas. Annuals do not normally have time to grow from seed in the short spring and summer of the tundra. However, milder conditions on the Sierran peaks have allowed tough desert annuals to invade the high mountains. Some of the desert plants found above the Sierra Nevada timberline are phlox (*Phlox*) and milk-vetches (*Astragalus*). These mix with alpine flowers such as buttercups (*Ranunculus*) and gentians (*Gentiana*).

Wildlife of the Sierra Nevada

Wildlife in the Sierra Nevada range is similar to wildlife on other West Coast mountain ranges. Several different species inhabit the lower elevations throughout the year.

MAMMALS Resident mammals of the Sierra Nevada include the gray fox (*Urocyon cinereoargenteus*), bobcat (*Felis rufus*), California ground squirrel (*Spermophilus beecheyi*), striped skunk (*Mephitis mephitis*), spotted skunk (*Spilogale putorius*), and deer mouse (*Peromyscus maniculatus*).

Mule deer (*Odocoileus hemionus*) and black bears (*Ursus americanus*) are commonly seen large mammals of the forested middle slopes during the summer; they move to lower elevations in winter.

The high country has fewer animals than any other part of the mountains. Here, however, one may find the wolverine (*Gulo gulo*) and the rare

Sierra race of the bighorn sheep (*Ovis canadensis*). The bighorns spend the summer high in the mountains and descend to the desert at the eastern foot of the range for the winter.

BIRDS Those which can be seen at low altitudes include the California quail (*Callipepla californica*), California towhee (*Pipilo crissalis*) and Bewick's wren (*Thryomanes bewickii*).

Birds teem amidst the forests during the summer. They include the beautiful western tanager (*Piranga ludoviciana*), with its red head, black wings and yellow body, the yellow, black-capped Wilson's warbler (*Wilsonia pusilla*) and the elusive hermit thrush (*Catharus guttatus*).

The few birds that are abundant in summer in the high country are Clark's nutcracker (*Nucifraga columbiana*) and the gray-crowned form of the rosy finch (*Leucosticte arctoa*).

REPTILES AND AMPHIBIANS The western rattlesnake (*Crotalus viridis*) and western whiptail lizard (*Cnemidophorus tigris*) are among the reptiles on lower slopes; reptiles are not particularly abundant in the forests, but the California mountain kingsnake (*Lampropeltis zonata*) and rubber boa (*Charina bottae*) can be found there.

THE GREAT BASIN MOUNTAINS

The mountains of the Great Basin lie between the Sierra Nevada and the Rockies on a high desert plateau (*see Deserts*). Some rise over 10,000 feet above sea level and are covered with coniferous forest that contrasts sharply with the desert below. The mountain ranges, which include the Spring Mountains and Shoshone Mountains of Nevada, tend to be broken ranges, unlike the Rockies and the Sierra Nevada.

The geological history of the mountains in the Great Basin is not fully understood. Scientists believe, however, that about 60 million years ago, the earth's crust in the Great Basin region cracked (mostly on a north-south axis) in many places, separating the rock into great blocks. About 30 million years ago, disturbances deep within the earth, such as volcanism, uplifted many of the blocks along the cracks, so the rocks rose above the landscape. The risen rocks became the ranges, separated by broad, long valleys, characteristic of the region today.

During the Pleistocene ice ages, most of the mountains in the Great Basin were capped by glaciers. Only one glacier remains, on Wheeler Peak of the Snake Mountains, on the Nevada–Utah border. The Wheeler Peak glacier barely classifies as a glacier because most of the snow that accumulates there melts during the summer.

About 100 ranges occupy the 128,000,000-acre Great Basin. Some have peaks that rise to a great height, including 14,246-foot Mountain Peak in the White Mountains, which lie just east of Sierra Nevada, and Wheeler Peak, at 13,063 feet above sea level.

The mountains of the Great Basin are the most arid in the west due to the fact that winds coming in from the Pacific Ocean have released almost all their moisture by the time they pass over the crest of the Sierra Nevada, the eastern flank of which marks the Great Basin's western boundary.

The vegetation on lower slopes of the Great Basin Mountains is that of the sagebrush (*Artemisia*) desert.

Generally the Great Basin mountains are sparsely forested, often covered only with desert vegetation. In some areas, however, the ponderosa pine (*Pinus ponderosa*) grows on higher slopes. Towards the timberline grow stunted whitebark pine (*Pinus albicaulis*) and bristlecone pine (*Pinus aristata*). In the White Mountains of the Great Basin there are bristlecone pines believed to be more than 4,500 years old, and thought to be the oldest living organisms on earth.

Bristlecone pines grow in scattered alpine areas of the mountainous west. Their name comes from a prickly covering on the scales of their cones.

THE OLDEST LIVING TREE

*B*RISTLECONE pines (*Pinus aristata*) can grow to 60 feet tall, but in high, windswept areas they can be stunted, gnarled shrubs. Some bristlecone pines in the White Mountains, on the California side of the Great Basin, are believed to be the world's most ancient trees, almost 5,000 years old.

The White Mountains, where the oldest bristlecone pines grow, reach a height of more than 14,000 feet. Bristlecone pines grow slowly and have dense heads of branches. Their leaves are clustered in fives, and their cylindrical cones are approximately 3 inches long.

BRISTLECONE PINE

DISTRIBUTION MAP

GRASSLANDS

In the 16th century the first Spanish explorers saw the vast expanse of the grasslands, and called it 'the sea of grass.' The grass stood taller than a man, and in many places, a horseman venturing into the prairies had to stand on his saddle to get his bearings. All he saw, frequently, were the tops of grasses waving in the breeze, stretching like an unbroken sea to the far horizon.

The grasslands still looked the same some two centuries later when pioneers moved west. In western Kentucky, Indiana and Illinois, forests gradually diminished into parkland with scattered groves of trees and patches of open woodland. Between the wooded areas, bands of the greater western grasslands encroached on the margins of the Eastern Mixed Forest.

The sun is about to rise over the shortgrass prairie of Badlands National Park in South Dakota. Shortgrass prairie is the most arid of the three prairie types and tallgrass prairie the most moist of the three.

A tiger swallowtail butterfly (Papilio glaucus) alights on the prairie. This hardy butterfly ranges as far north as Alaska. Swallowtails of different species have a worldwide range, but are most abundant in the tropics.

ALTHOUGH now vastly changed by agriculture, grassland once stretched from central Alberta and Saskatchewan far into Mexico, and from the eastern slopes of the Rocky Mountains to Missouri. An eastern belt of grassland extended as far as western Ohio. Elsewhere islands of grassland were situated in the Central Valley of California (*see Mountains*) and, just west of the Rockies in Utah and Colorado, and in Arizona and New Mexico, lay desert grassland. The main areas of grassland, however, stretched across the prairies of the continent's middle section.

Prairies

The grasslands of the flat or rolling heart of the continent are known as prairies, meaning 'large meadows' in French. Prairies are divided into three types, according to the dominant grasses and the height to which they grow. Each prairie type runs in a north to south belt.

The easternmost prairie is the tallgrass prairie, which edges into the Dakotas, Nebraska and Kansas, and arcs into Alberta to the north. Here, grasses can grow to more than 8 feet high. The central prairie is the midgrass prairie, the most extensive prairie, with a maximum grass height of 4 feet. The boundaries of the prairie types are not clearly defined, and some areas of midgrass extend eastwards as far as Illinois. The midgrass prairie gives way to shortgrass on the windswept, semi-arid High Plains of the west. The shortgrass and midgrass prairies are commonly known as the Great Plains.

Lack of sufficient rainfall renders most of the prairies treeless. Winds blowing eastward across the Rocky Mountains release moisture over the mountains. Thus the area immediately east of the Rockies is arid, lying in the mountains' rain shadow. Here, where rainfall is less than 20 inches a year, is the shortgrass prairie. Grasses reach a maximum height of about 1½ feet.

Further east, the moisture content of the winds very gradually increases, coming from the Gulf of Mexico, to the south. As warm, moist air moves northward from the Gulf and meets cool, dry air from the north, fronts are formed, along which rain falls. Rainfall in this region surpasses 20 inches per annum, giving rise to the midgrass prairie. Still further east, rainfall increases to more than 30 inches annually, where the tallgrass prairie begins.

CONSERVATION OF THE PRAIRIE

THE tallgrass prairie has the richest agricultural soil in the world. Wheat grows well in the midgrass prairie and all prairies make superb grazing land. As a result, most of North America's prairies have been turned over by the plow or overgrazed by cattle and sheep. Remnant prairies remain, in places such as Badlands National Park and Prince Albert National Park, but most of the prairies are gone. Conservationists are making efforts to restore prairie, re-establishing prairie vegetation. However the vast virgin prairies are a thing of the past.

Here, in a protected area of north-western Iowa, is virgin tallgrass prairie. Many years ago, this type of prairie covered most of the continent's midsection.

Although winters can be bitterly cold, summers are baking hot. High summer temperatures and winds that sweep across the open country together create a high evaporation rate. The resultant lack of moisture contributes to minimal tree growth on the midgrass and shortgrass prairies. The tallgrass region, however, has enough moisture to support forests, and forest and prairie wage a continual war for supremacy on the easternmost margins of the grasslands.

Scientists believe that the vast herds of American bison (*Bison bison*) that once grazed all over the prairies prevented the growth of trees in the tallgrass by crushing seedlings under their hooves. Fires also prevented tree growth, while promoting the health of grasses. Driven by wind, a prairie fire moves so rapidly that heat does not penetrate beneath the soil to damage the roots of the grasses.

Roots make up by far the greatest part of the biomass of grasses, and penetrate the soil to a greater depth than the grass is tall. Since most of the living tissue of a grass is underground, when only the surface grass is burned the plants are not killed and regrowth will occur.

Fire also destroys the dead plant material that accumulates among the grasses. If dead vegetation builds up, it smothers the growth of new grass in the spring. (Research indicates that an accumulation of dead plant material is the most important factor in stopping the growth of tallgrass.) Experiments with prairie grasses show that if a prairie is burned on a yearly basis, the growth of grass is more abundant both above and below the ground.

Wildfires on the prairies are commonly caused by lightning, especially during dry summers when the grasses easily ignite. Indians also set the prairies on fire to drive game, and sometimes fires are caused accidentally. A prairie fire consumes everything in its path as grasses inflame almost instantaneously.

Dominant grass types

Tallgrass prairie is dominated by grasses such as the towering big bluestem (*Andropogon gerardii*) and switch grass (*Panicum virgatum*). Dominant midgrass plants are western wheatgrass (*Agropyron smithii*) and little bluestem (*Andropogon scoparius*). Buffalo grass (*Buchloe dactyloides*) and blue grama (*Bouteloua gracilis*) are among the key plants on the shortgrass prairie.

Although grasses dominate, they are by no means the only prairie plants. One study of prairie plant life conducted near Lincoln, Nebraska, located 237 different species of plants within one square mile of prairie. During the spring and summer, the prairies are studded with the colors of wildflowers such as prairie-smoke (*Geum triflorum*), Indian paintbrush (*Castilleja sessiliflora*), blazing star (*Liatris punctata*) and long-headed coneflower (*Ratibida columnifera*).

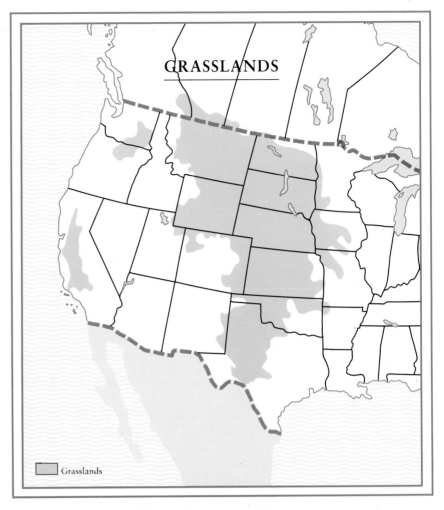

GRASSLANDS

Grasslands

Prairie-smoke, or purple avens (Geum triflorum), is one of the many wildflowers that from early spring through the summer splash the prairies with gorgeous colors. Wildflowers grow especially lush on the moist tallgrass prairie. Many prairie wildflowers have been propagated by cultivation.

Vegetational communities

The prairie plants form a distinct community. On the margins of the prairies and sometimes within them, changes in climate and geography bring the grasslands into contact with other plant communities: the eastern edge of the prairies confronts mixed deciduous forest, and the western edge meets the Rocky Mountains. To the north, the prairies meet the boreal forest, while the south-western prairie border gradually becomes semi-desert (*see Deserts*).

In parts of Arizona desert grassland grows between 3,500 and 5,000 feet above sea level, with true desert below. From 5,000 to 7,000 feet lies shortgrass prairie grassland.

Within the prairie region, the grasslands of western South Dakota and eastern Wyoming rise into the Black Hills. The slopes of these low mountains are covered by coniferous forests. A unique plant community exists within the midgrass prairie, in the Sandhills region of south-central Nebraska, covering 20,000 square miles. Scientists believe that the Sandhills were once barren, but today they are anchored by vegetation representative of all three prairie types. The Sandhills comprise the largest dune formation in the Western Hemisphere. Some of the dunes reach a height of more than 200 feet.

As aridity increases to the west and south-west, the prairie vegetation includes plant species that are found in semi-desert areas (*see Deserts*). Various types of sagebrush (*Artemisia*) appear, as do several species of cacti, including the prickly pear (*Opuntia*).

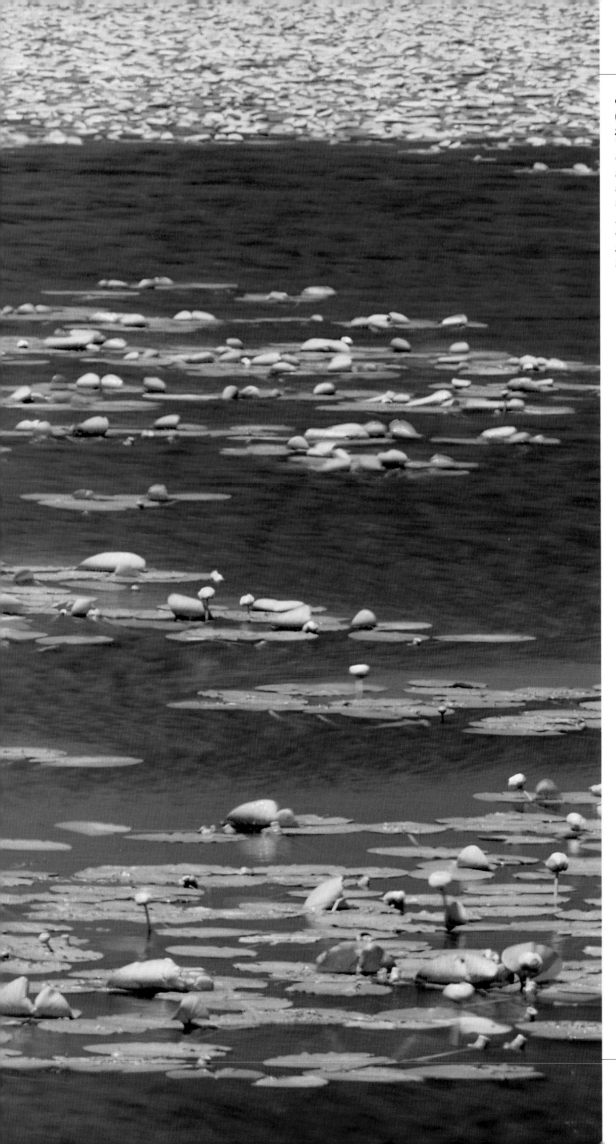

OPPOSITE: *Junipers (*Juniperus*) mix with grasslands in Arizona's Tonto National Forest. Grasslands extend from the main prairie region into Arizona, especially at middle elevations, between 5,000 and 7,000 feet. There are also extensive tracts of grassland in the eastern part of the state.*

LEFT: *A lake shimmers in the Sandhills region of south-central Nebraska. Lakes and wetlands are scattered through this region of sand dunes that have been stabilized by prairie grasses of several types. The wetlands of the Sandhills are an important resting and feeding area for millions of waterfowl and other aquatic birds.*

SAGE GROUSE AND PRAIRIE CHICKEN DISPLAY

*T*HE greater prairie chicken (*Tympanuchus cupido*) and related sage grouse (*Centrocercus urophasianus*) both conduct highly ritualized courting dances during the spring breeding season. The birds gather on display grounds, or 'leks', where the males perform dances to attract mates. The sage grouse puffs up white air sacs on its breast. The prairie chicken inflates orange sacs on either side of its neck. In both birds the sacs serve as resonance chambers to increase the volume of vocalization emitted during the courtship dance.

With its chest expanded by inflated air sacs, a male sage grouse performs on the display grounds (left). During display, the male raises and spreads its tail feathers.

Orange neck sacs bulging, a male greater prairie chicken bows and dances during its courtship ritual (above). Raising of feathered tufts above the ears is part of the display.

Wildlife of the grasslands

Some grasslands wildlife has adapted to all three types of prairie. The American bison is one of these. Other creatures demonstrate a preference for a particular kind of prairie.

The prairie chickens (*Tympanuchus*) and the sage grouse (*Centrocercus urophasianus*) are closely related ground birds that all live on open grasslands and behave in similar fashion. The greater prairie chicken (*T. cupido*) inhabits tallgrass and midgrass prairies, while the lesser prairie chicken (*T. pallidicinctus*) is largely restricted to shortgrass. The sage grouse is a shortgrass bird, too, but, as its name suggests, is most common where aridity favors the growth of sagebrush.

In their virgin state, grasslands support a tremendous number of large mammals, as the abundance of grasses provides them with so much food. Grasslands, however, make a very specialized habitat, and many of the 200 or so plant species on the prairies are alike. The greater the variety of vegetation the more diverse the species of herbivores within a region. To survive in the grasslands, herbivorous animals must specifically be grass eaters, hence grasslands support fewer species than, for example, forests.

THE AMERICAN BISON

The story of the American bison (*Bison bison*) shows how human action can benefit or harm a species. When Europeans first colonized North America, it was the home of 60 million American bison. At that time the bison was probably the most common large terrestrial mammal on earth. By 1895, however, fewer than 1,000 bison remained, and these were mainly in zoos and private preserves. The only wild herds consisted of about 20 animals in and around Yellowstone National Park (established 1872) and a few hundred animals on the present site of Canada's Wood Buffalo National Park, in Alberta and the Northwest Territories. The bison had been slaughtered relentlessly (primarily for its hide but also, to a lesser degree, for its flesh). Today, as a result of one of the first major efforts to save a species on the brink of extinction, about 50,000 bison exist in and around parks and preserves in the United States and Canada.

Bison are the largest of North American mammals. An adult bull has a massive, shaggy head and curved horns. It can measure 6 feet high to the shoulder and weigh more than 2,000 pounds. Cows

are smaller, but can still weigh up to 1,100 pounds and reach a shoulder height of more than 5 feet.

The ancestor of the American bison probably originated in southern Asia about 400,000 years ago. Prehistoric bison are thought to have arrived in North America less than 40,000 years ago, when, during the last Pleistocene glaciation, a decrease in sea level left a bridge of land between Siberia and Alaska. The prehistoric bison of North America were larger than the modern species. One ancient bison, *Bison latifrons*, had horns measuring 9 feet from tip to tip.

At their peak, modern bison ranged over a third of the continent. They could be found from the northern shores of Great Slave Lake, in Canada, to Mexico, in the south, and from the Rocky Mountains in the east to western New York state. The bison in the eastern forests were slightly larger than

the plains bison and similar to those that inhabit Wood Buffalo National Park today. Plains bison were much more numerous, and migrated across vast distances as they grazed.

Eastern bison became extinct as pioneers moved westward through the eastern forest. The first major bison hunts were not organized until the 1830s; then the unrestricted slaughter of the plains bison began. So numerous were the bison, however, that millions still roamed the prairies in 1870. In the following decade, however, the trade in bison hides reached its peak, when as many as 250,000 hides could be auctioned in a single day.

It was almost too late to save the remaining wild bison, but conservationists alerted federal governments in Canada and the United States, and by the middle of the 1890s, both had passed legislation prohibiting the killing of bison.

An American bison (Bison bison) braves the harsh weather of a western winter. Bison are found in the Canadian north almost at the northern limits of the boreal forest. In a winter storm, bison turn their heads into the wind and wait it out. The most difficult winter conditions for bison occur when a warm spell causes the surface of deep snow to melt, and then cold weather turns it to an icy crust which is difficult to break through to obtain food.

In 1905, a group of conservationists met at the Bronx Zoo in New York City and formed the American Bison Society to continue to work to save the species. That same year a tract in Oklahoma (now the Wichita Mountains National Wildlife Refuge) was declared a wildlife preserve by United States President Theodore Roosevelt, a former bison hunter. Two years later, 15 bison from the Bronx Zoo were transplanted to the preserve. This gesture marked the first of efforts to re-establish bison. Gradually, bison were released in national parks and refuges scattered across the western United States, and became a classic conservation success story. In 1922, Canada established Wood Buffalo National Park to protect remaining bison and the herd flourished (*see The High Arctic and Tundra*). Although there are nowhere near as many bison as there were in the past, they can once more be seen roaming the western grasslands. In the areas that can support them, the bison must be carefully managed, and removed if populations exceed the capacity of the habitat to support them. In some places, surplus bison are rounded up and sold. In other areas, hunting is used to control them.

About 15,000 bison inhabit Wood Buffalo National Park. More than 2,500 live in and around Yellowstone National Park. South Dakota's Custer State Park has almost 1,500, and Badlands National Park, South Dakota, has 500 of them. Three hundred graze in Theodore Roosevelt National Park, also in South Dakota. Montana's National Bison Range has a herd that fluctuates in number between 300 and 500 animals. Parks and refuges such as these, supporting populations of bison and other western wildlife, provide an indication at least of what the western grasslands were like in their pristine state.

The National Bison Range

The National Bison Range covers 18,541 acres in the Flathead Valley, between the Cabinet Mountains on the west and the Mission Range on the east in the Rocky Mountains of north-western Montana. Elevation above sea level ranges from 2,582 feet to 4,885 feet. The refuge provides a graphic example of the combination of grasslands and mountains, with a resultant mixture of plant communities and wildlife.

VEGETATION Seventy-eight per cent of the range is native shortgrass prairie, with prairie grasses typical of the region, such as wheatgrass (*Agropyron*) and fescues (*Festuca*). Higher elevations in the mountains are painted in many hues during spring and summer by wildflowers, among them asters (*Aster*) and wild lupines (*Lupinus perennis*). The forested slopes consist mainly of Douglas fir (*Pseudotsuga menziesii*) on northern exposures and ponderosa pine (*Pinus ponderosa*) on south-facing slopes. Other trees grow in the bottomlands along streams, in a thick tangle of cottonwoods and aspens (both *Populus*), willows (*Salix*), alders (*Alnus*) and junipers (*Juniperus*). Creek backwaters and scattered potholes provide a few wetland areas.

LEFT: *A mule deer* (Odocoileus hemionus) *buck, showing his full rack of antlers, is ready for breeding. The mule deer roams western grasslands, mountains and semi-desert.*

ABOVE: *A coyote* (Canis latrans) *consumes a freshly caught sage grouse* (Centrocercus urophasianus). *Coyotes are highly adaptable and able to live on a wide variety of prey.*

MAMMALS Mammals of the range present a cross-section of western prairie and mountain wildlife. The bison herd roams the grasslands area, together with pronghorn antelopes (*Antilocapra americana*). Whitetail deer (*Odocoileus virginianus*) haunt the wooded bottomlands while mule deer (*O. hemionus*) and elk, or wapiti (*Cervus elaphus*), live on the slopes. Higher up the mountainside bighorn sheep (*Ovis canadensis*) share their territory with a handful of mountain goats (*Oreamnos americanus*). Coyotes (*Canis latrans*) live throughout the range, hunting small rodents such as red squirrels (*Tamiasciurus hudsonicus*) in the mountain forests and Columbian ground squirrels (*Citellus columbianus*) on the grasslands.

BIRDS Bird life is similarly diverse because of the variety of available habitats. More than 180 species have been observed in the refuge. Although wetlands account for less than one per cent of the area, they provide nesting for several species of waterfowl, including mallards (*Anas platyrhynchos*), green-winged teal (*A. crecca*), common goldeneyes (*Bucephala clangula*) and common mergansers, or goosanders (*Mergus merganser*). The streamside bottomlands offer food and shelter for warblers, such as the common yellowthroat (*Geothlypis trichas*), willow flycatchers (*Empidonax traillii*) and common flickers (*Colaptes auratus*). The grasslands are inhabited by vesper sparrows (*Pooecetes gramineus*) and horned, or shore, larks (*Eremophila alpestris*), as well as prairie falcons (*Falco mexicanus*), red-tailed hawks (*Buteo jamaicensis*) and ferruginous hawks (*B. regalis*). Rough-legged hawks (*B. lagopus*) visit the region in winter.

Forest species inhabit mountain slopes. Among them are Lewis' woodpecker (*Melanerpes lewis*), Clark's nutcracker (*Nucifraga columbianus*) and blue grouse (*Dendragapus obscurus*). A major avian attraction is the golden eagle (*Aquila chrysaetos*), which is often seen flying above the range. Snow geese (*Chen caerulescens*) sometimes visit the area during spring and fall migrations.

*Snow geese (*Chen caerulescens*) rising from a prairie lake during migration. Wetlands of the prairie region are extremely important as migratory stopovers for waterfowl. Snow geese breed in the Arctic and winter mostly along the Pacific and Gulf coasts. These birds must cross over the grasslands during their migrations.*

THE BADLANDS

The name 'Badlands' has ominous connotations. It comes from the words French-Canadian trappers used to describe the area when they first arrived in the early 19th century – *les mauvaises terres à traverser* ('bad lands to travel across'). The trappers were not the first to give this region of rugged, unusual topography a menacing name. The Sioux Indians called the region *mako shika*, meaning 'land of no good'. But this spectacular area, eroded out of the rolling prairies of western North and South Dakota, is not as forbidding as its name implies, and parks there preserve some of the essence of the prairies of the past.

The Badlands is a region of magnificent vistas, sometimes stretching from horizon to horizon. Mazes of steep, bisecting canyons cut through the land and in places spires of rock looking like wizards' towers, ridges with knife-edge crests and isolated buttes rise out of the landscape. In some areas, the prairie lies on islands of uneroded tableland surrounded by canyons. It was on one of these tablelands, Stronghold Table, that the Sioux held their Ghost Dances in 1890, which contributed to their massacre at Wounded Knee by the United States Cavalry in the same year.

The Badlands were carved out of the earth by wind and water which eroded the rock and exposed layers of rock dating back to the Oligocene epoch, during the Age of Mammals. The geological history of the Badlands, however, goes back beyond the Age of Mammals, to the Mesozoic era, when dinosaurs walked the land. Mesozoic rocks can still be seen in both Badlands National Park in South Dakota and Theodore Roosevelt National Park in North Dakota.

The oldest rock in Badlands National Park is Pierre shale. It is formed from layers of sediment that settled on the bottom of the shallow Pierre Sea that cut north to south through the middle of the continent from about 100 million until 65 million years ago. As the Rocky Mountains were beginning to form, so was the sea retreating, until it disappeared.

When the Rockies rose on the west, sediment was deposited by streams and turned what had been sea bottom into a rich alluvial plain. Plants grew on the plain, forming jungle-like vegetation. The ancient shale began to weather, but during the Oligocene epoch, 37 million to 23 million years ago, water from highlands to the west began to wash in volcanic ash, mud and sand that accumulated several feet thick. Plants grew profusely in the subtropical climate, including conifers similar to the sequoias. Some of these grew in swamps. When they died they fell into the swamp and were buried by sediment. This happened so rapidly that they decayed very little. Over a long period of time, the overlying sediments created

The terrain of Badlands National Park in South Dakota is almost surrealistic in appearance. Erosion by wind and water has carved the Badlands landscape into mazes of canyons, ridges, spires, domes and buttes. Large areas of tableland in the Badlands are covered by prairie grasses.

pressure that compacted the woody material of the dead trees. Chemical changes transformed the woody material into soft lignite coal. Lignite coal is clearly visible today in parts of Theodore Roosevelt National Park.

Roving the great, swamp-filled plain during the Oligocene were a fantastic assortment of prehistoric mammals. Pig-like entelodonts the size of cows galloped over the landscape, which was also populated by herds of titanotheres. These were huge creatures not unlike rhinoceroses. They had horns branching from the nose, and stood 8 feet high to the shoulder. A ferocious saber-toothed cat, *Eusmilus*, stalked its prey among the herbivores. Today, the Badlands contain a wealth of Oligocene fossils which have left a clear imprint in the soft, exposed rock formed of muddy sediments. The Badlands area is recognized by paleontologists as one of the most important in the world.

After the Oligocene, the climate cooled, the land became more arid and the swampy forests were replaced by grass, which requires less moisture to grow. The area remained much the same until glaciers in the Pleistocene era moved south. Although they never reached the Badlands, they contributed to the erosion that shaped the area: rivers running north to south through the region, such as the Little Missouri, were blocked. The flow of the Little Missouri was diverted south-eastward and, since the slope to the south-east was steeper, the river and its tributaries, flowing faster, cut more deeply into the soft rock, creating the landscape of Theodore Roosevelt National Park.

The world-wide cooling of the climate during the ice ages generated wild weather and heavy rains. New streams formed, which also eroded the plain, a process which continues today. Although erosion is changing the Badlands landscape, man has done little to change it. It is too rugged to plow and is less heavily grazed than any other area of the western grasslands, making it a haven for grasslands wildlife.

Badlands National Park

Badlands National Park is in the heart of the Badlands region, where midgrass prairie becomes shortgrass prairie. It has only about 16 inches of precipitation per annum. Most of the rain falls during torrential spring and summer storms. Plants in this region have adapted to long periods without rain. Barr's milkvetch (*Astragalus barrii*) is a perennial that has a long root, which anchors the plant against the strong prairie winds and reaches deep into the soil for water. It can live for 50 years. Visher's buckwheat (*Eriogonum multiceps*) is an annual that drops seeds in the fall. They lie dormant in the crumbly soil and then sprout during spring rains. Prairie grasses in the park include big bluestem, typical of tallgrass regions (*Andropogon gerardii*), and blue grama (*Bouteloua gracilis*),

while the aridity of the region is demonstrated by the presence of narrowleaf yucca (*Yucca glauca*) and the prickly pear cactus (*Opuntia compressa*).

Wildlife of the Badlands

Badlands National Park covers more than 240,000 acres and contains a cross-section of wildlife typical of the western prairies, although the elk, or wapiti (*Cervus elaphus*), the grizzly bear (*Ursus arctos*) and the gray wolf (*Canis lupus*) no longer survive here.

MAMMALS Along with the bison, bighorn sheep (*Ovis canadensis*), which were once extirpated from the Badlands, have been reintroduced among the crags and cliffs. Mule deer (*Odocoileus hemionus*) prefer woodlands, but can occasionally be seen in bare Badlands areas and on prairies. Whitetail deer (*O. virginianus*) come out of woodlands to feed at the edges of meadows. Pronghorn antelopes (*Antilocapra americana*) roam meadows and prairies.

The pronghorn antelope is one of the fastest land mammals in the world, able to rocket across the prairie at 60 miles per hour. Although not as numerous as the bison, before the west was settled pronghorns by the millions ranged grasslands and deserts from Canada to Mexico. Hunting greatly reduced their numbers, and when the grasslands were fenced off the territory available to pronghorns was restricted, further limiting their numbers. By 1908, only 20,000 pronghorns existed

A pronghorn antelope (Antilocapra americana) buck stands guard over his harem of does. Pronghorn antelopes breed in the fall. Each buck attempts to drive females into his harem group. The buck must make a great effort to keep his does together, away from other males that attempt to steal the females. The herd usually numbers up to half a dozen, although some dominant bucks gather more than a dozen does. When a buck in charge of a group of females confronts a challenger, the two animals push and shove until the weaker one breaks off the combat.

COYOTE FAMILY

Coyotes (*Canis latrans*) breed in mid-winter, with the pups born in the spring. The number of pups in a litter can vary from as few as two to as many as a dozen. The pups are born in a den, which is a burrow either vacated by some other animal or dug out by the parents. For about two weeks, the pups feed exclusively on the mother's milk, but after that are gradually weaned as both parents regurgitate meat for the youngsters. The coyote family remains together through the summer and often until the next breeding season.

RIGHT: *The coyote family is tight knit. Pups walk about a month after birth. Their first prey are usually insects.*

COYOTE DISTRIBUTION MAP *showing the vast range of this predator.*

LEFT: *A coyote investigates a prairie dog burrow. Coyotes hunt both alone and in family groups. Pups learn hunting techniques from their parents.*

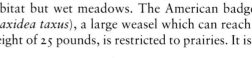

north of Mexico. Like the bison, however, they have since been protected. Today, more than 200,000 pronghorns roam the west, both in and around parks and refuges. So many of them now exist that sport hunting of these animals – which are prized for the excellent flavor of their meat – is allowed in several states.

Among the predators, the adaptable coyote (*Canis latrans*) hunts in virtually every Badlands habitat but wet meadows. The American badger (*Taxidea taxus*), a large weasel which can reach a weight of 25 pounds, is restricted to prairies. It is a

The thirteen-lined ground squirrel (Spermophilus tridecemilneatus) ranges throughout the heart of the prairie region. Ground squirrels live in burrows and forage near their homes. Many other animals, such as hawks and snakes, prey on them.

powerful excavator and can dig rodents out of their burrows. The rodents it eats include the thirteen-lined ground squirrel (*Spermophilus tridecemlineatus*) and the black-tailed prairie dog (*Cynomys ludovicianus*).

The ecological role of prairie dogs

The black-tailed is one of four prairie dog species inhabiting the west, the others being the white-tailed (*C. leucurus*), the gunnison (*C. gunnisoni*) and the Utah (*C. parvidens*). The range of the black-tailed prairie dog covers most of the mid- and shortgrass prairie region from southern Alberta and Saskatchewan to the Mexican border. The eastern edge of the species' distribution approximately coincides with areas that receive less than 30 inches of precipitation a year. Although they live on grasses and other plants, prairie dogs do not prosper on the eastern tallgrass prairies, because the dense growth of the tallgrass makes burrowing difficult and makes it hard to see predators. The three white-tailed species range from southern Montana to parts of Utah and Colorado, central Arizona and New Mexico.

The black-tailed prairie dog usually inhabits plains, while the white-tailed prefers mountain meadows 5,000–8,500 feet in elevation. In some places, however, such as the Black Hills of South Dakota, black-tailed prairie dogs live in both types

of habitat. The rodents weigh 2 to 3 pounds each.

Prairie dogs, especially the black-tailed, were once numerous on the grasslands. According to some estimates there were as many as 25 billion of them before agricultural practises encroached on their territory. The black-tailed species live in colonies, some of which cover vast areas. One colony of 400 million rodents, observed in 1900 in Texas, covered more than 25,000 square miles.

Today, prairie dog colonies, known as 'towns', are widely scattered, and have vanished from most of the areas they once occupied. Their disappearance is a result of the disruption of the delicate natural balance of the plains by humans.

Before the grasslands were altered for agricultural purposes, and before the great bison herds disappeared, there was an intricate relationship between the prairie, prairie dog and bison. Prairie dogs, in addition to eating plants, chew them down to prevent their view of predators from being obscured. Even shortgrass prairie has such thick root systems that it makes burrowing hard work for the rodents, and discourages their establishment. However, as the bison migrated over the prairie, the vast herds grazed down the vegetation, providing a better habitat for prairie dogs. When the bison moved on, the prairie dogs, by burrowing, aerated the soil that had been trampled on by the herds. As a result, the grasses regenerated.

INSIDE A PRAIRIE DOG BURROW

THE burrow of a prairie dog (*Cynomys*) is composed of several tunnels and chambers. The network of tunnels can be quite long, covering more than 30 feet. Chambers serve as listening posts, turn-arounds, nests and dens. The arrangement of a burrow can vary according to the individual prairie dog. Prairie dogs spend more than half of their lifespan underground in their burrows, which are their chief means of defense against the many predators that like to feed on them.

RIGHT: *Black-tailed prairie dogs* (C. ludovicianus*) have emerged from their burrow to feed. Prairie dogs obtain most of their water from plants.*

BELOW: *A cross section of a burrow shows a typical arrangement of tunnels and chambers excavated by prairie dogs.*

KEY TO BURROW
A Safety hatch
B Plunge hole
C Nesting chamber
D Listening post

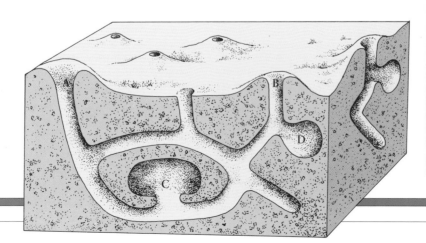

Cattle are confined and do not migrate. As herds were introduced to particular areas they disturbed the grasslands to the point of overgrazing, enabling prairie dogs to prosper. The grass had no time to rejuvenate and dwindled. Ranchers, believing that the loss of the grasses was due to the prairie dogs, instigated eradication campaigns. As a result, prairie dogs are scarce where they once were abundant. Fortunately, control now occurs on a very selective basis.

Prairie dog towns

Prairie dog families live in remarkably well-engineered, extensive burrows. The burrows have a number of chambers, an entrance and, about 10 yards away, an escape hatch, loosely sealed with mounded soil that can be cleared away in a flash. A mound of dirt is erected around the entrance to serve as a levee against flooding in times of heavy rain. If the barrier breaks and the burrow is flooded, the prairie dogs retreat to the mounded escape hatch, which is above ground level and, except in extreme weather, does not fill with water.

The burrow also provides a safe retreat from predators, not only mammals but many birds of prey, including the golden eagle (*Aquila chrysaetos*), red-tailed hawk (*Buteo jamaicensis*), Swainson's hawk (*B. swainsoni*) and ferruginous hawk (*B. regalis*), which tend to target the young.

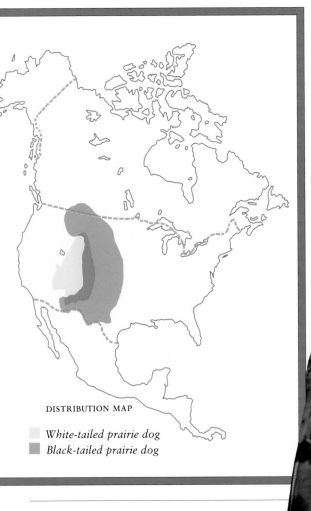

DISTRIBUTION MAP

White-tailed prairie dog
Black-tailed prairie dog

*A Swainson's hawk (*Buteo swainsoni*) soars over the Montana grasslands. This hawk is exclusively a western species. Its main prey consists of rodents. Although found in mountains and coniferous forest all the way to the southern margins of the tundra, it is most common in grasslands.*

Colonial life provides advantageous means of defense for the prairie dog. Multiple eyes, ears and noses are alert for danger. If a prairie dog sees, hears or smells danger, it stands on its hind legs and emits a loud, shrill alarm call. Nearby members of the colony then stand and sound the alarm as well.

If a predator approaches a burrow, all those prairie dogs on the surface which inhabit the burrow bolt for cover. The end of a threat is signaled by a whistle, after which the prairie dogs carefully emerge from their underground havens.

However, the prairie dogs do not have a cooperative community organization (such as ants have, for example). There is no organization of labor or system of dominance within the town as a whole. The prairie dog town is not so much a society as a gathering of individual, extended families, called coteries, each with its own group of burrows. Except during the breeding season, when the young may wander beyond territorial boundaries, families preserve the integrity of their burrows and do not go from one territory to another.

Within the family, however, there is a strong social order, usually headed by a dominant male. Members of the family reinforce their relationships with one another by a variety of behaviors, such as grooming, and even 'kissing'.

A number of other animals live in and around prairie dog towns. The small burrowing owl (*Athene cunicularia*) lives and nests in abandoned prairie dog burrows. Adult owls sometimes feed on young prairie dogs while adult prairie dogs in turn eat owls' eggs and nestlings. Young prairie dogs are also sometimes the victims of the western rattlesnake (*Crotalus viridis*), which, like the owl, inhabits vacant burrows.

No predator is more closely associated with prairie dogs than the black-footed ferret (*Mustela nigripes*), a relatively large member of the weasel family with a body length of up to 18 inches and a 6-inch tail. No ferrets are known to exist in the wild because of the extermination of prairie dogs and subsequent disappearance of their towns. Several hundred, however, have been bred in captivity (*see Conservation*). The black-footed ferret has never been common and has suffered proportionately more losses from the war waged by humans against the prairie dog than the prairie dog itself.

Wild horses

Nothing evokes stronger images of the Old West than herds of wild horses galloping across the prairie. Although wild horses lived in North America during prehistoric times, they died out after the Pleistocene epoch. Those roaming the prairies today are not native wild horses, but the feral descendants of escaped domesticated stock, *Equus caballus*, which came from Spain.

The horse arrived in North America with the Spanish in the 16th century. Escaped horses thrived on the western grasslands, and by the 17th century herds numbered in the thousands. The first escapees roamed Mexico and the south-west and gradually spread into Canada. As they spread north, Indians of the plains, who were hunter-gatherers with no beast of burden but the dog, captured and learned to breed and ride them as war ponies. Some of the Indian ponies escaped, adding once more to the wild herds. A century or so later, the plains tribes could boast some of the most expert horsemen on earth.

The horse dramatically changed the Indians' way of life. No longer did they stalk bison on foot, but could pursue their prey on the backs of fleet ponies. The Comanche, who chiefly inhabited an area from Colorado to Texas, were considered by some to have the finest horsemen in the world.

With the advent of modern ranching, the wild horse was regarded as a nuisance and a grazing competitor for cattle. The horse, like the prairie dog and bison, became the victim of extermination programs. Today, however, the descendants of those that survived are protected by law.

One of the surviving wild horse populations lives in the Badlands of Theodore Roosevelt National Park, where, during the 1880s and 1890s, Roosevelt was the owner of two ranches. The park is one of the few places where wild horses can still be observed.

The Roosevelt herd numbers about 50 animals, kept at that level by periodic roundups. Wildlife managers believe 50 horses is the maximum number the park can support. Surplus horses are sold at public auction.

Roosevelt himself observed, while living on his home ranch:

> In a great many – indeed, in most localities, there are wild horses to be found which, although invariably of domestic descent, being either themselves runaways from some ranch or Indian outfit, or else claiming such for their sires and dams, yet are quite as wild as the pronghorn antelopes on whose domain they have intruded.

Photographs and drawings of horses that roved the Badlands a century ago indicate that those of the national park today are their descendants. The horses of yesteryear had large heads and short backs, were often blue or roan in color, and many had white faces and patches on their sides. Called an apron, this color pattern is not common nowadays except in the Roosevelt herd.

Wary, with good vision, hearing and smell, wild horses live in small family bands of about 5 to 15 individuals. Young stallions live in bachelor groups until they can secure mares for themselves.

The family band is led by a dominant stallion, and the rest of the herd consists of his mares and their young, although it is not unknown for a

OPPOSITE: *A burrowing owl (Athene cunicularia) peeks out of the burrow in which it nests. The owls occasionally prey on young prairie dogs. The adult prairie dogs turn the tables and eat owl nestlings and eggs.*

THIS PAGE: *The breeding range of the short-eared owl (Asio flammeus) is immense. It covers much of North America, the West Indies, Eurasia and various islands in the Pacific. This owl is even found in the Galapagos and other Pacific island groups. Its range extends from the frigid climate of Siberia to the steaming heat of Borneo, and it is most abundant in open country, especially grassland. Short-eared owls sometimes nest in small and loose colonies. They are ground nesters, preferring to set up housekeeping among tallgrass. Rodents and other small animals are their prey. The name of the short-eared owl comes from the tiny tufts of feathers above its eyes.*

second male to run with the group. Stallions herd their mares with head and neck extended close to the ground. When a band is fleeing danger, a dominant mare leads and the stallion brings up the rear to ensure that stragglers do not fall behind and to act as rear guard.

Colts and fillies are driven from the band when they reach sexual maturity, which is between the age of two and three years. Bachelor stallions can establish their own harems by either mating with the fillies or challenging a dominant stallion. If a bachelor tries to steal mares from a band, a ferocious battle, with teeth and hooves, is likely to result as the lead stallion defends his herd.

BIRDS Teeming with small mammals, especially rodents, and insects, the prairies draw many resident and nesting birds. Since the grasslands span the continent from the border between Mexico and the United States, moreover, they contain myriad stopping places for migratory birds (*see Rivers, Lakes and Wetlands*).

Above the prairie several birds of prey often circle overhead. Red-tailed (*Buteo jamaicensis*), Swainson's (*B. swainsoni*) and ferruginous (*B. regalis*) hawks all hunt rodents on the grasslands. Small mammals are also the prey of the swift prairie falcon (*Falco mexicanus*), a light brown bird with a maximum wingspan of 43 inches, but at least half of its prey consists of other birds. Although the prairie falcon is a bird of open areas, it nests on cliffs and buttes. The Badlands, with their combination of rugged and level terrain, provide the ideal habitat for this bird.

Another bird that seeks its prey in open country but nests where the landscape is rugged is the cliff swallow (*Hirundo pyrrhonota*), found in both Badlands and Theodore Roosevelt national parks. The cliff swallow makes a gourd-shaped nest of mud, which it plasters to a vertical surface, such as a canyon wall, a cliff face or a man-made equivalent (such as the side of a building). Cliff swallows were made famous for their regular return to the mission at San Juan Capistrano in California, where they return every year almost at the same time and on the same day.

Another unusual bird's nest found in the grasslands is that of the black-billed magpie (*Pica pica*). Positioned on or close to the ground, the magpie nest is a huge assemblage of sticks, usually about 2 feet in diameter but sometimes as much as 4 feet. Inside the construction, the magpie builds a mud cup lined with grass and animal hair, where it lays its eggs and broods.

The short-eared owl (*Asio flammeus*) is also an open country bird and found through most of the grasslands, although in winter some of these owls migrate further east. They nest in tallgrass, lining shallow depressions with feathers and pieces of vegetation. Sometimes they nest in loose colonies.

CLIFF SWALLOW COLONIES

THE banks of canyons and cliffs in areas such as the Badlands provide ideal sites for nesting colonies of the cliff swallow (*Hirundo pryrrhonota*), a bird primarily of open country. Colonies of cliff swallows may consist of thousands of birds. They are similar to Cave Swallows (*H. fulva*) in appearance.

The cliff swallow builds a round nest of mud and clay which it attaches to a vertical surface such as the side of a cliff or even a building. This swallow has a dark chestnut and blackish throat and a pale forehead. Juveniles are much duller and grayer.

ABOVE: *Magpies (*Pica pica*) are common grassland birds. The magpie is characterized by its long tail, longer than its body, and its white wing patches. It belongs to the same family (Corvidae) as crows and jays.*

DESERTS

As the ability of the air to evaporate water exceeds annual rainfall, the shortgrass plains gradually – ever so gradually – merge into desert. Such a transition occurs in West Texas on the barren Staked Plains, in the lower Rio Grande Valley of South Texas, and west of the Rocky Mountains on the vast Colorado Plateau.

Between grassland and true desert lie various intermediate environments, their boundaries blurred and difficult even for ecologists to define precisely. Typically, in a transition that can be vertical, with altitude, or horizontal, with latitude, as moisture decreases, shortgrass plains give way to thinly vegetated desert grassland, also known as arid steppe. This is followed by woody scrub, sometimes called semi-desert, and then by true desert.

The saguaro cactus (Cereus giganteus) grows only in the Sonoran Desert, and is protected at preserves such as Saguaro National Monument near Tucson. Other species shown here at the Monument include the teddy bear cholla (Opuntia bigelovi) and paloverde (Cercidium microphyllum).

THE chief characteristics these environments share with one another and with true desert is that all are short of water. True desert differs from desert grassland and semi-desert in its ecological definition, which describes it as an area that receives less than 10 inches of rainfall annually. True desert may be accurately termed high desert, low, cool desert or hot desert, with a number of subdivisions.

DESERT CHARACTERISTICS

For a desert to exist, almost all the water that falls from the clouds must be lost. Sometimes this occurs before the raindrops even spatter on the ground. It is not necessarily caused by high air temperatures. Each of the North American deserts lies in the rain shadow of mountains. Moist air flowing eastward from the Pacific Ocean is forced aloft as it meets these mountains, and as it rises, it cools. The moisture in the air then condenses, and rain falls, usually on the western slopes of the mountains. By the time air flows out over the lowlands to the east it has lost its moisture, and could not produce moisture even if air temperatures were lower. If rain does reach the land, often during brief, torrential cloudbursts, it rapidly runs off the ground surface through ravines and gullies, causing typical desert flash floods, which evaporate in a flash off the surface of the soil. Hardly any moisture from rainfall remains available to plants and animals, although they can glean some moisture from dew that condenses during the night.

The searing heat of deserts is by no means constant. They can be places of climatic extremes,

Blue yucca. Yuccas (Yucca) grow throughout the North American deserts, and have stiff leaves with sharp points. Indian tribes used the plants' tough fibers to weave baskets and similar items.

during the course of a single day as well as seasonally. Without the thick layer of vegetation common to non-desert areas, their surfaces lose tremendous amounts of heat through radiation at night. Even in the hottest deserts, temperatures drop to chilly levels after dark. High-altitude deserts can be frigid in winter throughout both day and night.

How plants and animals survive in the desert

There are many fascinating ways in which plants and animals have adapted in order to survive in the desert environment. Seeds of desert plants do not readily dry out, and the seeds can last long periods in a dormant state. However, during brief but drenching seasonal rains, they sprout, grow and flower within weeks, briefly turning the barren landscape into a multi-colored natural canvas.

SAGEBRUSH

ABOUT 20 species of sagebrush or wormwood (*Artemisia*) grow in arid parts of western North America from northern Canada and Alaska to Mexico. Clothed in grayish-green leaves, sagebrush is a tough plant able to suck water from the soil even when its moisture content is very low. When sagebrush requires water, it shuts pores in its leaves, setting up suction in the roots which draws water from the soil. Some animals, including the mule deer (*Odocoileus hemionus*), eat sagebrush.

Sagebrush is adapted to conditions of extreme seasonal temperature change and aridity. Evergreen, it has two sets of leaves annually.

Many desert plants have spongy or fleshy tissues that store moisture, and thick-skinned leaves, some waxy coated, which prevent its loss. Leaves are often small, reducing the area from which water can evaporate, or covered with tiny hairs that reflect sunlight. Other plants bear leaves only during rainy episodes. Shallow but extensive root systems, close to the surface, allow many desert plants to absorb water quickly from a large area before the surface water evaporates. Other plants have roots which extend 30 feet deep or more, thereby enabling the plants to tap underground water supplies.

Desert animals stay out of the sun during the heat of the day, many sheltering underground. Reptiles, whose body heat is governed by the temperature of their surroundings, are especially vulnerable to temperature fluctuations. During the day, they may spread their bodies, or bodily structures such as throat pouches, increasing their surface area. They bask and soak up warmth before the night brings unduly cool temperatures. Otherwise throat pouches are generally used for territorial display and courtship, for short display durations.

The metabolism of desert animals reduces excretion of water, promotes its storage and, in some cases, actually produces water. Kangaroo rats (*Dipodomys*) have a modified kidney that concentrates urine to a paste, almost solid. Natural heat exchangers in their nasal passages minimize moisture loss while breathing. These creatures do not need to drink free water, but can derive moisture from metabolism of seeds.

In other desert species which do not drink free water, the water contained in food is their only source, which, for carnivores, is the fluids of prey. Herbivorous desert animals can masticate and digest the toughest and thorniest of plants. Fat, deposited when food is plentiful, provides energy for myriad desert animals when food is scarce. No better example exists than the fat-laden hump of the Arabian camel. An example from the American desert is the gila monster (*Heloderma suspectum*), one of only two venomous lizards in the world, which stores fat in its chunky tail.

THE GREAT AMERICAN DESERT

The 19th-century pathfinder Zebulon Pike named the arid interior which lies west of the Rocky Mountains the Great American Desert. It consists of four different desert regions, with transitional environments between them. The regions are similar, but each has its distinct characteristic plant communities.

Almost all of this vast 440,000-square-mile desert complex lies between the Rockies and the Sierra Nevada of California. To the south, flanking

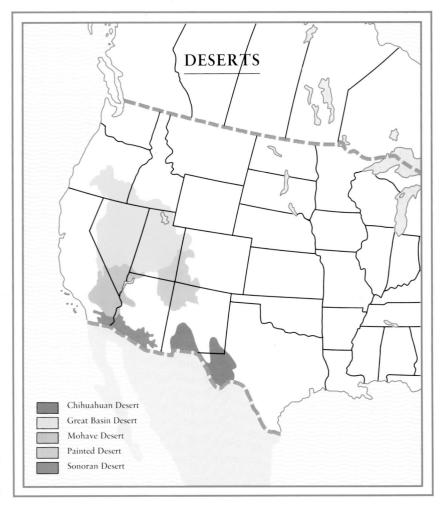

DESERTS

Chihuahuan Desert
Great Basin Desert
Mohave Desert
Painted Desert
Sonoran Desert

the Rockies, stretch the northern limits of deserts that extend into Mexico. Most of the Great American Desert lies on plateaux which are often more than a mile high. This tableland is broken by isolated mountain ranges, sometimes peaking at about 12,000 feet. The true desert of Nevada, however, lies largely in broad, flat valleys flanked by mountains.

Dry, sun-seared desert may be separated from cold, moist northern coniferous mountain forest by only a few thousand feet, vertically (*see Mountains*). Temperature drops with altitude, whilst moisture increases – but not as a result of the drop in temperature. Peaks standing in desert may receive three times the amount of rain as the landscape from which they rise.

THE SONORAN DESERT

The Sonoran Desert, which covers 120,000 square miles and extends from Mexico into south-western Arizona and south-eastern California, is a hot desert, where summer temperatures average 90°F and winter temperatures are usually over 40°F. Winter highs, however, often approach 70°F, while between May and September the temperature often reaches 100°F.

RIGHT: *These woody ribs remain after a saguaro cactus (*Cereus giganteus*) dies. When the plant is alive, they serve as a skeleton for the fleshy tissue, which can absorb a lot of water.*

FAR RIGHT: *The collared peccary (*Dicotyles tajacu*) frequents the deserts of southern Arizona and New Mexico and south-western Texas. Peccaries live in small herds and are omnivorous.*

The true Sonoran Desert lies below 4,500 feet, and is the most spectacular of American deserts for plant life. Only here does the towering saguaro cactus (*Cereus giganteus*) grow, which motion pictures have made characteristic of the west. In fact it has a very restricted range, not just geographically but according to terrain. In Arizona the saguaro grows only in rocky or gravel soils between about 2,000 and about 4,500 feet, mostly on slopes with a southern exposure.

Saguaro National Monument

A remarkable plant, the saguaro can live for 200 years and may weigh several tons, most of the weight due to stored water. The best site of this giant cactus and the plant and animal communities of the Sonoran Desert is Saguaro National Monument, which covers more than 64,000 acres near Tucson, Arizona.

The zonation of desert and desert-like communities stands out vividly on the Monument's 8,666-foot-high Mica Mountain. Below 3,000 feet, the sandy desert is dominated by widely spaced and low growths of creosotebush (*Larrea divaricata*), as well as saltbush (*Atriplex polycarpa*) and burr sage (*Franseria dumosa*). Relatively moist areas, such as washes, support stands of mesquite trees (*Prosopis*), which grow thickly on the arid grasslands to the east of the desert.

Above 3,000 feet, the Sonoran Desert marker community, dominated by saguaro and shrubby paloverde (*Cercidium*) trees, begins. Along with the saguaro myriad other cacti grow – the Sonoran has more species of cacti than any other of the American deserts – such as barrel (*Echinocactus*), prickly pear (*Opuntia*) and cholla (*Opuntia*). Ascending, the saguaro zone ends where it meets a narrow belt of desert grassland, which in turn is followed by a mixture of dominant scrub live oak (*Quercus turbinella*), manzanita (*Arctostaphylos*) and sundry other plants that together form nearly impenetrable thickets known as chaparral.

Above the chaparral the forest zones begin, culminating in high-altitude stands of firs.

The cactus forest

Saguaro belts such as that in the National Monument are in a sense cactus forests. Indeed, from a distance they look like forests of great branched green columns rising from the rocky, gravelly slopes, and spilling over into ravines. Here and there stand the skeletons of dead saguaros, with only the longitudinal woody ribs that served as the framework of the plant remaining.

The saguaro, threatened by habitat destruction and collectors of cacti, is important to the life cycles of myriad animals. Its seeds sustain numerous small creatures, including desert kangaroo rats (*Dipodomys deserti*) and the white-winged dove (*Zenaida asiatica*).

Most of the saguaro seeds are eaten by animals, but a few manage to sprout. The cactus grows very slowly, and after five years is no longer than a finger. After 75 years, it stands about 20 feet high and develops arms. When full grown, it can reach 50 feet high and weigh 10 tons.

Inside the hard skin of the saguaro, pulpy tissues swell with water absorbed by its fanned-out root system during rare periods of rainfall. The trunk is pleated like an accordion, and expands in order to accommodate the swelling interior.

In April and May, the tips of the saguaro arms flower with clusters of creamy, cup-shaped blossoms, each in bloom for only 24 hours. During the day, white-winged doves flock to the nectar of the flowers. Their feathers become dusted with pollen from the flowers, which they inadvertently carry to fertilize other saguaros. At night, insects and the nectar-feeding big longnose bat (*Leptonycteris nivalis*) carry out a similar function. The saguaro fruit ripens by mid-summer, when many birds feed on the red pulp and seeds.

MAMMALS Fallen saguaro fruit is gobbled by creatures large and small, among them coyotes (*Canis latrans*), mule deer (*Odocoileus hemionus*), round-tailed ground squirrels (*Spermophilus tereticaudus*), and collared peccaries (*Dicotyles tajacu*), the American relatives of pigs. Occasionally the desert race of the bighorn sheep (*Ovis canadensis*) ventures down from the montane pastures to sample the cactus fruit.

Due to the wide spectrum of environments created by altitude, both desert and non-desert mammals range the region. Those not specifically adapted to the desert include the coatimundi (*Nasua nasua*), the raccoon (*Procyon lotor*), and the ringtail (*Bassariscus astutus*). Although not in the same family as the coatimundi and the raccoon, the ringtail is closely related. The cougar (*Felis concolor*) regularly visits the desert from higher elevations.

BIRDS So many creatures domicile in the saguaro it is called the 'apartment house of the desert'. Red-tailed hawks (*Buteo jamaicensis*) and great horned owls (*Bubo virginianus*) build nests among its arms. The gila woodpecker (*Melanerpes uropygialis*) depends mainly on the saguaro for nest holes. Pecking away at the spongy tissue, the woodpecker drills deep pockets in which it houses its young. The gilded flicker (*Colaptes auratus chrysoides*) does likewise.

The abandoned holes of these birds are occupied by other small birds such as purple martins (*Progne subis*), American kestrels (*Falco sparverius*) and the sparrow-sized elf owl (*Micrathene whitneyi*). The range of the elf owl parallels that of the giant cactus.

In all, about 250 species of birds inhabit Saguaro National Monument and adjacent areas. The largest of these birds is the majestic golden eagle (*Aquila chrysaetos*), and the smallest are hummingbirds, represented by half a dozen stunning species.

AMPHIBIANS AND REPTILES Not surprisingly, few moisture-loving amphibians make their home in the desert. Some, like Couch's spadefoot toad (*Scaphiopus couchi*), estivate beneath the desert surface, except when breeding during the summer rainy season.

Reptiles, on the other hand, abound, and many are highly adapted. Found only in sandy parts of the Sonoran Desert, the fringe-toed lizard (*Uma notata*) has feet that act like snowshoes, enabling it to whiz across the sand, even on its rear legs. Using its toes, the lizard can also 'swim' in sand. Loose-skinned chuckwallas (*Sauromalus obesus*) are found throughout the deserts of south-eastern California, western Arizona and southern Utah and Nevada.

The desert iguana (*Dipsosaurus dorsalis*) roves the hottest creosotebush country, and has such tolerance of high temperatures that it remains active throughout the day. Like many lizards, the desert iguana can change its hue. Scientists have suggested an interesting correlation between the changing color of the desert iguana and external temperature. When the lizard is light in color, it can absorb more visible and ultraviolet light than when it is darker. The color of a desert iguana that emerges from a cool burrow into sunlight may start to lighten in order for it to absorb heat more quickly. At that point, the lizard begins to bask. As its body temperature rises, the iguana becomes active. From then on, its color relates not to temperature but to the color of its surroundings.

One reptile of the Sonoran Desert that has attracted considerable attention because of its rarity is the desert tortoise (*Gopherus agassazi*). More than 14 inches in length, this tortoise digs long burrows where it hides from enemies, shelters from the sun and deposits its eggs.

INVERTEBRATES Invertebrate life of the Sonoran Desert is spectacular and includes some desert monsters. The venomous giant desert centipede (*Scolopendra heros*) is 8 inches long and hunts insects and even small mammals by night. Other gargantuans of the Sonoran world are the tarantula hawks (*Pepsis*). These wasps grow up to 5 inches long and hunt tarantula spiders (Theraphosidae).

BELOW LEFT: *The chuckwalla (*Sauromalus obesus*) ranges widely throughout the deserts of the South. When alarmed, these lizards inflate by filling themselves with air, then wedge themselves into a crack or cranny to prevent predators from extricating them.*

BELOW: *The Joshua tree (*Yucca brevifolia*) gives its name to Joshua Tree National Monument in the Mohave Desert. This big yucca is characteristic of the Mohave.*

LOOKS DON'T KILL

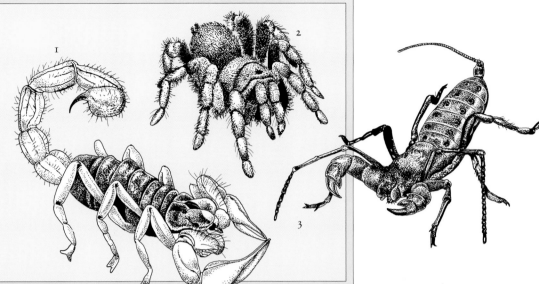

Of the many desert species of spiders and scorpions, a few are sufficiently venomous to endanger humans. Although fierce looking, the tarantula spider (Theraphosidae) and giant hairy scorpion (*Hadrurus arizonensis*) are not deadly, and the whip scorpion (*Mastigoproctus giganteus*) is non-venomous.

DESERT ARACHNIDS
1 *Giant hairy scorpion*
2 *Tarantula spider*
3 *Whip scorpion*

The tarantula spiders themselves are almost as large as a hand.

The giant hairy scorpion (*Hadrurus arizonensis*) is 5 inches long and venomous, but not as dangerous as its smaller relative, the bark scorpion (*Centruriodes sculpturatus*), the sting of which can be fatal to humans. Not a true scorpion, the largest non-venomous whip scorpion, *Mastigoproctus giganteus*, which can grow to 4 inches in length, is a voracious insect-eater, catching insects with its large pincers.

THE MOHAVE DESERT

The desert at Twenty-nine Palms, California, is the hot, dry Mohave, which touches extreme western Arizona and south-western Utah, part of southern Nevada and a large part of south-eastern California. The Mohave, which gives its name to the dangerous rattlesnake *Crotalus scutulatus*, has many plants in common with the Sonoran Desert, which lies to the east and south. The creosotebush and saltbush, for instance, cover many parts of the Mohave. Towering over all is the Joshua tree (*Yucca brevifolia*), which can reach 40 feet in height. This large yucca, which is only found growing at elevations above 3,000 feet, forms extensive scrub forests. These forests thrive in the 556,800-acre Joshua Tree National Monument near Twenty-nine Palms.

The Mohave Desert contains one of the most legendary regions on the face of the planet, Death Valley. Straddling the California–Nevada border, Death Valley National Monument comprises more than 2,000,000 acres of land and contains the lowest-lying spot in the Western Hemisphere; it is probably one of the hottest places in the world after the Danakil Desert of Ethiopia. Badwater, in the Valley, is 282 feet below sea level; the ground

The desert tortoise (Gopherus agassazi) dens and nests in burrows. Desert tortoises are related to the giant tortoises of the Galapagos.

DESERTS

PREVIOUS PAGES: *Although bone dry and baking in the sun most of the year, the desert of Death Valley blooms gorgeously during the brief spring rains. Here, a field of desert gold* (Linanthus aurens) *blooms in Death Valley National Monument, with Corkscrew Peak, of the Grapevine Mountains, in the background.*

RIGHT: *Wind has sculpted the Mesquite Flat Dunes of Death Valley National Monument. In the background are the Grapevine Mountains. Death Valley is in the Mohave Desert, not far west of the eastern flank of the Sierra Nevada.*

OPPOSITE TOP: *The greater roadrunner* (Geococcyx californiana), *a member of the cuckoo family, is a common desert bird. It preys on lizards, snakes, birds' eggs and small birds, and insects. About 2 feet long, the roadrunner seldom flies.*

FAR RIGHT: *Sagebrush or wormwood* (Artemisia) *dots the landscape of the Great Basin Desert in Nevada. During the Pleistocene ice ages the Great Basin was the site of huge lakes, which filled with meltwater from the glaciers that topped the region's mountains.*

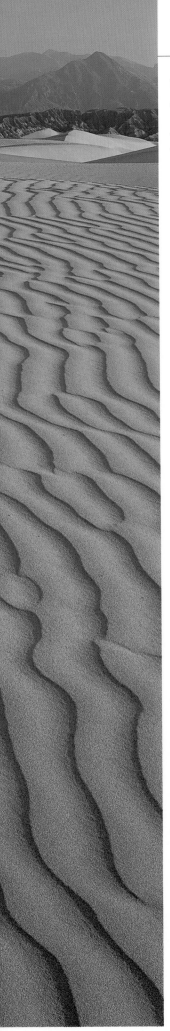

temperature at Death Valley's Furnace Creek on July 15 1972 was an astonishing 201°F.

Walled by mountains on all sides, Death Valley receives only about 2 inches of rain annually. Although winter temperatures are moderate, the summer is scorchingly hot, with air temperatures sometimes surpassing 130°F. Ironically, this baking desert is only a short distance from the cool forests of the High Sierras and the lush vegetation of the Giant Sequoia groves. Mount Whitney, which rises to 14,400 feet above sea level, is less than 100 miles from the lowest point of the continent at Badwater.

Despite the heat and aridity, Death Valley contains many of the animal species that inhabit the Mohave area. Desert bighorns (*Ovis canadensis*) roam the mountain rim. At night desert woodrats (*Neotoma lepida*) wander in search of cactus pulp and seeds. The gray fox (*Vulpes cinereoargenteus*) and kit fox (*Vulpes macrotis*), a desert race of the grasslands swift fox (*Vulpes velox*), stalk the rodents.

More than 200 species of birds have been seen at one time or another in the valley. As elsewhere in the south-western deserts, one of the most active birds is the roadrunner (*Geococcyx californiana*), a terrestrial cuckoo that speeds across the desert on long, strong legs. Its call is similar to that of other cuckoos, descending in pitch. Unlike most species in the Old World, it is not a brood-parasite but builds its own nest, incubates its own eggs, and then raises its own young.

The Mohave Desert serves as a transition zone between the Sonoran and the largest desert area of the continent, that of the Great Basin.

THE GREAT BASIN DESERT

Geologically and ecologically, the term 'Great Basin' can be confusing. Geologists define the Great Basin as an internally drained region between the Sierra Nevada and the Wasatch Mountains of central Utah. The region, however, belies the normal concept of a basin. It lies on a high plateau, much of which is above 4,000 feet, and contains parallel mountain ranges which are separated by immense valleys, as in Nevada.

The expanses between the mountains are Great Basin desert, which is high, cool-to-cold desert characterized by big sagebrush (*Artemisia tridentata*) and distinguished from other American deserts by a dearth of cacti. The Great Basin desert does not look at all like the popular conception of desert, and is often described as desert scrub.

The desert extends northwards beyond the geological limits of the Great Basin into Oregon and Wyoming. To the east and south-east, desert scrub covers much of the 130,000-square-mile Colorado Plateau, which extends through south-western Colorado, northern New Mexico, Arizona and southern Utah.

The Colorado Plateau consists of horizontal strata of sedimentary rocks uplifted to 7,000 feet or more. It has been etched by flowing waters into geological spectacles such as the Grand Canyon and Bryce Canyon, famed for the gorgeous colors of their worn-away rock faces.

The vegetation of the mid-elevations of the Colorado Plateau is dominated by low, arid woodlands of pinyon pines such as *Pinus edulis* and *P. monophylla* and junipers (*Juniperus*), standing in semi-desert grasses. Already contrasting with the desert below, above the pinyon pines and junipers grow big pines such as the ponderosa (*Pinus ponderosa*), then spruces (*Picea*) and firs (*Abies*); on the highest peaks is alpine tundra.

Higher elevations on the North Rim of the Grand Canyon receive up to 11 feet of snow annually. To the east of Grand Canyon National Park, however, as altitude decreases and precipitation lessens, true desert appears. This area has been labeled the Painted Desert because of the vivid colors of its rocks.

Great Basin National Park

The diversity of habitats and wildlife in the Great Basin can clearly be seen at Great Basin National Park, established in 1986. A 76,800-acre tract in eastern Nevada, the park's lowest elevations are sagebrush desert, while Wheeler Peak, at 13,063 feet above sea level, is topped by the only glacier in the Great Basin.

MAMMALS In desert areas of the park, the black-tailed jackrabbit (*Lepus californicus*), Townsend's ground squirrel (*Spermophilus townsendii*) and the Great Basin kangaroo mouse (*Microdipodops megacephalus*) are abundant mammal species. Other mammals favor higher, forested elevations.

BIRDS At 7,000 feet above sea level in the Lehman Caves vicinity of the park live a number of desert birds. They include the yellow-breasted chat (*Icteria virens*), rock wren (*Salpinctes obosletus*), black-throated sparrow (*Amphispiza bilineata*), sage grouse (*Centrocercus urophasianus*), and sage thrasher (*Oreoscoptes montanus*). The desert birds exist here alongside coniferous forest birds, such as Clark's nutcracker (*Nucifraga columbiana*), and

ABOVE: *The black-tailed jackrabbit (*Lepus californicus*) ranges over prairies and deserts throughout the western United States. It can run at 35 miles an hour.*

LEFT: *A cactus wren (Campylorhynchus brunneicapillus) perches near its nest. The largest North American wren, it can be 7 inches long.*

PETRIFIED TREES OF ARIZONA

*I*N the Painted Desert of Arizona lies Petrified Forest National Park, site of the largest concentration of petrified wood in the world. Perhaps 200 million years ago huge conifers, much like the sequoias, were toppled and covered by water. The water permeated the wood and deposited minerals in it. Over the ages, the minerals turned to stone. The sections of petrified logs – some of which are more than 9 feet in diameter and 36 feet long – are exact replicas of the ancient tree trunks.

A copy in stone of a section from a prehistoric tree trunk. Erosion has broken down some of the trunks; the smallest chips will eventually be converted into grains of quartz.

OPPOSITE: *Erosion caused by precipitation and rivers has worn away soft rock in many parts of the western deserts and Colorado Plateau into beautiful bridges and arches. Here, Delicate Arch in Utah's Arches National Park is covered with winter snow. The park contains hundreds of spectacular rock formations, including pinnacles and pedestals.*

RAPID REPRODUCERS: SPADEFOOT TOADS

S PADEFOOT toads (*Scaphiopus*) are named for the horny edge of the inside of their hind feet, used to dig burrows. Spadefoots inhabiting deserts may stay underground in a state of dormancy for months during dry spells. When the rains come, from April to July, Great Basin spadefoots (*S. intermontanus*) emerge in vast numbers and go to temporary pools to breed. The young hatch as tadpoles and metamorphose into adults in a few weeks – an adaptation to breeding patterns that results from desert pools drying up rapidly under the hot sun.

Spadefoot toad tadpoles (left) become adults within a few weeks. This reduces the risk of the water evaporating while they still cannot breathe air.

Adult Great Basin spadefoot toads emerge from burrows to breed during rains in such numbers that the desert appears to be crawling with them.

those that prefer pinyon-juniper, such as the northern shrike (*Lanius excubitor*) and loggerhead (great grey) shrike (*L. ludovicianus*). The loggerhead shrike comes from the Arctic to spend the winter in the Great Basin. This bird is known for its habit of impaling small birds, mice and other prey on thorns to make them easier to eat.

REPTILES AND AMPHIBIANS Desert reptiles include the desert night snake (*Hypsiglena torquata deserticola*), which is rear fanged (has venomous fangs in the rear of the jaw) with very weak venom, and the sagebrush lizard (*Sceloporus graciosus*). The western rattlesnake (*Crotalus viridis*) of the Great Basin is very adaptable in its range and can be found on the desert floor as well as at heights up to 11,000 feet above sea level.

CHIHUAHUAN DESERT

The transition between plains grassland and desert in southern and western Texas leads through mesquite semi-desert to the other major desert area of North America. This, the Chihuahuan Desert, spreads across from Mexico into the south-western corner of Texas, southern New Mexico and south-eastern Arizona. Higher than the Sonoran but lower in elevation than the Great Basin, the Chihuahuan Desert is in places grassy or covered with thick scrub. Typical plants are the tarbush (*Flourensia cernua*), mesquite (*Prosopis glandulosa*), the ubiquitous creosotebush (*Larrea*

divaricata), yuccas (*Yucca*), chollas and barrel cacti (both *Opuntia*) and, except for Arizona, yellow-flowered agave, or lechuquilla (*Agave lechequilla*), which is as symbolic of the Chihuahuan Desert as the Joshua tree is of the Mohave.

Most of the Chihuahuan is located on the Mexican Plateau, and, as are the other western deserts, it is studded with mountain ranges. Among the grandest of these are the Guadalupe Mountains, which rise on either side of the Texas–New Mexico border.

Once a stronghold of the fierce Mescalero Apaches, these mountains exhibit zonation ranging from ponderosa pine (*Pinus ponderosa*) at the top to true desert below. The grandeur of the mountains is preserved in the 77,440-acre Guada-lupe Mountains National Park of Texas, site of Guadalupe Peak which, at 8,751 feet above sea level, is the highest point in the state.

Another national park in the region is Big Bend, which covers an area of more than 704,000 acres on the Rio Grande in Texas. Again, the typical mountain desert zonation exists here, with forests on the peaks descending to hot, sandy desert. Big Bend National Park is the home of the world's population of the Chisos Mountain variety of the hedgehog cactus (*Echinocereus reichenbachii* var. *reichenbachii*), with about 1,000 plants in all. The northern reaches of the Chihuahuan are overlain by white gypsum sands, which form immense 50-foot-high dunes in White Sands National Monument, New Mexico.

ABOVE: *Mesquite (Prosopis) grows along desert washes and other moist areas. It spreads rapidly and, where conditions are favorable, can dominate the landscape.*

OPPOSITE: *A claret cup cactus (Echinocerus triglogchidiatus), in Big Bend National Park, Texas, adds a touch of gorgeous color to the Chihuahuan Desert when in bloom.*

The white-tailed antelope ground squirrel (Ammospermophilus leucurus) *is so named because when it runs with its tail curved over its back it evokes the white rump of the pronghorn antelope* (Antilocapra americana).

MAMMALS Chihuahuan wildlife is surprisingly varied. Black bears (*Ursus americanus*), cougars (*Felis concolor*), pronghorn antelopes (*Antilocapra americana*), collared peccaries (*Dicotyles tajacu*) and mule deer (*Odocoileus hemionus*), are among the larger mammals, which may also include the extremely rare Mexican race of the timber wolf (*Canis lupus*). Black-tailed prairie dogs (*Cynomys ludovicianus*) survive in some

areas. Nervous and quick, the white-tailed antelope ground squirrel (*Ammospermophilus leucurus*) forages for plant matter and also for insects.

The bat flight
Unquestionably, the most spectacular wildlife spectacle of the Chihuahuan – and one of the finest anywhere – arises from Carlsbad Caverns, in Carlsbad Caverns National Park at the edge of the

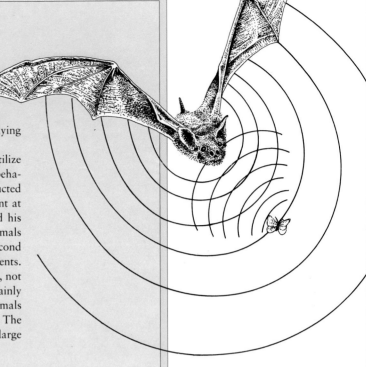

ECHOLOCATION BY BATS

BATS navigate and pinpoint the location of flying insects by a form of natural sonar called echolocation. The bat emits a series of high-pitched sounds – up to 200 per second – then listens to the echoes when they bounce back off objects. Scientists believe that some bats, at least, use echolocation so precisely that they can distinguish between different types of insects, their speed and flight pattern. In less than a second, a bat can emit a pulse of sound, listen for and analyze the echo off an insect, then chase and catch it.

Some of the moths upon which bats feed seem to have a defense mechanism specifically adapted to the sounds bats make to echolocate. Under experimental conditions, certain moths subjected to pulses of sound in the high frequencies

Bats can pinpoint insects as tiny as mosquitoes using sonar-like echolocation.

used by bats take evasive action by flying erratically.

Credit for proving that bats utilize echolocation goes to famed animal behaviorist Donald R. Griffin, who conducted research in the 1930s while a student at Harvard University and announced his findings in 1941. Bats, the only mammals capable of true flight, are the second largest mammalian order, after rodents. There are about 2,000 types of bats, not all of which eat insects. Some live mainly on fruit while others catch small animals such as birds and even other bats. The vampire bats exist on the blood of large mammals and even birds.

Guadalupe Mountains. Two hundred feet below the surface of Carlsbad Caverns, about 600 feet from its natural entrance, lies a passageway called the Bat Cave. Here, from early spring to October, 300,000 Mexican free-tailed bats (*Tadarida mexicana*) roost during the day.

A maternity roost, and a haven during the heat of the day, the Bat Cave's ceiling is covered by these flying mammals. The adult bat has a wingspan of more than 10 inches. The bats migrate from Mexico each year to give birth and rear their young, usually only one per female, which are born in June.

Like their elders, the youngsters cling to the ceiling, with as many as 300 bats per square foot of space. At dusk, the masses of bats begin to stir, fitfully fluttering. It is time for them to leave the cave and hunt the insects on which they feed.

At first, only a few bats wing from the cavern mouth. Minutes later, however, hordes of them surge forth like a living whirlwind that spirals into the darkening sky. As they gain altitude, an elongated cloud of the flying mammals snakes across the heavens towards the south-east where they go to feed over the valleys of the Pecos and Black rivers.

Dawn signals the return of the bats, flitting back in small groups or even singly. Their re-entry into the cave, like their exit from it, is spectacular, but performed on an individual basis. While still high in the air, each bat folds its wings close to its body and plummets earthward. Unerringly, it then opens its wings and flies into the mouth of the cave and disappears into the roost until evening falls.

BIRDS As the bird life of the Salton Sea testifies, any water area in a desert draws immense numbers and species of birds. The simple reason for this is that there is no other place for them to go.

The birds of Bosque del Apache
One such desert water area, on the northern fringes of the New Mexico desert, is the Bosque del Apache National Wildlife Refuge. Here, 9 miles from the Rio Grande, wildlife managers have created an extensive wildlife refuge that offers an ideal wintering habitat for waterfowl and other aquatic birds, plus a variety of perching birds.

In all, nearly 300 different species of birds have been seen on the refuge. Canada geese (*Branta canadensis*) and northern pintails (*Anas acuta*) migrate to the refuge from northern prairie breeding grounds. Mallards (*A. platyrhynchos*) dabble in the water all year round. Herons, especially the great blue heron (*Ardea herodias*), wade through the shallows. Ring-billed gulls (*Larus delawarensis*) wheel overhead. Such great flocks of water birds surviving in the desert may seem surprising, but they emphasize that deserts, although they may seem barren, really throb with life.

REPTILES The western diamondback rattlesnake (*Crotalus atrox*), which reaches its northern limits in the south-western desert, can be found in the Chihuahuan, as can numerous non-venomous snakes, such as the bullsnake (*Pituophis melanoleucus*). This desert is also the realm of the famed Texas horned lizard (*Phrynosoma coronatum*), more popularly known as the horned toad.

RIVERS, LAKES
and
WETLANDS

Every ecological community in North America, even in deserts, is influenced in some way by rivers, lakes and wetlands. They have far-reaching effects on the plant and animal life of disparate environments. The Colorado River and the Rio Grande flow through desert for much of their length, providing a green belt of plants and a feeding ground for wild creatures that spill over into the country beyond.

The lower Mississippi River contains myriad islands and sand bars. Rivers and river valleys are important thoroughfares for the dispersal of terrestrial wildlife as well as aquatic animals. Mammals move through the valleys and birds follow them on migration.

Inland lakes and wetlands are the breeding grounds of many different animals, including waterfowl which, when they migrate, enrich the fauna of areas sometimes thousands of miles from where they hatch. Many sea creatures breed in coastal marshes. Others breed in the sea, but the young go to the coastal marshes.

Wetlands, rivers and lakes are often linked. Lakes and wetlands give rise to rivers, and they are frequently formed when backwaters of rivers are cut off by sediment. Wetlands exist on the fringes of lakes and rivers (*see also South-eastern Forests and Subtropical Wetlands*).

MAJOR LAKES

Of the 50 largest lakes in the world, North America has 15, which is more than any other continent. The interconnected Great Lakes shared by the United States and Canada form the largest fresh-water area in the world, with a total surface area of almost 90,000 square miles. Of these, Lake Superior, covering 20,600 square miles in the United States and 11,100 square miles in Canada, is second only to the Caspian Sea as the Earth's largest freshwater lake.

North America contains lakes larger than some of the Great Lakes, however. Of the Great Lakes only Superior, Huron and Michigan lakes are larger than Great Bear Lake and Great Slave Lake, which are both in the Northwest Territories and cover 12,096 and 11,031 square miles respectively. Manitoba's Lake Winnipeg, at 9,417 square miles, is larger than Lake Ontario.

Other huge lakes of the North American continent include Athabasca in Alberta and Saskatchewan (3,064 square miles in area); Lake Nettilling on Baffin Island (2,140 square miles in area); Lake Winnipegosis in Manitoba (which covers 2,075 square miles) and nearby Lake Manitoba (covering 1,799 square miles).

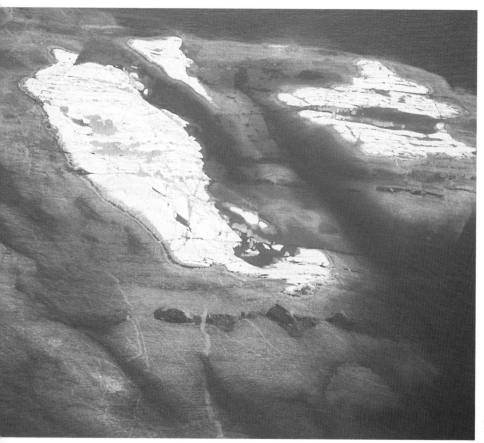

ABOVE: *Georgian Bay Shoals in Lake Huron. The Great Lakes contain 18 per cent of the world's fresh water. Thirty-eight million people live around the Great Lakes, which conservationists are trying to save from pollution.*

RIGHT: *The Fraser River flows beneath the majestic peak of Mount Robeson in the Rocky Mountains of British Columbia. The Fraser empties into the Strait of Georgia at Vancouver.*

MAJOR RIVERS

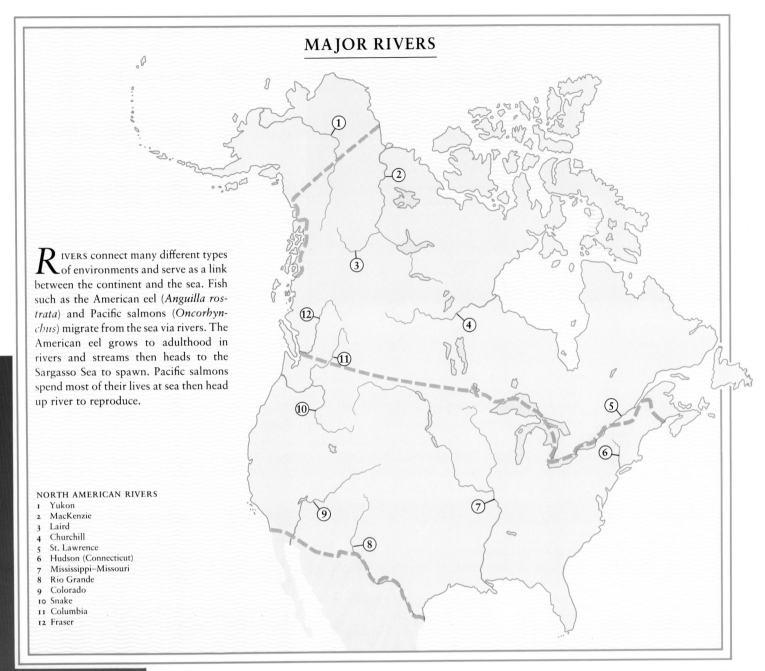

RIVERS connect many different types of environments and serve as a link between the continent and the sea. Fish such as the American eel (*Anguilla rostrata*) and Pacific salmons (*Oncorhynchus*) migrate from the sea via rivers. The American eel grows to adulthood in rivers and streams then heads to the Sargasso Sea to spawn. Pacific salmons spend most of their lives at sea then head up river to reproduce.

NORTH AMERICAN RIVERS
1 Yukon
2 MacKenzie
3 Laird
4 Churchill
5 St. Lawrence
6 Hudson (Connecticut)
7 Mississippi–Missouri
8 Rio Grande
9 Colorado
10 Snake
11 Columbia
12 Fraser

GREAT RIVERS

The rivers of North America include some of the longest in the world. The length of a given river sometimes takes tributaries into account. Thus the combined length of the Mississippi and the Missouri is about 3,700 miles, making the third longest river on earth, after the Nile and the Amazon.

A major river and its tributaries are collectively known as a river system. Besides the Mississippi–Missouri river system, which drains the heartland of the United States, other key North American river systems include the Mackenzie, which starts at Great Slave Lake and empties into the Arctic Ocean more than 2,600 miles away; the Columbia, beginning in Columbia Lake, British Columbia, and flowing more than 1,240 miles to the Pacific Ocean between Washington and Oregon; the Yukon, arising in the Coast Ranges of British Columbia and running for nearly 2,000 miles to the Bering Sea on the Alaskan coast; the Rio Grande, which has its source high in the Rocky Mountains of Colorado and continues for more than 1,700 miles to the Gulf of Mexico; and the Arkansas, which also has its source in Colorado, and meets the Mississippi almost 1,500 miles away.

Where many major rivers meet the sea great cities have arisen: New York lies at the mouth of the Hudson River; New Orleans and Louisiana are at the mouth of the Mississippi; and Vancouver is at the Fraser River's mouth. Environmental conditions at the source of a great river often contrast with those at the mouth. For example, the Fraser and the Missouri rivers begin west and east of the continental divide respectively, in remote areas of the Rocky Mountains.

ABOVE: *Lake Tear of the Clouds on the slopes of Mount Marcy in the Adirondack Mountains is the source of the Hudson River.*

RIGHT: *Captain's Rock along the Columbia River in Washington. The Columbia, which has been extensively dammed, is the major river of the Pacific North-west.*

OPPOSITE: *The lower falls of the Yellowstone River in Yellowstone National Park roar into the Grand Canyon of the Yellowstone. The canyon formed because the rock was weakened by thermal processes beneath the surface and was then eroded by the river.*

River sources

The Mississippi begins its life in northern Minnesota as a mere stream flowing from a small lake, while the source of the Hudson River is the tiny Lake Tear of the Clouds, which lies 4,293 feet above sea level in New York State.

Occasionally the sources of several rivers are not far from each other. On the eastern side of the continental divide in Yellowstone National Park both the Yellowstone and Snake rivers begin. On the western slope, the Snake River descends towards its confluence with the Columbia River in Washington State.

River drainage basins

Great rivers drain and influence vast areas. The Mackenzie river basin covers an area of almost 422,800,000 acres which is bounded on the north by the Arctic Ocean and on the south by the Canadian prairies. The river basin encompasses the Great Slave Lake, the Great Bear Lake, Lake Athabasca and many rivers, including Slave and Peace rivers.

Rivers course through many disparate environments. The Colorado River wells out of the high country of Colorado, starting in a cold climate among coniferous forests. It later cuts through the Colorado Plateau, carving the 220-mile Grand Canyon out of the multi-hued rock (*see Appendices*). The Colorado traverses the desert on the Arizona–Nevada border and ends in the Sonoran Desert (*see Deserts*) in the Gulf of California. Like many other big rivers, particularly in the western United States, the Colorado has been dammed and diverted for irrigation, recreation and other purposes. Where man intervenes, the land, flora and fauna that depended on the original river course are threatened.

The Rio Grande, another great western river, begins in the high country of Colorado in mountain coniferous and aspen (*Populus*) forest. It flows on through the Chihuahuan Desert of New Mexico and reaches the sea through patches of subtropical Mexican palmetto (*Sabal mexicana*) woodlands, which were once extensive.

The palm forest

In the United States sabal palm woodlands exist only in extreme south Texas, although the palms have an extensive range in adjacent Mexico. Little remains of the 40,000 acres of sabal woodlands that once grew along the lower Rio Grande; they have largely been cleared for agriculture. However, a portion of the woodland has been preserved in the 32-acre Sabal Palm Grove Sanctuary near Brownsville, Texas, owned by the National Audubon Society.

Sabal Palm Grove Sanctuary is on the flood plain of the Rio Grande. The plant community of the sanctuary has both temperate and tropical elements, and it hosts many species of wildlife that range no further north into the United States: biologists believe that two endangered tropical cats, the ocelot (*Felis pardalis*) and the jaguarundi (*F. yagouaroundi*) may be found there. Several birds that reach the northern end of their range on the southern fringe of Texas also inhabit the sanctuary. They include the black-bellied whistling duck (*Dendrocygna autumnalis*), the great kiskadee (*Pitangus sulphuratus*) and the groove-billed ani (*Crotophaga sulcirostris*).

WETLANDS

The term wetland encompasses many types of wet environments. In North America these environments include salt marshes, freshwater marshes, coniferous bogs, wooded swamps, seasonally flooded tundra ponds and bottomland hardwood forests, and prairie potholes.

Wetlands are now recognized as important ecological resources that support wildlife and vegetation. Wetlands soak up water like a sponge, thus promoting natural flood control, and also serve as watersheds.

Millions of waterfowl breed in northern wetlands and overwinter in wetlands to the south. Wading birds and shorebirds depend on wetlands for their survival, feeding, resting and reproducing where water meets land.

Frogs are common in wetlands, including wood frogs (*Rana sylvatica*), which live in and around tundra ponds or north-eastern swamps. The surface of the quiet water churns with the breeding frogs in early spring.

Wetlands tend to occur in low-lying areas along rivers, beside lakes or in coastal estuaries which contribute to their existence. However, they can also occur on higher ground, where water seeps

Yellow water lilies (Nuphar polysepalum) *and water shield* (Brasenia schreberi) *grow in an Oregon pond. These plants of lakes, ponds and wetlands root in the bottom and send up long stalks that sprout leaves at the surface.*

PHRAGMITES INVASION

Phragmites greens and grows swiftly in spring and early summer. During the late summer and autumn it becomes dormant and turns brown.

THE reed phragmites (*Phragmites australis*), which can grow up to 20 feet tall, thrives in marshes that have been drained or filled. The reason is that this plant needs soil that is soggy but not waterlogged. Its leaves do not receive enough light underwater for photosynthesis to occur so it cannot live where it is regularly submerged to two thirds its height. Thus, phragmites cannot survive in the middle of a healthy marsh, but can at its edge. When a marsh is drained or filled, however, the conditions change in the favor of phragmites.

Scientists believe that phragmites evolved around the end of the Cretaceous period, about 65 million years ago — about the same time that the dinosaurs are thought to have died out. (The first land plants are now believed to have evolved around 420 million years ago, at the same time as the first land-based invertebrates, such as worms and arthropods.)

Phragmites may be the most widespread of all flowering plants, although it appears to be an introduced species in North America. In the Americas as a whole, phragmites grows from coast to coast from the middle of Canada to southern South America. It is found across Eurasia, in much of Africa and in Australia. Highly adaptable, its habitats include hot springs in Japan and 16,000-foot-high mountains in Central Asia.

SMOOTH CORDGRASS

S MOOTH cordgrass (*Spartina alterniflora*) can survive in salt water because it has glands that remove the salt after the water enters its roots. Its roots, and rhizomes (underground reproductive structures), help stabilize the marsh by anchoring the mud in place.

Smooth cordgrass reproduces both by seeds and by rhizomes. The rhizomes spread underground and give rise to new shoots. This dual system of reproduction helps make it one of the most successful plants worldwide.

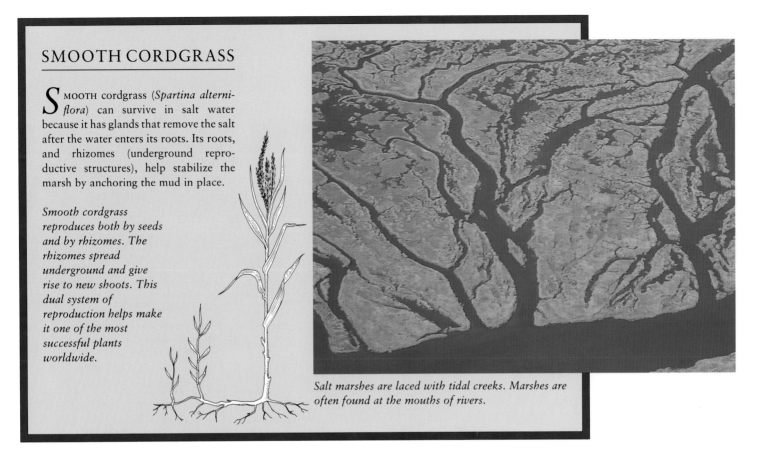

Salt marshes are laced with tidal creeks. Marshes are often found at the mouths of rivers.

from the ground, such as from a spring. Wetland types are defined by climate, vegetation, soil type and the hydrology of the ground.

Few habitats have suffered more from man's intervention than wetlands, which have been thoughtlessly drained, filled and polluted for the best part of the 20th century. By the middle of the 1970s, almost half of the original 215,000,000 acres of wetlands in the contiguous United States had vanished. Between the middle of the 1950s and the mid-1970s more than 500,000 acres of wetlands were destroyed annually. In the past 20 years or so in some areas of Canada, about 40 per cent of the wetlands have disappeared and wetlands conservation laws have recently become more stringent, but the battle to save the wetlands that remain is a continuing one.

Salt marshes

Coastal estuarine wetlands often lie behind barrier islands. The most common type of estuarine wetland is salt marsh, which lies in brackish or salt water. Salt marshes closest to the edge of the sea are flooded every high tide, while those on higher ground are flushed by the sea during peak periods of the tidal cycle and in storms. The most extensive salt marshes are situated on the east coast.

On a typical salt marsh on the Atlantic Coast the dominant type of vegetation changes as water salinity decreases and as the ground rises. Regularly flooded salt marsh is characterized by smooth cordgrass (*Spartina alterniflora*), a plant that is

highly tolerant of saline conditions. This latter sort of marsh furnishes food for many animals, including waterfowl and muskrats (*Ondatra zibethicus*) and, living among the grasses, skitter rails, small relatives of cranes. Common species include the Virginia rail (*Rallus limicola*) and clapper rail (*R. longirostris*). The former also inhabits freshwater marshes, while the latter is only found on coastal marshes.

As salinity decreases, vegetation becomes more varied and salt hay or saltmeadow grass (*Spartina patens*), related to smooth cordgrass, takes over. Inland, rushes such as blackgrass (*Juncus gerardii*) and spikegrass (*Distichlis spicata*) appear, along with switchgrass (*Panicum virgatum*) and the pretty pink gerardia (*Gerardia maritima*).

Large salt marshes situated behind barrier islands can offer a spectacular array of birds as well as scenic vistas. Nauset Marsh, behind the Atlantic Ocean barrier islands of the Cape Cod National Seashore, is a vast area of mud flats and marsh vegetation. The marsh lies directly below low hills, and is visited by vast assemblages of migrating shorebirds in spring and fall. Beyond the marsh, white-crested waves crash onto the shores of white sand barriers.

At low tide on Nauset Marsh, when the mud flats are exposed, the shorebirds feed in droves on invertebrates. The birds include black-bellied, or gray, plovers (*Pluvialis squatarola*), greater yellowlegs (*Tringa melanoleuca*), willets (*Catoptrophorus semipalmatus*), dowitchers (*Limnodromus*),

LEFT: *A young osprey (Pandion haliaetus) stretches its wings on its nest in Montana. Ospreys prey on fish, diving on them from great heights. Possessed of excellent eyesight, an osprey can spot a fish from a height of hundreds of feet.*

THESE PAGES: *Snow geese (Chen caerulescens) paddle through the mist rising from the salt marshes at the Jamaica Bay Wildlife Refuge. Most snow geese migrate through the western part of the continent but those that breed in western Greenland, Ellesmere Island and Bylot Island migrate almost due south, down the Atlantic coast.*

small sandpipers and stints (*Calidris*) of all species. Great black-backed gulls (*Larus marinus*), herring gulls (*L. argentatus*) and fish-eating ospreys (*Pandion haliaetus*) wheel overhead.

Not all wetlands wildlife is confined to the countryside. Within New York City, on the margins of the John F. Kennedy International Airport, the Jamaica Bay National Wildlife Refuge hosts a multitude of migratory and nesting birds. Much of this complex of islands and salt marshes, which is part of the federal Gateway National Recreational Area, has been filled and dredged. However, more than 300 species of birds have been seen here, about 250 of them on a regular basis.

Freshwater wetlands

There are many types of freshwater wetlands, although only 1 per cent of the total available water on earth is freshwater. Ninety per cent of this is locked up in ice. Marshes, border rivers or lakes often occur in shallow depressions or even on tundra. Typical freshwater marsh plants include cattails (*Typha*), bulrushes (*Scirpus*), water lilies (*Nymphaea*), pond lilies (*Nuphar*) and wild rice (*Zizania aquatica*). Insectivorous plant species such as sundews (*Drosera*) and pitcher plants (*Sarracenia*) are sometimes found in bogs. Skunk cabbage (*Symplocarpus occidentalis*) is one of the first herbs to appear in northern woody swamps in spring. Its large, green leaves resemble cabbage leaves and, if bruised, emit a powerful odor reminiscent of a skunk's. In many places, the skunk cabbage is one of the earliest flowering plants, and thus among the first visited by bees when they emerge from the hive in spring.

Pothole wetlands

The Prairie Pothole Region stretches from south-central Canada to the north-central states of the United States, covering an area of about 192,000,000 acres in total. Potholes are shallow depressions, often only a few feet deep, gouged out by Pleistocene glaciations and now filled with

RIGHT: *A least sandpiper (Calidris minutilla) stops at Jamaica Bay Wildlife Refuge in New York City while on its southern migration. This bird breeds in the Arctic and Subarctic and winters along the south-eastern and Gulf coasts of the United States.*

ABOVE: *A freshwater marsh in New England. Wetlands such as this one provide a home for many types of wildlife and act as buffers against floods by soaking up runoff from rainwater. Many marshes have been drained for agricultural uses and development but, more recently, laws have been enacted to protect them.*

water. Pothole ponds are among the most important marshes to waterfowl. The region in which prairie potholes exist on average produces half of the ducks hatched annually, although it covers only 10 per cent of the continent's duck breeding area.

The prairie pothole wetlands are primary breeding areas for mallards (*Anas platyrhynchos*), redheads (*Aythya americana*) and northern shovelers (*Anas clypeata*), among other duck species.

Unfortunately, many potholes have been drained for agricultural purposes and the original 7,000,000 acres of prairie pothole marshes in North and South Dakota have been more than halved. Research in Alberta and Saskatchewan indicates that agriculture is adversely affecting about 50 per cent of the prairie pothole basins and 79 per cent of the wetland plants surrounding the potholes.

The loss of prairie wetlands has necessarily paralleled the destruction of grasslands in which they lie (*see Grasslands*). In recent years, moreover, long periods of drought have further diminished pothole wetlands. Drought and increased agricultural use of land resulted in the loss of 40 per cent of pothole habitats between 1980 and 1988. As

ABOVE: *The round-leafed sundew (*Drosera rotundifolia*) is an insect-eating plant of the wetlands. The bright-colored hairs on the sundew's leaves are covered with a sticky substance resembling honey. This attracts insects, which stick and are digested by the plant.*

a result, duck populations have severely diminished. In the 1970s, the United States and Canada had a breeding duck population of about 62 million, producing a fall flight of 100 million birds. By 1988, the breeding population was greatly reduced, evidenced by a fall flight of only 66 million. Conservation efforts in the United States and Canada now aim to preserve and improve the prairie wetlands habitat and reverse this downward population trend.

Bogs

Bogs are sometimes found near large bodies of water, or are isolated in poorly drained depressions – usually these were once ponds or lakes. The surface of a bog is covered with mosses and other live vegetation. Underneath is dead, decaying vegetation which eventually compacts and becomes peat. A bog is often circular and surrounded by trees, which encroach as the bog continues to fill in with rotting vegetation and they are able to take root.

Bogs are common in coniferous forests (*see Coniferous Forests*). Northern bog plants include stunted black spruce (*Picea mariana*) and larch (*Larix laricina*), insectivorous sundew (*Drosera*), leather-leaf (*Chamaedaphne calyculata*) and cranberry (*Vaccinium*). Among southern bog plants are shrubby pond pine (*Pinus serotina*), sweetbay (*Magnolia virginiana*), marsh St. John's-wort (*Hypericum densiflorum*) and Venus' fly trap (*Dionaea muscipula*).

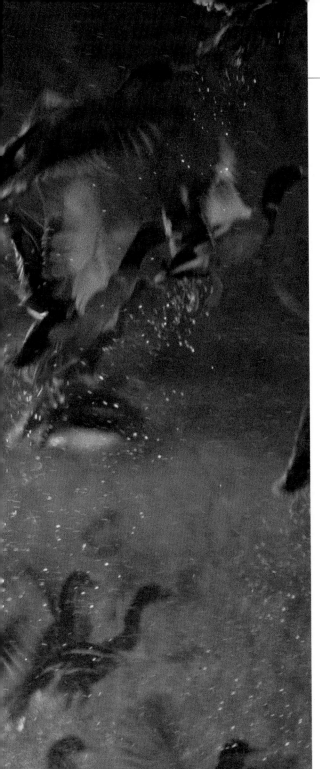

WILDLIFE REFUGES

A number of wetlands wildlife refuges are important for the survival of plant and animal species, especially birds.

Rice Lake National Wildlife Refuge

This 18,065-acre refuge, located in east-central Minnesota, is drained by the Rice River, which flows into the Mississippi River 20 miles away. In the middle of the refuge is Rice Lake, 7 square miles in area; after the last ice age, more than 10,000 years ago, ridges of glacial rubble, called moraines, prevented water drainage, and the lake formed on the flat landscape. Year after year rotting vegetation and sediment are trapped in the lake, developing it into a peaty bog. Much of the Rice Lake refuge has already turned to bog, with scattered islands of forested upland.

The Rice Lake refuge lies in a transitional zone between the boreal and Eastern Mixed forests, with the eastern edge of the prairie region. Trees in the refuge include the quaking aspen (*Populus tremuloides*) and black spruce (*Picea mariana*) – *see Coniferous Forests* – as well as red oak (*Quercus rubra*) and red maple (*Acer rubrum*) – *see The Eastern Mixed Forest*. Patches of grassland edge many wetland areas.

The watery expanses of the refuge support extensive stands of wild rice (*Zizania aquatica*), an annual, which is still harvested by local Chippewa Indians. Just before dying in fall, the mature plant produces seeds, which sink to the bottom of the water, and sprout the following spring. In winter, the water is usually low in oxygen and cold enough to freeze. In spring the ice melts and the water is rippled by the wind, increasing the oxygen supply. Without these winter and spring conditions, the wild rice seeds will not sprout. Alternatively, if the water level is abnormally high in spring, not enough oxygen reaches the seeds and they will remain dormant, sometimes for up to 10 years.

Wildlife of the Rice Lake refuge

Wild rice and other aquatic plants that grow profusely in the refuge provide food for the wide variety of wildlife in the woodland, grassland and wetland habitats.

MAMMALS More than three dozen species of mammals inhabit the refuge. Commonly seen are eastern gray squirrels (*Sciurus carolinensis*) of deciduous woodlands, ground squirrels (*Spermophilus*) of the prairies, and varying hares (*Lepus americanus*) of cold coniferous forests, beavers (*Castor canadensis*) and muskrats (*Ondatra zibethicus*). Whitetail deer (*Odocoileus virginianus*), black bears (*Ursus americanus*) and moose (*Alces alces*) are also present. Mink (*Mustela vison*), which subsists on frogs, fish and other

*Mallards (*Anas platyrhynchos*) are among the most widespread North American ducks. Like other species of ducks, mallards have decreased in numbers because of drought in the western prairies, where many of this species breed. Mallards feed in shallow, marshy water. The male can be identified by its bright green head and the white band on its neck.*

Forested wetlands

These occur throughout forested regions of the continent. Some retain water almost all the year round and others are flooded seasonally during periods of heavy precipitation. This usually occurs in the winter and spring. The trees of forested wetlands reflect those of the surrounding woodlands. Red maple (*Acer rubrum*) swamps, for instance, are common in the north-eastern United States and south-eastern Canada. The South-eastern United States (*see South-eastern Forests and Subtropical Wetlands*) has baldcypress (*Taxodium distichum*) and overcup oak (*Quercus lyrata*) swamps. In the Pacific North-west forest wetland trees include western hemlock (*Tsuga heterophylla*) and willows (*Salix*).

aquatic creatures, prowl the watersides, and coyotes (*Canis latrans*) hunt prey on the grasslands and in the woodlands.

BIRDS Rice Lake refuge is inhabited by more than 200 species of birds, including a large, established flock of Canada geese (*Branta canadensis*). Thousands of geese and ducks breed there in the spring and rest there during migrations. Nesting ducks include mallards (*Anas platyrhynchos*), blue-winged teal (*A. discors*), American wigeon (*Anas americana*) and wood ducks (*Aix sponsa*).

American white pelicans (*Pelecanus erythrorhynchos*) occasionally visit the refuge on migration between their wintering grounds on the Gulf Coast and breeding territory on lakes in Canada. Ruffed grouse (*Bonasa umbellus*), which tend to favor transitional forests, are common. Less common are spruce grouse (*Dendragapus canadensis*) of boreal forests, and sharp-tailed grouse (*Tympanuchus phasianellus*) of northern prairies occasionally make an appearance.

Many avian predators hunt in the refuge. Almost two dozen species of hawks and owls frequent the area, including the northern, or hen, harrier (*Circus cyaneus*), which flies close to the ground over marshes and open areas, and the eastern screech owl (*Otus asio*). Bald eagles (*Haliaeetus leucocephalus*) travel through the refuge on migration. They are attracted to wetlands because of their fish-eating habits.

Mississippi wildlife refuges

Separate tracts distributed sporadically over more than 284 miles along the upper Mississippi River between Wabasha, Minnesota, and Rock Island, Illinois, are all administratively part of the Upper Mississippi National Wildlife Refuge. Covering 200,000 acres, the refuge has bottomland forested swamps, grasslands, backwater lakes, marshes, and wooded islands as well as river front.

The refuge is within the Mississippi Flyway (*see Appendices*), over which millions of waterfowl migrate each year and for which it is a key resting and feeding area. Open water areas in marshes attract diving ducks such as canvasbacks (*Aythya valisineria*), greater scaup (*A. marila*) and ring-necked ducks (*A. collaris*), as well as thousands of tundra swans (*Cygnus columbianus*). Shallow marshes draw mallards (*Anas platyrhynchos*) and blue-winged teal (*A. discors*). Wood ducks (*Aix sponsa*) nest in the bottomlands swamps, where large trees grow in the seasonally flooded lowlands. These trees provide breeding places for a wide variety of wading birds, including the great blue heron (*Ardea herodias*).

In Mississippi, along the lower Mississippi River, lies the Mississippi Sandhill Crane National Wildlife Refuge (covering 17,000 acres). This was one of several preserves originally set aside to protect a remnant of one of North America's most spectacular birds, the sandhill crane (*Grus canadensis*). The refuge is the home of about 50 members of one non-migratory subspecies of sandhill crane, the Mississippi sandhill crane, which is today considered endangered.

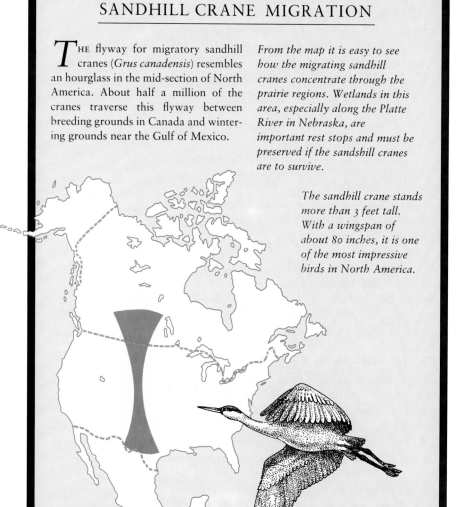

SANDHILL CRANE MIGRATION

T HE flyway for migratory sandhill cranes (*Grus canadensis*) resembles an hourglass in the mid-section of North America. About half a million of the cranes traverse this flyway between breeding grounds in Canada and wintering grounds near the Gulf of Mexico.

From the map it is easy to see how the migrating sandhill cranes concentrate through the prairie regions. Wetlands in this area, especially along the Platte River in Nebraska, are important rest stops and must be preserved if the sandshill cranes are to survive.

The sandhill crane stands more than 3 feet tall. With a wingspan of about 80 inches, it is one of the most impressive birds in North America.

TYPICAL CREATURES OF THE WETLANDS

Two prominent wetlands species are the sandhill crane and the beaver (*Castor canadensis*).

The sandhill crane

The elegant sandhill crane is more than 3 feet high with a wingspan of 6 feet. Gray as ash and capped with scarlet, it is one of the most magnificent of North American birds. There are six subspecies of sandhill crane, which range North America from the Arctic tundra to the Gulf Coast and the tip of Florida. They prefer open marshes, tundra and prairies and can be found nesting both in the Arctic and on the edges of the tropics. The sandhill crane is predominantly found in the west; its range ends in the prairie states and provinces. However, south-eastern cranes live along the Gulf of Mexico and Florida.

Most sandhill cranes are migratory, breeding in northern areas and wintering in the south. Some, such as the south-eastern crane, live throughout the year in the south. Once, scattered resident colonies of the southern cranes existed from Louisiana to Florida. Today, they survive only in Mississippi and Florida, with a few just north of Florida's border in Georgia.

The majority of migratory sandhill cranes travel from points as far apart as Alaska and Mexico. Four of the six subspecies of sandhill crane are rare. More common are the lesser and the Canadian subspecies, which travel over the greatest distances between nesting and wintering grounds. The majority of lesser and Canadian sandhill cranes migrate from wintering havens in Texas, New Mexico and Mexico to Canada and Alaska, and a few reach Siberia. As they head north in the spring, most of these cranes stop to rest and feed along the Platte River of Nebraska, where they can be seen around the junction of the South and North Platte from early March to the middle of April.

About 2.5 million waterfowl depend on wetlands along this 70-mile stretch of river, including an estimated 80 per cent of North America's sandhill crane population. The staging (preparing for migration) of these 500,000 sandhill cranes on the Platte River is considered one of the world's greatest wildlife spectacles.

The Platte River flows across western Nebraska and eventually joins the Missouri River. It was once a broad, shallow stream described as 'a mile wide and a foot deep'. Bordered by marshes and wet prairie, it is one of the most important way stations for migratory birds on the continent. Settlers transformed the land for agriculture, however. Further developments, including the diversion of the Platte's water for irrigation purposes and for the generation of hydroelectric power, altered the course, character and size of the stream. In places the channel width shrank by 90 per cent and the flow decreased by 70 per cent, and thus the river's wildlife was vastly diminished.

Sandhill cranes feed in river and lake shallows and on prairies, where they eat worms, insects, amphibians and vegetable matter. They usually roost on sandbars and in shallows where the river channel is at least 300 feet wide. Alteration of the riverside environment has reduced crane feeding areas. In places, the reduction in the river's flow has curbed flooding, which previously kept the roosting areas free from woody vegetation. The cranes shun overgrown roosting areas. Crowded into the few remaining roosting areas, the cranes become vulnerable to disease and the number of cranes affected by storms is greater. A sanctuary along the

Platte River has been established by the National Audubon Society to protect native prairie and preserve an area for the cranes. Much more land must be set aside, however, if the traditional resting area for this magnificent bird is to survive.

Beavers

One wild creature that creates wetlands is the American beaver (*Castor canadensis*). The largest rodent in North America, it can weigh up to 60 pounds. The beaver literally changes the landscape by building dams on streams. Streams overflow behind the dams and flood the landscape, creating ponds and larger areas of wetland. Dams several hundred feet long and more than 10 feet high, the work of generations of beavers, are not uncommon. There have been reports of beaver dams measuring over half a mile in length.

The rodents make the dams out of small tree trunks, branches, mud, aquatic plants and stones. Beaver dams, like many of those built by human engineers, are wide at the base and narrower along the top, which is level. The rodents also create spillways to relieve the pressure of water building up behind the dam, and construct auxiliary dams to help reduce the stress on the main structure. A beaver colony will work on a dam with great tenacity, carrying sticks and stones to the structure, plastering on mud, and patiently repairing breaks.

*A beaver (*Castor canadensis*) enjoys a meal of leaves. Beavers are natural engineers, building elaborate systems of dams that back up water and provide them with a place to live. The home of the beaver is a large, partly submerged lodge built of sticks and mud. The entrance to the lodge is underwater. By damming streams, beavers create wetlands that in turn provide habitats for other creatures, such as waterfowl and fish.*

ABOVE: *Painted turtles (Chrysemys picta) bask in the sun at the Wellfleet Wildlife Sanctuary on Cape Cod. This turtle feeds on aquatic plants, insects, crayfish and other small invertebrates. During the winter, the turtle hibernates in the mud of the bottom.*

RIGHT: *A green frog (Rana clamatans) eyes the world through a film of duckweed (Lemna). This frog has a call that resembles the sound made when a loose banjo string is plucked.*

FRESHWATER CREATURES

The freshwater areas of North America – rivulets, small ponds, lakes and rivers – provide habitats for aquatic and semi-aquatic ectothermic vertebrates and invertebrates.

REPTILES AND AMPHIBIANS The painted turtle (*Chrysemys picta*) ranges along coastlands, even managing to survive in the arid south-western United States. Most frogs, toads and other amphibians begin their lives as eggs in fresh water, then metamorphose into gilled larvae and from gilled larvae into air-breathing adults. Some frogs, such as the green frog (*Rana clamitans*), spend a great deal of their lives in or near the water. It can be found in the eastern half of North America from the Maritime Provinces of Canada to Texas and Florida. Others, such as the pickerel frog (*R.*

HOW FISH SWIM

MOST fish use their fins as rudders, not for motive power. They swim by contracting and relaxing muscles in sequence from head to tail, so fast the human eye cannot detect it. The thrust that pushes the fish ahead is provided by the tail, which pushes against the water when the undulations of the muscles reach it. The typical fish has a stream-lined, torpedo-like shape, an adaptation

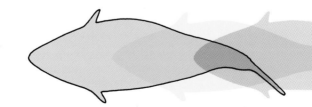

to moving through the dense medium of water. This shape helps a fish wedge itself through the water, which offers substantial resistance to movement.

1. *Tail moves left, pushing the fish ahead.*
2. *Another series of undulations ensues.*
3. *Tail moves right, providing more thrust.*

palustris), can be found in meadows and fields far from water, over a similar range.

Certain types of tree frog, such as the spring peeper (*Hyla crucifer*) and the gray tree frog (*H. versicolor*), leave the water after breeding and spend the summer in the woodlands; they hibernate in the woodland floor during the winter.

FISH Species of fish in the freshwaters of North America range in size from the immense white sturgeon (*Acipenser transmontanus*) of West Coast rivers, which can grow to more than 12 feet long and weigh approximately 1,000 pounds, to small fish such as the naked sand darter (*Ammonrypta beani*), which inhabits streams in the lower Mississippi Valley.

Perhaps the most elegant fish of the continent are the salmonids of the salmon family, trout and their relatives. The king of freshwater gamefish, the Atlantic salmon (*Salmo solar*), is a silvery, sleek creature that has been recorded at over 100 pounds in weight, but usually averages about 5 pounds. Like many other salmonids, the Atlantic salmon breeds in freshwater rivers on both sides of the Atlantic, but spends most of its life at sea, returning to its natal waters to mate. Pollution, dam construction and too much commercial fishing have threatened the existence of the Atlantic salmon, and it has vanished from most of the rivers in which it once bred. However, rivers are being cleansed of pollutants, and fishways and fish ladders are being built on dams, as conservation agencies attempt to propagate and release the salmon, in the hope that they will return in large numbers to reproduce.

Pacific salmon (*Oncorhynchus*) also live as adults in the sea and return to native streams to breed. Unlike the Atlantic species, however, they make but one trip up river to mate, after which they die. One of the most important of the Pacific salmon is the chinook (*Oncorhynchus tshawytscha*), which reaches 100 pounds in weight. It spawns in rivers of the Pacific North-west, such as the Fraser and Columbia.

The muskellunge (*Essox masquinongy*) is a huge pike that can reach about 70 pounds in weight and more than five feet in length. The muskellunge is native to a wide area in the middle section of the continent and is found in rivers such as the St. Lawrence and upper Mississippi as well as in the Great Lakes. It is a voracious predator, hunting fish as well as other creatures, including ducks.

One of the hardiest of North American fish is the largemouth bass (*Micropterus salmoides*), a fiesty predator with a huge mouth capable of swallowing sizeable snakes, small ducks and young muskrats, as well as fish and frogs. This fish can live in sluggish, warm waters which are low in oxygen. Native to the mid-west and the south, it has been widely introduced in other areas across the continent, and even overseas.

One of the continent's most unusual fish is the paddlefish (*Polyodon spathula*), a weird creature with a long, paddle-like snout that can grow more than 6 feet long and weigh as much as 200 pounds. The primitive paddlefish has a monstrous gape to its jaws, large enough to engulf a basketball, but feeds only on microscopic plankton and tiny crustaceans. Scientists believe that the spatulate snout may contain sensory organs and be used to stir up food from the mud. Paddlefish live in rivers throughout the Mississippi Valley region.

INVERTEBRATES Insects can be found in all kinds of freshwater niches both above and below the surface of water. The predatory larvae of dragonflies (order *Odonata*) search the floors of ponds and streams for other invertebrates and even small fish. Widespread water scorpions, such as *Ranatra*, are elongated insects that spend much of their time underwater. They breathe through an anterior air tube which they extend above the surface. Water striders, or pond skaters (family Gerridae), as their common names imply, merely skim the surface of the water.

AQUATIC INSECTS

MANY types of insects inhabit the fresh waters of North America, a few, such as the water striders of the genus *Halobates*, even venture out onto the ocean. Water insects are generally predacious. During the winter, many species hibernate in the mud and beneath the sand, rocks, weeds and other debris on the bottom.

Water striders (Gerridae) can literally walk on water. Their feet do not break the surface film, merely dimple it. Predacious diving beetles (Dytiscidae) take air from above the surface and store it in cavities under the body to help them breathe while they are diving after prey.

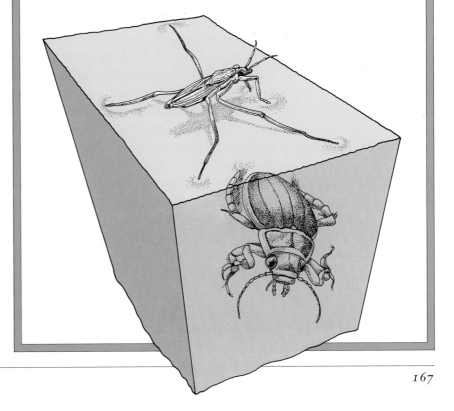

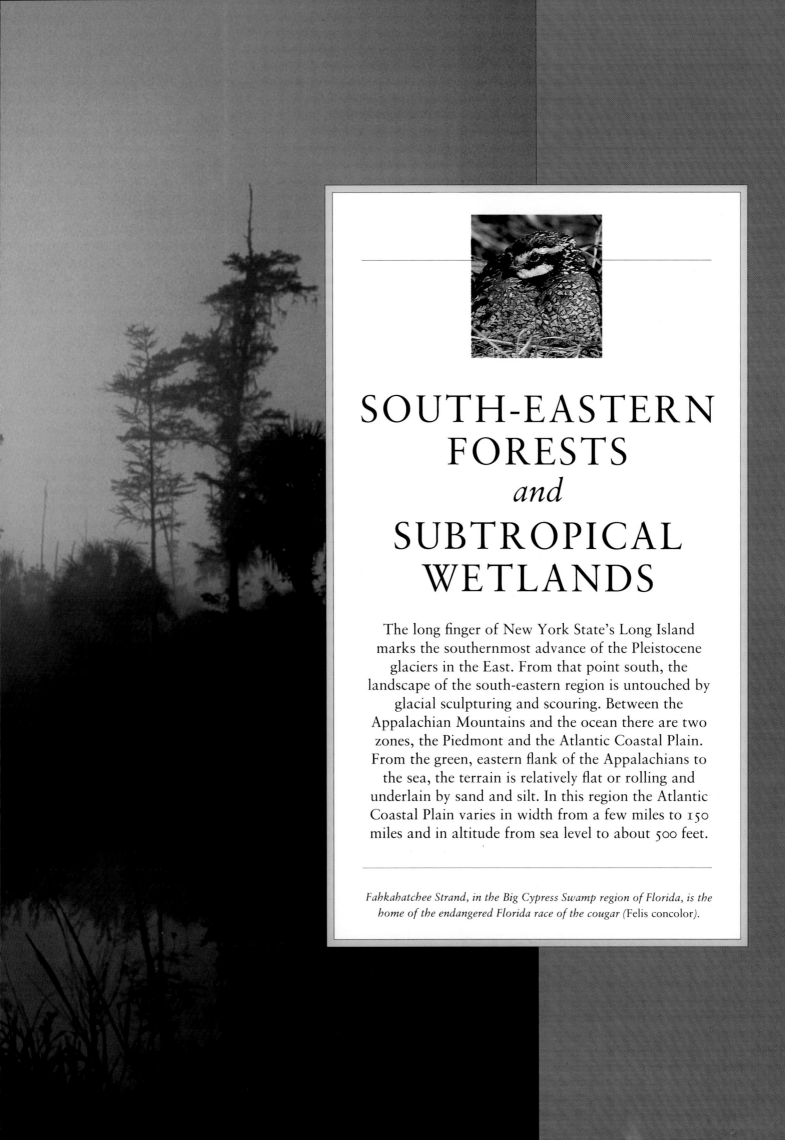

SOUTH-EASTERN FORESTS
and
SUBTROPICAL WETLANDS

The long finger of New York State's Long Island marks the southernmost advance of the Pleistocene glaciers in the East. From that point south, the landscape of the south-eastern region is untouched by glacial sculpturing and scouring. Between the Appalachian Mountains and the ocean there are two zones, the Piedmont and the Atlantic Coastal Plain. From the green, eastern flank of the Appalachians to the sea, the terrain is relatively flat or rolling and underlain by sand and silt. In this region the Atlantic Coastal Plain varies in width from a few miles to 150 miles and in altitude from sea level to about 500 feet.

Fahkahatchee Strand, in the Big Cypress Swamp region of Florida, is the home of the endangered Florida race of the cougar (Felis concolor).

An alligator (Alligator mississippiensis) swallows a heron chick that has fallen into the water. Alligators are the supreme predators of their environment. They feed on a host of creatures, including rodents, birds, turtles, fish, amphibians, and even, in coastal areas, crabs. Only rarely are alligators hazardous to people, but, even so, these large reptiles should not be approached too closely.

ALTHOUGH the Atlantic Coastal Plain as we know it today stops at the water's edge, its terrain actually continues under the sea to the continental slope, up to a hundred or so miles offshore. The underwater portion of the Coastal Plain is part of the East Coast's continental shelf, the submerged rim of the continent that juts seaward like a pouting lower lip.

Geologically, the shelf and the plain are one. During the Pleistocene glaciations, when sea level was lower than today, the plain extended to what is now sea bottom, 300 feet below the Atlantic. Prior to the glaciations, the sea reached far inland, beyond the present sites of Washington, D.C., and Baltimore, Maryland.

The Atlantic Coastal Plain extends into Florida and merges with a similar region across the Gulf Coast through eastern Texas. The Gulf Coastal Plain, centering on the Mississippi River, stretches far inland, as far as southern Illinois.

REALM OF THE ALLIGATOR

Except for its northern extremes, this coastal plain complex coincides with the historical range of one of the most impressive reptiles inhabiting the North American continent – the American alligator (*Alligator mississippiensis*). Crocodilians, the family to which the alligator belongs, are by and large tropical creatures. The alligator ranges further north than any of its New World kin, to north-eastern North Carolina.

The presence of the alligator in the coastal plain region signifies the gradual transition from a temperate to tropical environment within this realm. The transition is complete in South Florida and extreme southern Texas, which, although just above the Tropic of Cancer, verge on tropical conditions.

While much of the region described has been altered by human activity, the land was once

entirely clothed in what is known as South-eastern Forest. Because the dominant – but, by no means, only – trees in this vast expanse are pines, the forest is also known as the pine lands or, colloquially, as the 'piney woods'. Encompassed by this forest are some of the largest swamps on the continent.

In South Florida, the pine lands become replaced by subtropical forests and wetlands. Along the Gulf Coast, especially in Louisiana and eastern Texas, the South-eastern Forest is fringed by expansive marshes, which gradually grade from fresh to saline water. The seaside marshes of south-western Louisiana and eastern Texas lie in an area where the pine forest begins to give way to oak scrub and prairie, which marks the beginning of the western grasslands.

TREES OF THE SOUTH-EASTERN FOREST

Although rainfall is abundant throughout the year, the soils of the coastal plains drain quickly and thus tend towards aridity. The trees growing here are adapted to drier soils than those of the north-east and of the higher elevations of the south-east.

Besides pine, the forest contains myriad evergreen and deciduous broad-leaved trees. The composition of the forest varies geographically and according to the nature of the habitat. Some areas are almost exclusively coniferous, while in other areas broad-leaved forests proliferate. Deciduous woodlands cover the lands of the lower Mississippi floodplain, where alluvial soils have been drained from the interior of the continent. However, in the coastal plains the pines are the dominant species.

Pines thrive in the forests of the coastal plain not only because they have adapted to the soil but because they are resistant to fire. Historically, fires – triggered by lightning or ignited by man – have periodically burned through the woodlands. Even young pines, however, have thick bark that protects them from fire, while the broad-leaved trees, with their thinner bark, perish. Pine seedlings are also highly resistant to fire, whereas broadleaf seedlings are not. Fires in the forest understory discourage the growth of trees that otherwise would compete with the pines for dominance. For this reason, in pine forests forestry managers sometimes conduct controlled burns or allow natural fires to spread, within bounds.

Pines
More than half a dozen different species of pine grow in the South-eastern Forest. Most widespread are the shortleaf pine (*Pinus echinata*) and the loblolly pine (*P. taeda*), both important in the timber industry and growing to 100 feet high. They reach further inland than other species of pines of the coastal plain.

The loblolly pine favors loamy soils. Where the soil is sandy, the loblolly gives way to the longleaf pine (*P. palustris*), another key lumber tree, which can grow to 120 feet high, and also has an extensive range. Slash pine (*P. elliottii*), at 100 feet, is found in the southernmost part of the region, its range extending to the tip of Florida. Fast growing (thus widely used for reforestation), it thrives in moist soils and is the most subtropical of these pines.

Scrub pines include the sand pine (*P. clausa*), which grows in poor soils in Florida and the edge of the Gulf Coast, and the swamp-dwelling pond pine (*P. serotina*). The spruce pine (*P. glabra*) is a large tree which grows alongside hardwoods in an area stretching from South Carolina through northern Florida to Louisiana.

Broad-leaved trees
Oaks are among the most numerous broad-leaved trees mixing with the pines. The scrub turkey oak (*Quercus laevis*), myrtle oak (*Q. myrtifolia*) and bluejack oak (*Q. incana*) are strictly southern and prosper in sandy soil. The wide-crowned live oak (*Q. virginiana*), an evergreen which grows to 50 feet, is the most stately of the region, and can be twice as broad as it is high.

Other broad-leaved trees of the south-east include several hickories (*Carya*), dogwood (*Cornus florida*), sweetgum (*Liquidambar styraciflua*), and, less commonly, witch hazel (*Hamamelis virginiana*). Palms start to appear in the Carolinas, sporadically at first, then with increasing frequency. The northernmost palms are the cabbage palmetto (*Sabal palmetto*), which can be up to 80 feet tall, and the saw palmetto (*Serenoa repens*). The latter can reach 25 feet, but is usually found growing as a shrub in thickets beneath the pines and oaks.

*Slash pines (*Pinus elliotti*) and saw palmetto (*Serenoa repens*) in Everglades National Park typify the vegetation that grows on high ground throughout much of southern Florida. This region is the southernmost extension of the pine forests of the south-eastern United States.*

WILDFLOWERS

The South-eastern Forest shares many wildflowers with the deciduous forests of the east, although they do not grow in such profusion there as in the moist, rich woods of the east. Wildflowers in the pine woods are quite sparse. Among the wildflower species are the downy false foxglove (*Aureolaria virginica*), spotted wintergreen (*Chimaphila maculata*), cross vine (*Bignonia capreolata*) and the pink lady's slipper (*Cypripedium acaule*),

an increasingly rare member of the orchid family.

Other rare wildflowers of the South-eastern Forest include the Harper's beauty (*Harperocallis flava*), which can be seen only in a small area of the Apalachicola National Forest in north-western Florida; the coastal parnassia (*Parnassia caroliniana*), a white-flowered swamp dweller peculiar to the coastal plain region; the 5-foot-high Indian plantain (*Cacalia floridana*) of north-eastern Florida; and the tuba milkweed (*Asclepias tomentosa*), a plant of sandy pine barrens.

PREDATOR PLANT: VENUS' FLY TRAP

When the leaf of a Venus' fly trap snaps shut, the spines interlock and, unless the insect within is so small that it can slip through them, it is imprisoned.

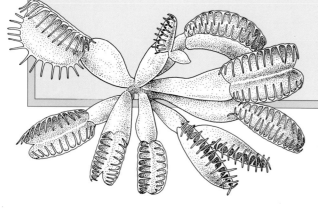

THE rare Venus' fly trap (*Dionaea muscipula*) lives in a few areas of the coastal plain of the Carolinas. It is a carnivorous, insect-eating plant with reflexes that are almost aggressive. Each of the plant's two-bladed leaves is a trap, hinged down the middle and edged with spines. The bright red inner lining of the blades is covered with minuscule hairs, which serve as triggers. Insects are lured into the trap by the plant's color and a scented secretion. An insect only has to trip two or more trigger hairs, and the blades immediately snap shut and the insect is digested.

TYPICAL WILDLIFE

The fauna of the South-eastern Forest is varied and abundant although most species are not unique to the region, particularly the mammals and birds.

MAMMALS Typical mammals include the only North American marsupial, the Virginia opossum (*Didelphis virginiana*), the raccoon (*Procyon lotor*), the black bear (*Ursus americanus*), the whitetail deer (*Odocoileus virginianus*), and the red fox (*Vulpes vulpes*).

Common small mammals include the eastern gray squirrel (*Sciurus carolinensis*), which prefers nut-bearing hardwood areas, and the eastern fox squirrel (*S. niger*), whose range extends into the pine woods.

BIRDS The mixture of habitats afforded by the varied coastal plain forests and wetlands has promoted a diversity of bird life in the South-eastern Forest. By way of example, more than 280 species of birds, most of them frequently seen, have been recorded in Francis Marion National Forest, in the heart of South Carolina's coastal plain. The forest encompasses 250,000 acres, covering an area from the coastal marshes to the inland pine woods, and includes swamp as well as upland. Its birds thus range from aquatic species, such as herons and egrets, to woodland types, which include flycatchers, warblers and thrushes.

ABOVE: *The open south-eastern pinelands are prime habitat for the northern bobwhite (*Colinus virginianus*). The males have a white eye line and throat.*

RIGHT: *The great blue heron (*Ardea herodias*), largest heron in North America, frequents freshwater and saline wetlands in the United States and Canada.*

THE DESTRUCTION OF HURRICANE HUGO

WHEN Hurricane Hugo roared in off the Atlantic Ocean and into South Carolina, it took a tremendous toll on forests and wildlife. The 250,000-acre Francis Marion National Forest was especially hard hit, losing about half of its trees. The forest supports one of the largest populations of redcockaded woodpeckers (*Picoides borealis*), which was decimated. Perhaps even worse, almost all their nesting habitat – the woodpeckers nest in tree cavities – was destroyed.

Other South Carolina forests were hit nearly as hard. Eastern gray squirrels (*Sciurus carolinensis*) and fox squirrels (*S. niger*) suffered heavy losses. Many of their den trees and the oaks that provide them with acorns were toppled. Biologists fear a food shortage both for the squirrels and for wild turkeys (*Meleagris gallopavo*), which also depend heavily on the acorn crop. According to some estimates, half of South Carolina's bald eagle (*Haliaeetus leucocephalus*) population was destroyed. Biologists say it will take well into the 21st century for the forest to recover, especially the hardwoods such as oaks, which grow more slowly than pines. Some creatures, however, will benefit from the destruction. The northern bobwhite (*Colinus virginianus*) prefers open forests and the edges between trees and clearings, as does the eastern cottontail (*Sylvilagus floridanus*).

Hurricane Hugo devastated the forest of coastal South Carolina, blowing down trees and scattering them over the landscape.

Hugo hit late in the night of September 21 1989. With winds of 135 miles an hour, it cut a swathe through the center of the state.

Map showing point of impact with the mainland and direction.

Although, as elsewhere, human activities continue to encroach on plant and wildlife habitats on the south-eastern Coastal Plain, substantial wild areas, even expanses of true wilderness, still exist, mainly in the parks and other reserves. These untouched regions typify the natural history of this immense section of the continent.

DISMAL SWAMP

In 1842 in his poem *The Slave in the Dismal Swamp*, Henry Wadsworth Longfellow wrote of a wild land of forest and bog on the border of Virginia and North Carolina:

> *In the dark fens of the Dismal Swamp*
> *The hunted Negro lay;*
> *He saw the fires of the midnight camp*
> *And heard at times a horse's tramp*
> *And a bloodhound's distant bay.*

Today, despite two centuries of manipulation by man, the Dismal Swamp retains a wilderness atmosphere rivalling that of the wilderness areas of the West. Legend-haunted, once a refuge for escaped slaves, it is one of the northernmost great Atlantic Coastal Plain swamps. Covering about 256,000 acres, almost evenly divided by the state line, the Dismal Swamp dramatizes the transition from a temperate to a subtropical environment. In this area, certain key plant and animal species of the Deep South begin (or end) their range.

The swamp has been remarkably resistant to human exploitation. A lumber industry was begun here by George Washington in the 18th century, and since then virtually all of the swamp has been cut over at least once. Large tracts have been drained for development and for agricultural purposes. Yet the swamp remains wild – although a third of its original size. Today, 106,000 acres of the swamp lie within the bounds of a national wildlife refuge.

The Dismal Swamp is unusual in that, while most swamps are catch basins and receive the flow of streams, its streams flow out of it: instead of being a saucer-shaped basin, the Dismal Swamp is a gently-sloping hillside, with the shallow, 3,000-acre Lake Drummond on high ground in the center.

Scientists believe the swamp began to form between 6,000 and 9,000 years ago, when clay and then peat (now about 15 feet deep) built up over sediments deposited by the sea when it covered the area. Lake Drummond is about 4,000 years old, but its origin is a mystery.

The swamp area was once inhabited by the Nansemond Indians, who believed the lake was created by a firebird. The legend is supported by analyses of the lake bottom, which indicate that a peat fire – perhaps started by lightning – created the lake's circular depression. Few scientists accept the theory that the firebird was a meteorite.

The 150-foot-deep layer of impermeable clay beneath the peat prevents water from filtering through to the ground below. Most of the swamp's water is lost through evaporation and transpiration, which occur during the steamy summer when, paradoxically, rainfall is heaviest. During the cooler months, the swamp is wetter, even though there is less rainfall.

VEGETATION Unusual geology and hydrology make the forests of the Dismal Swamp vegetationally complex, with characteristics akin to marshier regions. The forest is like a patchwork quilt of evergreen shrub bogs, loblolly pine barrens, cypress swamps, hardwood forests and myriad other habitats.

The wettest parts of the swamp are dominated by red maple (*Acer rubrum*), tupelo (*Nyssa*) and baldcypress (*Taxodium distichum*).

Not a true cypress but a member of the redwood family, the latter grows in water and has conical woody knees projecting above the surface of the water from its roots. Drier areas of the swamp are characterized by loblolly pine and hardwoods such as oaks.

Dismal Swamp has some unusual plants, including swamp-pink (*Helonias bullata*) and the rare *Xanthoxylum clava-Herculis*. The latter is a member of the rue family, which is most abundant in Australia and Africa; the trunk of this small tree can be up to 40 feet in diameter and is studded with needle-sharp spines.

A TREE ADAPTED TO GROWING IN WATER

*T*HE baldcypress (*Taxodium distichum*) has adapted to growing in water. This tree is characteristic of swamplands in the south-eastern United States. Although most large baldcypresses were cut down many years ago, some still stand at their maximum height of 130–150 feet. Baldcypresses reach their greatest size in conditions where water is plentiful and the mucky soil is deep. Where water levels are low and soil thin, a smaller variety of the same species, the pondcypress (*T.d.* var *nutans*), more commonly grows. Overlapping scales on its trunk prevent water loss.

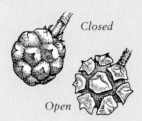

Closed

Open

Rounded cones open to disperse seeds.

BALDCYPRESS
DISTRIBUTION MAP
The baldcypress is largely found within the pine forests of the south-eastern United States, but it also extends up the Mississippi Valley.

☐ *Baldcypress*
(Taxodium distichum)

Large baldcypress trees have projections called knees growing upright from their roots. Cone shaped, the knees rise above the water level. It is thought that the knees may gather air or provide support for the tree. Muck accumulates among the roots and knees, creating soil that may eventually support other trees, as in the case of cypress strands.

Several plant species of the swamp are at or near the northern extreme of their range, an indication that this is an area of transition between different regions. Hanging from oaks and other trees hairy draperies of Spanish moss (*Tillandsia usneoides*) can be seen. This is not really a moss but a flowering plant growing as an epiphyte (epiphytes grow on trees and draw moisture from the air). Southwards from southern Virginia, Spanish moss, which is very closely related to the pineapple, is abundant.

MAMMALS Many of the mammals living in the Dismal Swamp are found throughout much of North America. The black bear, raccoon, opossum, gray squirrel and whitetail deer are common here and elsewhere. Some mammals, like the plants, evidence the transitional nature of the region. The marsh rabbit (*Sylvilagus palustris*) and the cotton mouse (*Peromyscus gossypinus*), typical of the south-eastern coastal plain, live no further north than the swamp.

BIRDS The bird life of the Dismal Swamp has not been studied extensively, but more than 75 species are known to nest, and over 200 have been recorded there. Perhaps the most unusual avian phenomenon is the annual winter invasion by 25 million blackbirds – red-winged (*Agelaius phoeniceus*) and rusty (*Euphagus carolinus*) blackbirds, and common (*Quiscalus quiscula*) and boat-tailed (*Q. major*) grackles. They find good pickings in peanut fields adjacent to the swamp, and at night roost high up in the forest canopy.

REPTILES AND AMPHIBIANS Reptiles and amphibians abound in the swamp. There are 21 species of snakes, five types of lizards and eight different kinds of turtles. The 23 amphibian species include six tree frogs.

The swamp marks the northern limit of the green anole (*Anolis carolinensis*), which used to be sold at circuses and carnivals as a chameleon, and the cottonmouth, or water moccasin (*Agkistrodon piscivorus*), an aquatic snake found throughout the south-east. Usually species are uncommon at the bounds of their range, but the cottonmouth thrives in the Dismal Swamp.

The cottonmouth, which lives largely on fish, frogs and small mammals, is a pit viper of the same family as rattlesnakes. Highly advanced in evolutionary terms, pit vipers are so-called because of the single pitted structure beneath each eye with which they sense the heat given off by warm-blooded prey.

FISH Two fish species inhabiting the swamp are especially interesting. Considered the most beautiful fish in the swamp, the blue-spotted sunfish (*Enneacanthus gloriosus*) is a dwarf that rapidly

TYPICAL PIT VIPER

A heat-sensitive structure between each eye and nostril enables pit vipers such as the cottonmouth (*Agkistrodon piscivorus*) to locate their prey. Pit vipers' fangs are hollow and have a hole at the tip like a hypodermic needle, through which poison, secreted from glands situated in the head, is ejected.

The fangs of a pit viper lie folded back in the jaw and pivot up and forward during a strike.

BELOW: *Wet prairies such as this are characteristic of the Okefenokee Swamp, on the border of Florida and Georgia. The Okefenokee contains open marshes, wooded swamps of baldcypresses, pine forests, lakes and many other habitats. It has a rich fauna.*

INSET: *Golden club (Orontium aquaticum), found in wetlands such as the Okefenokee, is named for its large, club-like, golden spathe.*

changes color, showing a variety of indescribable hues with every motion. Named after the swamp, but rarely seen there, is the swamp fish (*Chologaster cornuta*), a blind species of fish which is similar to the sightless fish that live in caves. It is logically found in the swamp, since the waters in which the swamp fish live are almost as dark as those of caves, stained to a dark coffee color by the accumulation of organic matter.

INVERTEBRATES The Dismal Swamp has a rich insect fauna, including the usual pests. Sand flies (Ceratopogonidae) and deer flies (Tabanidae) nip away at unprotected flesh. During the warm months, the air hums to the sounds of myriad grasshoppers, crickets and katydids.

OKEFENOKEE

In the Okefenokee the call of the alligators in the breeding season reaches the ear like a building thunderstorm. From a hidden corner of the swamp, the alligators' thundering cries build to a crescendo until the earth and air seem to tremble with sound.

Trembling earth is the name given to Okefenokee Swamp by the Indians. The swamp is a peat bog, situated in south-eastern Georgia and crossing the Florida state line. Four-fifths of the swamp, which is 38 miles long and 25 miles wide, lies within the Okefenokee National Wildlife Refuge.

VEGETATION More than a million years ago, during an interglacial period when surf boomed 75 miles inland from today's Georgia beaches, the Okefenokee was beneath the sea. Gradually, currents and infilling by wave action created a sandbar, a great spit that stretched for 100 miles on a north-to-south axis.

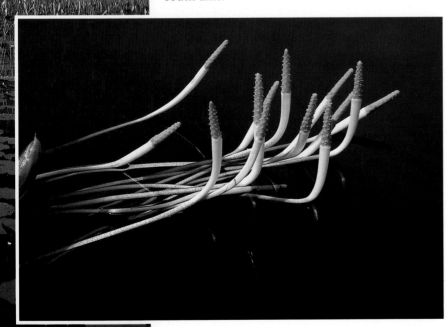

As new ice advanced in the north, the sea shrank back, leaving the bar high and dry. Over the ensuing period plants took root as the bar became a ridge. Behind the ridge, some of the sea had been trapped in a basin, and formed a salt lake. Eventually, with seasonal rainfall, the water lost its salinity and a freshwater lake was formed.

Remains of dead water plants sank to the bottom and formed peat, filling portions of the lake bed. Subsequently plants adapted to marshy conditions took root and grew. Any of their decayed vegetation added to the peat. Baldcypresses, gums and other wetlands trees appeared. The Okefenokee was born on a 20-foot foundation of peat, a foundation which is so unstable it sometimes trembles when stepped upon, giving rise to the Indian name for this swampy wilderness.

In many ways, the Okefenokee encapsulates the entire south-eastern wetland region. The swamp is surrounded by sandy forests of slash pine (*Pinus elliottii*) and longleaf pine (*P. palustris*), with uplands covered by hardwoods.

In the swamp, however, the environment changes. Spanish moss hangs like beards from baldcypresses over dark alleys of slow-moving water. The baldcypresses are shakily rooted in the peat, unable to reach the firm sand below. Stomp hard beside the baldcypresses and the trees will shake as though in gelatin. On the surface the ground is spongy, due to the growth of sphagnum moss (*Sphagnum*), the remains of which contribute substantially to the layers of peat.

The main water sources of the Okefenokee are springs, which bubble up into 60,000 acres of shallow, flooded marshes (the aquatic equivalent of the prairies). Plants growing on such prairies include waterlilies (*Nymphaea*), pipewort (*Eriocaulon*), maidencane (*Panicum hemitomon*) and a variety of sedges and grasses. Abundant in the Okefenokee is golden club (*Orontium aquaticum*), a shallow-water plant. The marshes are dotted with more than 50 islands, called hummocks, some of which are floating, and which support gums, maples and baldcypresses. They occupy a total area of about 25,000 acres.

Like the Dismal Swamp, the Okefenokee is in an area of transition. As in the Dismal Swamp, the Okefenokee has peat and piney woods and, like the Everglades to the south, it has areas of level land covered with water.

According to Indian legend, long ago an island in the center of the Okefenokee was inhabited by a tribe whose men were unbelievably cruel and whose women were incredibly beautiful. Tales of the Okefenokee abound – of swampers and outlaws prowling the interior, and of dangerous men living in a dangerous place.

Like any other wilderness, the Okefenokee cannot be taken lightly. If you step out of a boat on to a small peat island, the island might well float

ALLIGATOR RECOVERY

THE American alligator (*Alligator mississippiensis*) is a conservation success story. During the 1960s, poached for its hide and imperiled by destruction of its wetlands habitat, the alligator was declared an endangered species by the United States Department of the Interior. Once it and large areas of its habitat were protected, the alligator thrived. Numbers of alligators increased dramatically in states such as Louisiana and Florida, and by 1987 it was no longer considered endangered throughout its range. Where alligators are especially numerous, a moderate amount of legally controlled hide hunting is now allowed.

Alligators are imposing reptiles, reaching a length of 15 feet, although most are smaller. During the spring the bull alligator stakes out its mating territory and possibly attracts females by expelling air from its lungs with a booming bellow that can be heard for a mile or more. After mating, the female builds a nest of vegetation and deposits the fertilized eggs within it. She then guards the nest for about nine weeks, after which time the young alligators hatch from the hard-shelled eggs.

The only other species of alligator existing today, the Chinese alligator (*A. sinensis*), is smaller than the American one, measuring about 5 feet in length. It is endemic to China and also an endangered species. It inhabits rivers.

American alligators belong to the order of crocodilians, which also includes crocodiles, caimans and gavials. Fossils of prehistoric alligators have been found in both North America and Asia.

Young alligators have white markings when they hatch. As they grow the markings turn yellow and finally disappear. When it hatches, an alligator is about 8 inches long and weighs 2 ounces.

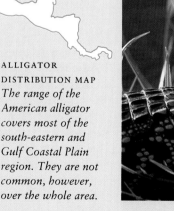

ALLIGATOR DISTRIBUTION MAP
The range of the American alligator covers most of the south-eastern and Gulf Coastal Plain region. They are not common, however, over the whole area.

away, carrying you with it. Danger dissolves in the beauty of the wilderness. Early in the morning by the edge of an Okefenokee swampland, where sphagnum moss carpets the ground, you might see fresh raccoon tracks in the mud, like elfin footprints still filling with water. From the watery prairie, the wind carries a rolling sound, low but powerful. From somewhere in the swamp, a sandhill crane (*Grus canadensis*) might call.

MAMMALS There are 41 species of mammals recorded in the Okefenokee. The black bear, which readily adapts to a range of habitats and climates, roves through all types of terrain in the region. Raccoons, which also make use of all habitats, are numerous, but are most abundant on the swamp edges. Red foxes are rare, although the omnivorous grey fox (*Vulpes cinereoargenteus*), which sometimes climbs trees to evade enemies, is fairly common in surrounding uplands.

BIRDS More than 210 species of birds have been recorded in the Okefenokee. Eleven species of herons, egrets and bitterns stalk fish and amphibians in the shallows. A common waterfowl is the wood duck (*Aix sponsa*), which nests in the cavities of aging and dead swamp trees. Logging practices in the south-east result in a lack of mature trees with red heart disease, the preferred nest site of the endangered red-cockaded woodpecker (*Picoides borealis*) which has found suitable sites in the swamp. Dead and dying trees are also removed, imperiling other hole nesters.

REPTILES AND AMPIBIANS Among Okefenokee amphibians and reptiles are typical south-eastern species as well as those which can be found in other areas of the continent. The common snapping turtle (*Chelydra serpentina*) lives in the Okefenokee, and in languid waters over virtually the entire eastern half of the country. The huge alligator snapping turtle (*Macroclemys temmincki*), on the other hand, is primarily a south-eastern species, although its range extends up the Mississippi drainage system. The biggest freshwater turtle of North America, the alligator snapper, also inhabits the region. It can weigh over 200 pounds, and wriggles its worm-shaped tongue to lure fish within reach of its horny jaws.

Like most other wetlands, the Okefenokee is a paradise for amphibians, and more than 30 species live there. South-eastern Georgia is the southern terminus of the range of the carpenter frog (*Rana virgatipes*). This amphibian of the Atlantic Coastal Plain, characteristic of sphagnum bogs, is brown in color and blends with peat-stained water. Its call sounds like the rapping of carpenters' hammers.

Another south-eastern frog inhabiting the Okefenokee is the highly aquatic pig frog (*R. gyrlio*), which grows up to 6 inches long and has a call closely resembling the grunt of a pig. A chorus of these frogs, in fact, can hardly be distinguished from a herd of pigs in full voice.

More than 60 reptile species live in the Okefenokee. The swamp has its complement of venomous snakes, including rattlesnakes and the cottonmouth. Harmless snakes include the glossy water snake (*Natrix rigida*), mud snake (*Farancia abacura*) and eastern hognose snake (*Heterodon platyrhinos*).

The hognose snake is noted for its ability to mimic the aggressive behavior of a venomous snake when threatened. If that does not frighten its foe, the hognose rolls over and plays dead. The act has one fault, however: if righted, the snake turns over once again, and the enemy knows the snake is not dead.

Like the scavenging lion on the African plains, the supreme predator of the Okefenokee – and of most south-eastern wetlands – is the American alligator. Adult alligators eat a wide range of prey, from crabs in brackish water to turtles, frogs, snakes, small mammals and birds.

More than 6,000 alligators are believed to inhabit the Okefenokee. They dig large holes in the soft muck of the swamp, nosing into the mud and pushing it aside with their flanks and tails until a saucer-shaped alligator hole forms.

THE EVERGLADES

South of the Okefenokee lies Florida which, with the fastest-growing population in the United States, has tremendous environmental problems, although it still has great natural areas, even wilderness. One national wildlife refuge, Merritt Island, is notable because its 46,530 acres of wetlands and pine woods constitute the buffer zone between the missile launching sites at the John F. Kennedy Space Center and the mainland. Most renowned of all Florida wild places, however, are the Everglades.

The Seminole Indians call the Everglades area 'Pa-Hay-Okee', meaning grassy waters. It has also been dubbed 'The River of Grass'. These names accurately describe what constitutes one of the largest marshes in the world. Associated with great swamps, the area is a truly subtropical wetland wilderness and is among the most spectacular natural areas on the continent. Although, as elsewhere, animal life is but a shadow of what it was in the past, the region still offers a wildlife spectacular, and is particularly renowned for its water birds.

The Everglades proper are freshwater marsh, dotted with tree-covered islands and pock-marked by ponds. They occupy about 5,000 square miles of South Florida, below the 700-square-mile Lake Okeechobee (the third largest freshwater lake in

Lobelias (Lobelia) are often found in wet soil in and around wetlands. Most, such as the glades lobelia (Lobelia glandulosa), bear brightly colored flowers.

ABOVE: *This natural cut in the surface of the Everglades shows vividly how the region is underlain with limestone, covered only by a thin coating of peat and clay-like marl. The limestone originates from sediments deposited when the area was under the sea.*

OPPOSITE: *Pickerelweed (Pontederia cordata), shown here in Everglades National Park, is one of the most common wetland plants in North America. It has lance-shaped leaves and bright blue flowers. This plant grows along the muddy edges of the shore and in shallows.*

the United States). The glades are at the heart of an even greater wetland that includes immense mangrove and baldcypress swamps, together spanning almost the entire southern tip of the Florida Peninsula.

Exposed by a retreating sea level after the last ice age, the landscape is quite flat and covered by limestone that was once sea bed. The lush plant life of the area is rooted only in a thin layer of marl and peat which lies over the limestone.

Most of the Everglades are barely above sea level, with the highest point at about 25 feet. Typically, an elevated tree-covered island stands just a foot or so above the marsh.

South of Lake Okeechobee, the land tilts 2 to 3 inches per mile towards Florida Bay, 100 miles away. Drenched by 50 inches of rain annually, the Okeechobee area is the most important source of water for the Everglades, which are annually flushed by the overspill.

Characteristic of the subtropics, South Florida has a wet season during the summer, and a dry season in winter. Water from Lake Okeechobee creeps down the gradually inclining slope of the

Everglades at about a tenth of an inch daily, creating the River of Grass. Fifty miles wide, this river averages 6 inches deep.

This thin sheet of water is the lifeblood of the glades, where the life cycles of plants and animals are timed to seasons of dry and wet. Poorly planned irrigation and draining for agricultural and other human purposes have destroyed large expanses of the glades and continue to threaten those that remain. Conservationists wage a continual war against these threats.

True Everglades

The true Everglades constitute a wet prairie dominated by the sawgrass *Mariscus jamaicensis*, which is really a sedge and can grow twice as high as a human being.

Channels, called sloughs, and ponds formed in sink holes and other depressions in the limestone contain open water, where marsh plants such as pickerelweed (*Pontederia cordata*) and cattails (*Typha latifolia*) grow.

Heads and hammocks

Irregularities of only a few inches in the limestone foundation of the Everglades or slight peat accumulations allow four different types of woodland to grow; the woodland is prevented from spreading by the wildfires that periodically burn through the surrounding sawgrass prairie.

Depressions which hold enough water to remain wet even in the dry season can be the sites of what are known as cypress heads: peat builds up in the center of these depressions where the water is deepest. The cypresses in the center of depressions are therefore taller than those growing near the less-fertile rim, and this creates a tree-top contour that is sometimes called a cypress dome. Cypress heads are dominated by baldcypresses and a smaller variety of this species, the pondcypress (*Taxodium distichum* var. *nutans*).

Sawgrass is lush in the wet season (above).

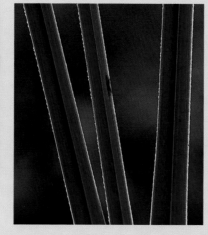

A PLANT THAT CUTS

SAWGRASS (*Mariscus jamaicensis*), dominates the Everglades, where it once covered 3,000,000 acres. In winter, its blades fall and decompose, adding to the wetland floor. Sawgrass is a freshwater species and, where the Everglades approach the coast and the marsh is saline, it dwindles then disappears.

Each blade of sawgrass has a row of sharp teeth on both edges and another down its midrib. The teeth can inflict deep cuts on unprotected flesh.

Areas where peat and marl accumulate high enough to stay above water during the dry season support bay heads and willow heads. Besides sweetbay (*Magnolia virginiana*), of the magnolia family, and redbay (*Persea borbonia*), a laurel, a bay head may also contain southern bayberry (*Myrica cerifera*), dahoon (*Ilex cassine*), icaco coco-plum (*Chrysobalanus icaco*) and an occasional cabbage palmetto (*Sabal palmetto*).

Willow heads are colonized by the coastal plain willow (*Salix caroliniana*), which, like all members of the family, prospers in moist conditions. The willows often take root around a water-filled sink hole or other depression. After dead willow vegetation creates a build-up of peat, shrubs and trees similar to those in bay heads are also able to find a footing.

Areas of land which are seldom below water support dense stands of tropical hardwoods, called hammocks. Within these jungle-like woodlands grow live oaks and tropical trees such as the willow bustic (*Dipholis salicifolia*), gumbo limbo (*Bursera simarouba*), Florida royal palm (*Roystonea elata*) and a few West Indies mahoganies (*Swietenia mahagoni*), none of which grow naturally further north than South Florida. Tropical hardwood hammocks were heavily felled for timber in previous years, so many of the truly large trees are gone, although some still rise to 60 feet or more.

Hardwood hammocks are also found on pine uplands at the eastern edge of the glades. The interior resembles a tropical rainforest, with air plants, including a profusion of orchids, perching on branches and clinging to tree trunks. Vines lace the canopy while the Florida strangler fig (*Ficus aurea*) is markedly tropical. The strangler fig grows as an air plant on another tree, sends out aerial roots that drop to the ground and anchor there, and, finally, cuts its host tree off from nutrients and sunlight, eventually killing the host.

Mangrove wilderness

On the shores of the Gulf of Mexico and Florida Bay, the freshwater sawgrass gradually gives way to a swamp forest of mangroves. Mangrove trees do not compete well with upland species but tolerate salt water. Mangrove swamps, the tropical ecological counterpart of salt marshes, grow no further north than Florida.

The mangroves create a forbidding but beautiful wilderness, accessible only by boat via the many creeks that wind through the thick growth of trees. Three different species of trees which are called mangroves, but which are in fact in different families, comprise the swamp. Closest to the sea are red mangroves (*Rhizophora mangle*). Standing up to 20 feet high in Florida, they can be recognized by their large prop roots, which arch outwards

OPPOSITE: *In the foreground stands a small variety of the baldcypress, called the pondcypress (*Taxodium distichum var. nutans*). In the distance can be seen a dome-shaped concentration of baldcypresses, called a cypress head. The trees rise above the sawgrass (*Mariscus jamaicensis*) that grows on flat 'prairies' throughout the true glades. The prairies flood during the wet season.*

THE ALLIGATOR PLAYS AN IMPORTANT ECOLOGICAL ROLE

ALLIGATORS often live in the water-holes within willow and cypress heads, and in sloughs, or channels, around the perimeter of bay heads. The big reptiles play an important ecological role by keeping the water open for other wetland creatures, including many bird species. In the sawgrass, alligators create their own holes by digging out the muck formed by vegetation that has decayed in limestone depressions. The muck, piled up alongside the hole, provides soil in which willows eventually root.

Water-filled holes in the middle of cypress heads (right) can provide homes for the alligator. It, in turn, keeps the water free of clogging vegetation.

With eyes high on its head and nostrils on top of its snout, the alligator can lie low in the water yet still see and breathe.

from the trunk down into the water. The roots firmly anchor the red mangrove on sand, oyster beds and coral.

Inland, red mangroves gradually give way to black mangroves (*Avicennia germinans*), which have a pencil-like projection of the root sticking above the mud. The white mangrove (*Laguncularia racemosa*) starts to grow at the high-tide mark, the inner boundary of the seashore.

The mangrove trees provide roosting and nesting sites for thousands of wading birds, such as herons and ibises, as well as the double-crested cormorant (*Phalacrocorax auritus*) and closely related anhinga (*Anhinga anhinga*). The anhinga's serpentine neck and head are the only parts of its anatomy exposed when it swims.

Myriad birds also use baldcypress forests for nesting and roosting purposes. Where the forests have been cleared, the number of nesting sites available to many species has been drastically reduced, with the resultant decline of several of these species.

Big Cypress Swamp

North-west of Everglades National Park lies Big Cypress Swamp, an immense, shallow basin that, together with Lake Okeechobee, contributes to the life-giving flow of water for the marshlands. As elsewhere in South Florida, much of the swamp habitat has been altered by human activity. Since 1974, however, almost 600,000 acres in Big Cypress National Preserve have been protected from further destruction, and at the northern tip of the swamp the National Audubon Society manages Corkscrew Swamp, an 11,000-acre tract, as an inviolate sanctuary.

Corkscrew is a microcosm of South Florida's characteristic habitats. The cypress swamps are bordered by wet sawgrass prairie, while at the other edge of the prairie grow low forests of slash pine (*Pinus elliottii*) and saw palmetto (*Serenoa repens*). Here and there are hammocks and heads. This part of Big Cypress Swamp has changed little over the years, and has the largest remaining stand of baldcypresses, the oldest trees in eastern North America. Some are 700 years old, and tower at 130 feet with a 25-foot girth.

The largest baldcypress stands grow along linear depressions. Most of these linear cypress 'strands' have been felled but a virgin cypress strand 3 miles long, which is part of a 20-mile strand, remains in Corkscrew.

The anhinga (Anhinga anhinga) is a bird seen throughout the south-eastern wetlands. It is also called the snake bird because of the unusual curve to its neck, caused by a hinge in its vertebrae. When the anhinga swims (right), with only neck and head visible, it does have a serpentine appearance. Anhingas dive from the surface of the water after fish. These birds are also strong fliers. They are commonly seen perching on tree branches with their wings outspread to dry in the sun.

TREES THAT HELP BUILD LAND

*T*HE red mangrove (*Rhizophora mangle*) is the most salt-tolerant and pioneering mangrove. The sprouted seeds of the red mangrove float, sometimes for months, until they are stranded in the shallows, such as upon a mud flat exposed at low tide. They root and begin growing. Little by little, red mangroves extend the coastline and build islands. Once mangroves are anchored in the mud and grow, soil, shells, and other debris carried by the tide are trapped in their roots and land begins to be formed.

Seeds of the red mangrove (top), germinate and sprout while still on the tree. When they drop into the water, they float until stranded, then start growing immediately.

A young red mangrove tree (right), readily shows the arching prop roots characteristic of the species. Small red mangroves dot the shallows in Florida Bay, at the Everglades' edge.

Red mangrove seeds germinating on parent tree

Prop roots of mature trees

Young tree with its prop roots

WILDLIFE OF GLADES, MANGROVES AND CYPRESS SWAMPS

Birds are one of the main tourist attractions of the Everglades area. Everglades National Park alone has 239 regularly seen species, with about 100 others recorded to have been seen there. However, the region also hosts a number of rare mammals and reptiles, including the almost extinct Florida race of the cougar (*Felis concolor coryi*) and the few remaining species in the United States of the American crocodile (*Crocodylus acutus*).

MAMMALS Fewer mammals are found in the Everglades area than in the Okefenokee and, naturally, many are adapted for a semi-aquatic existence. Some of the widespread mammals, however, can live among marshes and swamps. Typical examples of the latter are the raccoon (*Procyon lotor*), black bear (*Ursus americanus*) and whitetail deer (*Odocoileus virginianus*).

The otter (*Lutra canadensis*) and (rarely) mink (*Mustela vison*), relatives of weasels that focus on aquatic prey, find sufficient food in the Everglades wetlands. The round-tailed muskrat (*Neofiber alleni*), a small version of the muskrat (*Ondatra zibethica*), also thrives in wetlands, but does not occur in the Everglades.

In the fastnesses of the glades and cypress swamps lurks a creature known as the 'gray ghost', which is the long-legged Florida race of the cougar. Once this cat ranged over much of the south-east. Although a few may be found in other parts of Florida, the Everglades Big Cypress area is their last stronghold. Even here, however, scientists estimate that fewer than 50 so-called Florida panthers survive. Efforts to prevent the cat's extinction are under way at both state and federal levels. These include the recent creation of a 30,000-acre national wildlife refuge for the panther next to Big Cypress National Preserve.

Another imperiled mammal inhabits the estuarine waters of the Everglades area. The Caribbean manatee (*Trichechus manatus*), which can weigh up to 1300 pounds and measures almost 15 feet long, swims through creeks and rivers, grazing on aquatic vegetation. Timid and inoffensive, this totally aquatic creature often suffers death or injury because of collisions with motor boats.

BIRDS Winter brings large numbers of waterfowl and shorebirds from the north to the glades. Among the common wintering ducks are the blue-winged teal (*Anas discors*) and American widgeon (*A. americana*). When their northern breeding grounds are gripped by cold, greater yellowlegs

(*Tringa melanoleuca*) and lesser yellowlegs (*T. flavipes*) throng on the mudflats under the South Florida sun.

As feeding grounds, the marshes and ponds are ideal for herons and egrets. On a good day, an ornithologist can see a dozen or so different species of these long-legged wading birds, which range in size from the least bittern (*Ixobrychus exilis*), which is 11 inches in length, to the great blue heron (*Ardea herodias*), which is more than 3 feet high with a wingspan of almost 6 feet.

Other prominent wading birds of the region are the white ibis (*Eudocimus albus*) and glossy ibis (*Plegadis falcinellus*). Their relative, the spoonbill

(*Ajaia ajaja*), which is a coastal bird, has a pink body with red highlights, and a wingspan of more than 4 feet.

Big Cypress, particularly in the Corkscrew Sanctuary, is one of the last nesting strongholds of the only stork that ranges north of the Mexican border. Suffering decades of decline in the United States, the wood stork (*Mycteria americana*) has been adversely affected by human intervention with the waters in which it fishes, and because many of its nesting trees have been cut down. Corkscrew has the largest remaining colony of these black-and-white storks, although there are fewer than 1,000 breeding pairs.

ABOVE: *Great blue herons* (Ardea herodias) *and other wading birds roost in trees in and near wetlands. Mangroves, trees which can withstand saline conditions, provide sites for wading bird rookeries.*

RIGHT: *The rare and beautiful spoonbill* (Ajaia ajaja) *feeds by swinging its flat-tipped bill through the water to scoop up small aquatic creatures.*

SHARING A MARSH

S EVERAL types of herons can share a marsh without undue competition for prey because their feeding habits differ according to the birds' size. Large herons with long legs wade beyond the shallows when stalking food. Smaller species, with shorter legs, stick to the shallows and shoreline.

The tricolored heron (Egretta tricolor) is a medium-sized bird that often wades into deep water to hunt its prey (inset). It prefers to feed along the coastline.

The green-backed heron (Butorides striatus), a small species the size of a crow, creeps along the edges of streams, marshes and swamps, where it remains in the shallows.

The limpkin (*Aramus guarauna*), another long-legged bird which inhabits the cypress swamps of Florida and south-eastern Georgia, also stalks the waters of Big Cypress. It feeds mainly on large apple snails (*Pomacea*), extracting them from the shell with the hooked tip of its beak.

A similar adaptation of the beak enables the snail kite (*Rostrhamus sociabilis*), with the Wood Stork federally listed as an endangered species, to eat apple snails, upon which it depends for survival. This bird of prey has been decimated in Florida, where the wetlands have been drained, hence eliminating its food supply.

In contrast to the snail kite, the swallow-tailed kite (*Elanoides forficatus*) abounds, except during mid-winter when it migrates to the tropics. These kites often gather in large flocks, catching insects on the wing and reptiles and amphibians from the ground.

Reptiles and amphibians are the chief prey of the most common hawk in the Everglades area – and indeed in all of Florida – the red-shouldered hawk (*Buteo lineatus*). As evidenced by its diet, this hawk prefers moist areas.

The South Florida wetlands attract other birds of prey which are dependent on water. Fish-eating ospreys (*Pandion haliaetus*) and bald eagles (*Haliaeetus leucocephalus*) make huge nests out of sticks in the tops of palms and cypresses. The northern harrier, or hen harrier (*Circus cyaneus*), glides low over the sawgrass, looking for small mammals, reptiles and amphibians. Other hawks pass through the wetlands on migration, or tarry there during the winter.

REPTILES AND AMPHIBIANS Most of the Everglades reptile and amphibian fauna resembles that of other Deep South wetlands. Probably the most common snake in the region is the eastern diamondback rattlesnake (*Crotalus adamanteus*), a highly venomous pit viper, while the American crocodile (*Crocodylus acutus*) is unique to the Everglades. Along Florida Bay live the few remaining members of this species in the United States. More aggressive than the alligator, the crocodile (which grows up to 15 feet long in North America but up to 23 feet in areas of Central and South America) buries its eggs in sand – its alligator relative buries its eggs in vegetation.

Although the bullfrog (*Rana catesbeiana*) is traditionally thought of as an amphibian of the south-east, the southern limit of its range is central Florida. The similar pig frog (*Rana gyrlio*) can be found south of central Florida.

FISH Among the scores of fish species inhabiting the region's waters, the Florida gar (*Lepisosteus platyryncus*) and longnose gar (*L. osseus*) comprise the main diet for alligators. One of the most important fish species is no longer than 2 inches. It feeds voraciously on mosquito larvae and is hence named the mosquito fish (*Gambusia affinis*).

INVERTEBRATES Apart from mosquitoes, the most obvious insects of the Everglades region are butterflies and skippers, with about 250 species in all. Among them are the tiny but brilliant Miami blue (*Hemiargus thomasi*) and the large, spectacular black swallowtail (*Papilo polyxenes asterius*).

FAR LEFT: *The limpkin* (Aramus guarauna), *a relative of the crane, feeds on large aquatic snails.*

ABOVE: *Palmetto and pine woods are the favored habitat of the eastern diamondback rattlesnake* (Crotalus adamanteus), *which can reach a length of 8 feet.*

LEFT: *The zebra butterfly* (Heliconius charitonius) *is essentially a tropical species that ranges into the southern United States.*

From the arm of Florida to the Rio Grande in Texas, the coastal plain forest is influenced by alluvial soils deposited by rivers such as the Mississippi. These soils promote growth of hardwood forests within the pine lands. The low-lying nature of the land creates myriad forested swamps throughout the region. Along the Louisiana and Texas coast, the forest and swamps grade into a narrow band of coastal prairie which in turn merges with the coastal marshes.

Bottomlands and bayous

Vast tracts of the Gulf Coastal Plain forest lie in seasonally flooded areas, known as bottomlands. Like the Everglades, the bottomlands have been extensively drained. Of the original 24 million acres of bottomland forest on the lower Mississippi floodplain, less than 5,200,000 acres remain. The densest swamps of the region are around bayous, sluggish streams that wind interminably through stands of hardwoods, pines and baldcypresses.

Wooded gulf bottomlands constitute one of the prime wintering grounds for waterfowl of the Mississippi Flyway. Millions of both wood ducks (*Aix sponsa*) and mallards (*Anas platyrhynchos*) migrate to the forested wetlands of the lower Mississippi floodplain.

Coastal marshlands

The coastal marshes of Louisiana and Texas also draw immense numbers of wintering waterfowl. Louisiana possesses a third of the total number of coastal marshes in the lower 48 states. Fifty miles wide in some places, these wetlands resemble those of the Atlantic Coast, with smooth cordgrass (*Spartina alterniflora*) growing in saline waters and salt hay (*S. patens*) in brackish areas.

Edging the Louisiana marshes parallel to the coast are low ridges, which lie only a few feet above sea level. They are the remains of ancient beachlines. Dotted with oaks, these 'cheniers' serve as barriers against storms. Some cheniers are populated and support agriculture; smaller cheniers remain wild.

Extensive barrier islands rim the Texas coast. The longest is Padre Island, which stretches from Corpus Christi to the Mexican border and is the site of an 80-mile-long national seashore. Just north of Padre lies another barrier, Matagorda Island. On a peninsula behind Matagorda, near where it adjoins Padre, is the 54,829-acre Aransas National Wildlife Refuge, which is the wintering haven for the entire wild population of the whooping crane (*Grus americana*), here numbering only about 140 birds.

Rimmed by salt marsh, with grasslands and woodlands of live oaks (*Quercus virginiana*) and blackjack oaks (*Q. marilandica*), the Aransas

refuge has wildlife elements which parallel the interior grasslands, South-eastern Forest and wetlands. Attwater's greater prairie chickens (*Tympanuchus cupido*), typical grasslands birds, are found here. Whitetail deer (*Odocoileus virginianus*) and wild turkeys (*Meleagris gallopavo*) are usual forest species, coyotes (*Canis latrans*) and cougars (*Felis concolor*) are both forest and grasslands mammals. The south-eastern wetlands are represented by reptiles such as the American alligator (*Alligator mississippiensis*) and birds such as the roseate spoonbill (*Ajaia ajaja*).

The Big Thicket

East Texas marks the western boundary of the South-eastern Forest. Only a fraction of the forest remains today, and much of what persists lies

within the Big Thicket, a dense woodland that once covered 3,500,000 acres. The Big Thicket now covers only 300,000 acres, a third of which is federally protected.

Within the dense recesses of the Big Thicket live alligators of the south-east and roadrunners (*Geococcyx californiana*) of the arid south-west. Changes in climate and sea level, flooding and winds have carried plant life from the Great Plains, mountains of the East, tropics and the Mid-west to this unique area.

The Big Thicket has vegetative elements in common with the Everglades, the Appalachians, the Piedmont plateau, the Atlantic Coastal Plain and the jungles of Mexico. It has been called the biological crossroads of North America and the name is truly appropriate.

ABOVE: *Sabine National Wildlife Refuge on the coast of Louisiana is an immense fresh and salt marshland that has more than 300 species of birds.*

LEFT: *Now greatly reduced in size, the Big Thicket of Texas has environments representative of the South-eastern Forest and wetlands, Eastern Mixed Forest and western grasslands.*

CONSERVATION

The environment of North America has changed dramatically since Europeans first came to the continent. Wildernesses have been replaced by cities and farms. Entire species, such as the passenger pigeon (*Ectopistes migratorius*), which once numbered two billion birds, have disappeared due to the destruction of their habitat and over exploitation. Far-reaching and insidious harm continues to be done to the natural world because of society's technological needs and increasing human populations. At the same time, in this century people have demonstrated that they can also work on behalf of nature.

A bald eagle (Haliaeetus leucocephalus) *is a reminder that humans can help as well as harm a species. Bald eagles dwindled in numbers because their reproductive physiology was harmed by pesticides and by habitat destruction. Conservation measures have helped the eagle recover.*

The pitcher plant (Sarracenia purpurea) has become increasingly rare due to wetlands destruction. This one was photographed in the Pine Barrens of New Jersey, a sandy region covered by pine forests reminiscent of the pinelands further south. Many rare species of plants and animals are found in the Pine Barrens, which conservationists are trying to save from development.

HUMAN activity is only one contributing factor to changes in the environment. Long before man evolved, great environmental changes swept the globe. About 65 million years ago, conditions changed so drastically on a global scale that the dinosaurs and other great reptiles of the Mesozoic era perished.

The earth is always changing. Wind and water wear away mountains, forests grow where there were once marshes and marshes replace lakes. Sand swirls across deserts where the waves of long vanished seas once tossed.

Most such changes take millions of years. These alterations have an impact upon living species. To survive, a species must adapt to the changing environment, otherwise it can become extinct. In adapting, a species may remain essentially the same but sufficiently altered to survive, or evolve into an entirely different species.

Adaptation

Species adapt by chance genetic changes. To use an oversimplified example, imagine a species adapted to cold weather with a heavy coat of well-insulated hair. If the climate warmed, eventually it would not favor the shaggy coated species. The species might fade out of existence. However, if, before the species became extinct, individuals appeared among the species that had lighter coats, these individuals might find less covering advantageous in a warmer climate. They might produce offspring with shorter hair, which would have a better chance of surviving in a warm climate. As genes dictating a short coat were handed down through generations, the trend to less hair would intensify so that the descendants of the shaggy coated animals would look very different from their ancestors. On a much more complex level, this is how new species evolve from old ones.

With the exceptions of local catastrophes such as volcanic eruptions or floods, the length of time it takes for most environmental changes to occur allows species time to evolve. Natural extinction, however, is a fact of life on earth. Scientists estimate that 90 per cent of the species that ever lived have become extinct. Today, however, people have the capacity to influence the environment so rapidly that the pace of change is far greater than the pace of evolution.

Scientists believe that today human activity destroys between one and three species daily. Some predictions hold that by the beginning of the next century the rate of destruction will be one species per hour and that 15 per cent of those species which existed at the beginning of the 1990s will be gone.

Does the loss of a species of plant or animal always matter as far as the health of the environment and human welfare are concerned? Sometimes, the answer is easy. If a plant that has potential medicinal value becomes extinct, people will never reap its benefits. In other cases, it is impossible to demonstrate that the absence of a species will have adverse impact. Generally speaking, however, every species has its rôle to play in maintaining the delicate balance of nature, so if a plant or animal is suddenly removed because of human activity rather than natural processes, there is an imbalance, if only slight.

ENDANGERED SPECIES

The United States and Canada have governmental agencies whose job it is to prevent species from becoming imperiled and to save those that are endangered. The responsibility for this in the United States lies with the Department of the Interior, through its Fish and Wildlife Service, while in Canada the Federal-Provincial Wildlife Conference coordinates national wildlife conservation efforts. It is composed of representatives from federal, provincial and territorial governments, plus major conservation organizations.

Each of these groups has the power to place imperiled species or subspecies on its country's endangered species list for plants and animals. The species in the most critical peril are listed as officially 'endangered'. Those that are under threat, but less so, are listed as 'threatened'. Canada also has rare or vulnerable classifications (*see Appendices*). Classified species are given various forms of protection.

State endangered species lists also exist for species whose populations are dwindling within state boundaries, although not necessarily elsewhere. During 1989, for instance, Connecticut passed legislation creating its own list.

LEFT: *The bog turtle
(Clemmys muhlenbergi) is
an endangered species
living in scattered
populations from New
York to North Carolina.
This turtle likes spaghnum
bogs and clear, slow-
moving streams.
Destruction of wetlands
has contributed to its
decline. It has vanished
from many areas it once
inhabited.*

LEFT: *Oconee bells (Shortia
galacifolia) grow only in a
few sites in the rich
woodlands of the southern
Appalachians. This species
is endangered. The flower
pictured here was
photographed in the
Summer National Forest
of South Carolina.
Once thought extinct,
oconee bells need shade
to survive.*

ABOVE: *The timber
rattlesnake (Crotalus
horridus) is imperiled
throughout much of its
range, in the eastern half
of the United States. It is
particularly threatened in
the north-east, where it is
the only rattlesnake,
because urbanization
has decreased its
woodland habitat.*

Various programs have been implemented to help imperiled species recover. Some have been extremely successful. Programs may use several different tools to rebuild the health of a species' population, including captive breeding and re-releasing into the wild, taking individuals of a species from a place where they are abundant and relocating them in a habitat from which they have vanished, and the preservation of a habitat critical to a plant or animal's survival.

The wild turkey

A prime example of successful relocation is the wild turkey (*Meleagris gallopavo*). It was once abundant throughout most of the United States, but the woodland habitat it required was destroyed with agriculture and development. By the beginning of this century it had vanished from most of its range, especially in the north-eastern quarter of the country. As agriculture declined in the east, woodland once again began to cover large areas of turkey range. About 50 years ago, wildlife managers in states from which turkeys had vanished reintroduced turkeys from areas where they still existed (mostly in the south-east). Today, wild turkeys thrive in virtually every state in which they once lived.

The swift fox

The Canadian Wildlife Service is trying to reintroduce the swift fox (*Vulpes velox*) to Canada from the United States. The fox vanished from the Canadian prairies when its habitat was farmed, and also because it fell victim to poison set out for coyotes and other animals believed to be vermin. Widescale poisoning campaigns are no longer carried out and it is hoped that re-establishment will be successful.

The black-footed ferret

One of the rarest mammals in North America, the black-footed ferret (*Mustela nigripes*) – *see Grasslands* – is the subject of a major captive breeding program. Ferrets were captured from the only known population of these creatures, in Wyoming, and have been bred at research centers in Wyoming, Virginia and Nebraska. The aim of the program is to breed a total of 250 pairs before re-releasing the ferrets into the wild. Biologists are mapping prairie dog colonies in several areas (the ferrets live in and around prairie dog colonies and prey on prairie dogs) to find sites where the ferrets may be relocated.

The California condor

Captive breeding also seems to be the only hope of survival for the California condor (*Gymnogyps californianus*), one of the largest flying birds in the world. This condor has a 10-foot wingspan and is similar to the giant vultures that lived in California

*A wild turkey gobbler and hen. The wild turkey (*Meleagris gallopavo*) is a wildlife management success story. It was wiped out of most areas it once inhabited. However, it has now been reintroduced throughout much of its former range and is prospering. In many places wild turkeys exist in sufficient numbers for the species to be legally hunted.*

OPPOSITE TOP: *The whooping crane (Grus americana) remains endangered, but combined efforts by the United States and Canadian governments hold promise for possible recovery of this species, which has about 140 individuals in the wild.*

during prehistoric times. The condor has never been abundant, and its long reproductive cycle works against its survival in the modern world.

The giant bird does not first breed until it is 6 years old – it lives for up to 40 years – and thereafter nests only every other year. One egg is laid on a cliff-side nest. The parents care for the nestling for 7 months. Even a slight disturbance can cause the condors to leave the nest.

By 1950, the only 60 surviving condors lived along the rugged ridges of the Los Padres National Forest, north-west of Los Angeles. Part of the reason for the decline of these scavenging birds was that they ate poisoned baits set out by ranchers to kill predators. Numbers continued to dwindle and over the winter of 1984 to 1985, four out of the last five breeding pairs vanished. In 1982, however, the United States Fish and Wildlife Service began to remove young condors and condor eggs from the wild, having established breeding colonies at the San Diego Wild Animal Park and Los Angeles Zoo. The last wild condor was captured in 1987.

Supervised by the Fish and Wildlife Service, a condor recovery team is currently breeding the birds in the hope that, in the near future, condors propagated in captivity will be released in the Los Padres forest and once again become members of North America's fauna.

The peregrine falcon

Captive breeding and re-releasing has already helped to restore the wild population of the peregrine falcon (*Falco peregrinus*), which only a decade ago was in rapid decline. Although they are still not abundant, peregrines are nesting in several parts of North America, even on high buildings in some cities.

The whooping crane

There are times when the battle to save an endangered species requires combined governmental action. No better example of this exists than the whooping crane (*Grus americana*) – see *Southeastern Forests and Subtropical Wetlands*.

At almost 5 feet in height, the whooping crane is North America's tallest bird. The crane has a snow white body, black wing tips and a red and black head. Its wingspan is more than 7 feet.

Whooping cranes invariably mate for life. The close bonds between mates are further reinforced by elaborate courtship dances, during which the cranes emit loud, whooping calls, bow, leap high in the air and flap their massive wings.

*One of the fastest of all birds, the peregrine falcon (*Falco peregrinus*) was imperiled throughout much of North America because pesticides it ingested through the food chain interfered with its reproduction. Restrictions on pesticides and release of peregrines bred in captivity have helped this species toward recovery.*

Until the beginning of this century, whooping cranes ranged throughout western North America, although they have never been abundant. However, as the wetlands upon which they depended for food were drained for agricultural, industrial and residential purposes, the numbers of whooping cranes began to decline. By 1941, only 16 cranes remained in a flock that wintered in the Aransas National Wildlife Refuge in Texas. (The refuge was created in 1937 to protect the birds in their wintering grounds on the Gulf of Mexico.) The cranes left the refuge in the spring, and headed north to breed, although no one was sure exactly where. In 1984, the breeding grounds were discovered in Wood Buffalo National Park, in the Northwest Territories and Alberta. The distance between the Aransas refuge and Wood Buffalo park is more than 2,500 miles.

Scientists from Canada and the United States began studying the migrating cranes. In 1967, they created a captive flock at the United States Fish and Wildlife Service research center in Patuxent, Maryland, with the intention of keeping the species in captivity. Later, 22 birds raised at the Maryland site were transferred to a second center in Wisconsin. The present population of whooping cranes is about 200; the majority of these are in the wild and the remainder are in the captive flocks.

The joint effort to save the whooping crane was an unofficial arrangement between the two nations. In 1985, a formal memorandum of understanding was signed by both governments. It was renewed in 1990 and is now seen to represent international cooperation on behalf of an endangered species.

Important habitats

Historically, the greatest threats to the existence of species have been the destruction of the habitat upon which a species depends ,and over exploitation of a species, usually through uncontrolled market hunting. A few species in the past, such as the passenger pigeon (*Ectopistes migratorius*), suffered from sport hunting in addition to market hunting, but today, controlled, legal sport hunting endangers no species and is, in fact, a recognized and widely practiced means of controlling certain wildlife populations.

Poaching continues to devastate some creatures, such as Africa's rhinos. However, the overriding cause of a species' extinction today is habitat loss. The most vulnerable species of all are those that depend on a very specialized habitat that is limited in extent and is being further depleted by human activity.

Throughout Canada as well as the United States, and indeed in many other countries in the West, government agencies on a federal, provincial and state level, plus many conservation organizations large and small, are working to preserve and

One of the most beautiful of all amphibians, the pine barrens treefrog (Hyla andersoni) lives only in areas with sandy soils and acid waters. Its range is restricted to the Pine Barrens of New Jersey and perhaps a few small areas further south. It is particularly vulnerable to environmental disturbance because of its restricted habitat.

The Indiana Dunes. This fragile area of sand dunes, wetlands, prairies and beaches was protected as a National Lakeshore in 1966. The dunes lie close to the industrial center of Gary, Indiana. Local corporations that own areas of the dunes have helped the conservation initiative by setting aside tracts of land as preserves.

restore those habitats that are necessary for the survival of imperiled plants and animals.

National parks and preserves play a vital rôle in the preservation of habitat. Some environmental areas and the species that are adapted to living in them are particularly unusual. One example of such area is the Indiana Dunes, on the southern shore of Lake Michigan, not far from Chicago and the steel mills of Indiana.

Rising 180 feet above the shoreline, these dunes are part of a ribbon of land with a varying habitat that includes beaches, bogs, swamps and remnant prairies. The home of several rare plants, such as Mead's milkweed (*Asclepias meadii*), and an oasis of relatively unspoilt nature amidst industry, the Indiana dunes were almost lost to development. For years, conservation organizations and local residents fought what sometimes seemed like a losing battle to preserve them. Finally, their unceasing efforts were rewarded and the government declared the Indiana dunes a National Lakeshore. The Dunes now cover an area of almost 13,000 acres in total.

The protection of habitat for some species requires the application of stringent rules. For example, the piping plover (*Charadrius melodus*), which is numbered among the rarest of North American shorebirds, breeds on the Canadian prairies, on beaches around the Great Lakes and on coastal beaches from Newfoundland to North Carolina. The piping plover makes its nest on the ground. The breeding grounds on the prairies have been disturbed by the encroachment of agriculture and those on the shore are threatened by a host of factors which include cats preying on the young, bathers disrupting the plover's breeding ground, and marinas and condominiums being constructed in their habitat. In many places where piping plovers nest on publicly owned lands, and in those that are controlled by conservation organizations, the nest sites are declared legally out of bounds to the public and fences are erected to protect the nests from predators.

In some areas, it is not enough simply to preserve a habitat – efforts must also be made at manipulation in order to prevent a species from becoming extinct. The last remaining stronghold of the wood stork (*Mycteria americana*) is in southern Florida, where it breeds from October to March (*see Southeastern Forests and Subtropical Wetlands*). Traditionally, stork breeding areas were flooded during this period. However, in the 1960s a massive drainage project altered the flow of water in this part of the country. As a result, the period of high water now ends in January, and for the remaining two months of the nesting season the storks are short of fish and the other aquatic prey upon which they feed.

The National Audubon Society preserves a wood stork habitat at its Corkscrew Swamp Sanctuary. The society has constructed a levee to retard swamp drainage, put in an irrigation system, and built ponds and stocked them with fish in order to ensure the survival of the species.

ABOVE: *The piping plover (Charadrius melodus) is another beneficiary of conservation initiatives by the Canadian and United States governments, which protect many of the beaches where it nests.*

BELOW AND BELOW, LEFT: *The only North American stork, the wood stork (Mycteria americana) is in danger in the south-eastern United States because manipulation of water levels in its breeding habitat has adversely affected its feeding patterns. Within the United States, it is found primarily in Florida, especially in the Everglades and Big Cypress Swamp.*

Isle Royale National Park in Lake Michigan contains a pack of timber wolves (Canis lupus) that has been studied by scientists for many years. Northern Minnesota, Wisconsin and Michigan contain the largest numbers of timber wolves found south of the Canadian border. Conservationists hope to reintroduce wolves into Yellowstone National Park in Wyoming, from which they were exterminated in the 1920s.

Human intervention

Habitat preservation is the keystone upon which other methods of saving imperiled species are built. If a species' habitat ceases to exist, it has nowhere to rest, feed and breed and it cannot survive. On the other hand, even a multitude of apparently perfect habitats will not save a species if other factors, such as pollution, force its demise.

Sometimes the effort to re-establish a species depends heavily on changing human attitudes. The existence of the wolf (*Canis lupus*) in national forest and park lands (*see Coniferous Forests*) in northern Michigan, Minnesota and Wisconsin and Glacier National Park, Montana, demonstrates that there are habitats remaining in the lower 48 states where this creature can survive. Conservationists have been urging that wolves captured from the wild should be released in Yellowstone National Park. Ranchers in the area, fearful of the possibility that they might lose their livestock to wolves, have brought political pressure to bear against the effort.

MAJOR ENVIRONMENTAL THREATS

However much is done on behalf of imperiled species, their survival – and ultimately the survival of all life – depends on eliminating the poisoning of the environment on a broad scale by humans. Oil spills pollute the ocean and its shores, but are just one of many examples of human carelessness.

The Exxon Valdez Disaster

On March 24 1989, the *Exxon Valdez* tanker was wrecked and 11 million gallons of crude oil leaked into the pristine waters of Alaska's Prince William Sound. Eight hundred miles of shoreline, including some of the most beautiful wilderness anywhere, were fouled by the oil as it washed in from the sea.

Rich in salmon and other fish, Prince William Sound and its shores is the home of thousands of sea otters (*Enhydra lutris*), whales, approximately 100,000 seabirds and many other creatures, including 3,000 bald eagles (*Haliaeetus leucophalus*), making one of the largest populations of this bird on the continent. Thirty-three thousand seabirds, 1,000 otters and more than 100 eagles perished in the oil. These were measurable and immediate effects of the catastrophic oil spillage, but the long-term impact upon marine life may never be fully known.

The *Exxon Valdez* tragedy intensified the already volatile issue of just how much oil and gas development should be allowed in the wilderness areas of Alaska, including lands which have been designated as national wildlife refuges. Alaska is rich in oil and natural gas. It is also rich in wild lands and wildlife. Oil and gas are both essential to our modern society, yet wild habitats and the creatures that depend upon them must nevertheless be maintained. Eventually, methods must be found to meet society's energy needs without sacrificing our environmental heritage. However, there are increasingly hopeful signs that the corporate-industrial and environmental communities are finally discovering common ground, due to a growing realization that society will regress if the environment continues to degenerate.

The Alaska Range in Denali National Park, Alaska. National parks protect vast areas of wilderness in the United States and Canada. Environments in national parks of North America range from the subtropical Everglades to the Arctic tundra of Baffin Island.

Acid rain

One of the most serious long-term conservation problems on the continent is acid rain, a name given to rain, snow and fog that carries weak sulfuric and nitric acids stemming from industrial and vehicular pollutants. The acids form when sulfur dioxide and nitrous oxides combine with water vapor.

Sulfur dioxide has its origins in coal-fired power generating stations, mostly in the United States but also in Canada, and in various non-iron smelting operations, mostly in Canada. The main source of nitrous oxides is fuel combustion, especially in motor vehicles. Thus, the areas largely responsible for acid rain are those which are heavily populated and industrialized.

The chief states contributing to acid rain are those in the mid-western United States, such as Ohio and Indiana, and the provinces of Quebec and Ontario in Canada. Many other areas in both countries, however, also contribute to the problem. Florida, for example, has a high increase in emission levels of pollutants that cause acid rain.

The threats from acid rain

Regions far beyond those which are heavily polluted are adversely affected by acid rain, which is carried by the prevailing winds. Among the most vulnerable areas are New England, Ontario and Quebec, but the impact of acid rain is felt as far away as the Arctic. Areas with limestone rock are less affected because limestone, which dissolves in water, neutralizes the acids. The limestone once evident on the Canadian Shield, however, was eroded from the surface of underlying older rocks by the ice age glaciers (*see The Evolution of a Continent*). Thus, the heartland of the northern coniferous forest lies under severe threat.

Acid rain causes several types of environmental damage, and possibly human health problems, such as respiratory ailments, as well. The acids contained in the polluted precipitation acidify lakes and streams, killing fish and other aquatic life. The death tolls are staggering. In eastern Canada, 300,000 lakes are vulnerable to acid rain and 150,000 more lakes have been damaged by it. An additional 14,000 lakes in eastern Canada have been so acidified that they have lost virtually all of their fish species.

Lakes in 14 eastern states have acid rain levels high enough to harm aquatic life. More than 1,000 lakes in the eastern United States have actually lost most of their aquatic life due to acidity. Almost 4,000 others are already damaged by it, and 11,000 more are in danger if nothing is done soon to reduce acid rainfall. In the same region, more than 25,000 streams are also affected by the polluted precipitation.

The lakes that are most vulnerable to acid rain lie in areas such as the Canadian Shield where the rock and soil on lake floors and in surrounding areas do not contain sufficient limestone to buffer the acid. This means that half the total area of Canada is threatened.

Higher concentrations of acid can alter the body chemistry of fish, attacking the gills, and thus inhibiting respiration, as well as attacking the heart. Acid rain, however, not only harms fish directly. Even low levels of acids can kill microscopic plants and animals in the aquatic food chain, thus affecting the larger aquatic forms that consume them.

Sugar maples (Acer saccharum) tinge the fall forest of Vermont's Green Mountains with brilliant shades of red, crimson, orange, and gold as the leaves turn. The basis of the maple syrup industry – about 5 pounds of sugar are produced from the sap of one mature tree – sugar maples in areas such as the Green Mountains are being damaged by acid rain.

Damage to trees

Scientists suspect that acid rain also causes forest decline. It is believed that the acids speed up the leaching of nutrients in the soil and in the foliage of the trees themselves – nutrients that the trees need for growth. Acid rain may also promote the action of toxic metals in ground water. As a result, tree growth diminishes and the trees become weak, and hence susceptible to disease, drought and other such threats.

One tree that seems to suffer greatly from the effects of acid rain is the sugar maple (*Acer saccharum*), characteristic of transitional woodlands between the northern coniferous forests and the Eastern Mixed Forest. This tree, whose leaves blaze bright red in fall, provides sap for maple sugar and syrup. There are signs of decline in 40 per cent of sugar maples in Quebec. Red spruce (*Picea rubens*), another tree of transitional woodland areas, is faring poorly in New England and New York. More than 50 percent surveyed in some areas have died or been seriously damaged. Half the red spruces on the western flank of the Green Mountains in Vermont are reported to have died.

Efforts to control acid rain

Canada first took the lead in the campaign to combat acid rain several years ago, and the United States has followed, admittedly not as rapidly as many environmentalists would prefer. Key suggestions for fighting acid rain include the implementation of emissions control devices for industry and vehicles, as well as the use of fuels low in sulfur. Control programs have begun, and in some parts of eastern North America acid rain has lessened. Overall, however, the problem is far from solved and there is still much to be done.

THE RETURN OF THE BALD EAGLE

One example of how a widescale and pervasive form of pollution can imperil a species can be seen in the impact of the pesticide DDT on the bald eagle in the lower 48 states. After World War II, DDT was widely used in agricultural areas. The pesticide found its way into the aquatic food supply and hence into fish, a main dietary staple of eagles. The poison becomes more concentrated with each link in the food chain. The eagle, like other birds of prey at the top of the chain, was greatly affected by the DDT it absorbed via the fish, which found its way into the birds' systems and impaired reproduction. Birds poisoned by the pesticide laid eggs with thin shells which were easily crushed during incubation. The reproduction rate dropped dramatically, and by the 1970s only about 3,000 eagles remained in the lower 48 states, although they were still abundant in the wilderness areas of Canada and Alaska.

Pesticides, however, were not the only reason for the decline of the eagle. Eagles nest in tall trees, usually not far from the waters where they fish. They require solitude to nest successfully. Where forests had been cut down and areas of wilderness invaded by man, eagle numbers had already been gradually reduced.

In 1972, the eagle was declared a threatened and endangered species south of Canada. In the same year, a ban on the general use of DDT was put into effect in the United States. Meanwhile, the Fish and Wildlife Service, state conservation agencies and conservation organizations mounted a concerted effort to increase the number of bald eagles. Captive breeding projects were initiated, the eagles' habitat was protected and public education campaigns were mounted to enlighten the general public about the birds' survival requirements.

Slowly the bald eagle has recovered. By 1989, there were 2,660 nesting pairs in the lower 48 states, contrasting with only 400 nesting pairs in the early 1970s. Although its survival is still a matter of concern, the bald eagle has become a potent symbol of how humanity can help wildlife survive for the future.

*Bald eagles (*Heliaeetus leucocephalus*) are returning to areas from which they have long since vanished. They are breeding in increasing numbers south of the Canadian border, where they suffered most severely. During the last few years, several states have reported their first bald eagle nestings in decades. In other places, although eagles did not resume nesting, they visited during the winter, after migrating from northern breeding grounds.*

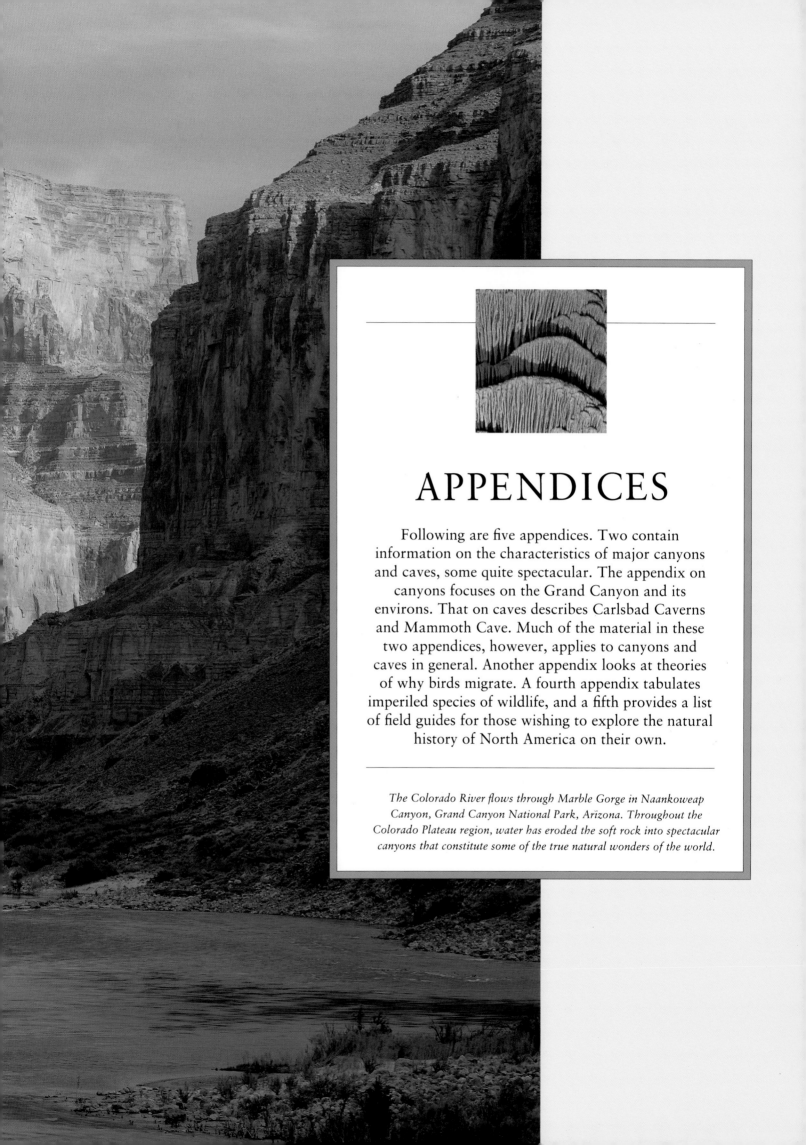

APPENDICES

Following are five appendices. Two contain information on the characteristics of major canyons and caves, some quite spectacular. The appendix on canyons focuses on the Grand Canyon and its environs. That on caves describes Carlsbad Caverns and Mammoth Cave. Much of the material in these two appendices, however, applies to canyons and caves in general. Another appendix looks at theories of why birds migrate. A fourth appendix tabulates imperiled species of wildlife, and a fifth provides a list of field guides for those wishing to explore the natural history of North America on their own.

The Colorado River flows through Marble Gorge in Naankoweap Canyon, Grand Canyon National Park, Arizona. Throughout the Colorado Plateau region, water has eroded the soft rock into spectacular canyons that constitute some of the true natural wonders of the world.

CANYONS

THE Colorado Plateau is a vast tableland that covers about 83,200,000 acres in south-western Colorado, north-western New Mexico, north-eastern Arizona and south-eastern Utah. The high plateau ranges from 4,000 to 12,000 feet above sea level, and contains some of the most spectacular canyons anywhere. These include the Grand Canyon, where the Colorado River has cut through the earth's surface in Arizona.

Grand Canyon National Park marks the southern limit of a series of five immense cliffs, collectively known as the Grand Staircase because they are arranged in steps, which ascend northwards. At the top of the staircase lies Bryce Canyon National Park, and near its center, Zion Canyon National Park.

Great canyons have formed in this region because the plateau is composed of soft rocks (including shale and sandstone) which originate from sediments deposited when the area was under a sea, about 250 million years ago. The sea disappeared, and about 10 million years or so ago the area was uplifted during a period when many mountains, such as the Rockies, were being formed. This was when the Grand Canyon was created. As the plateau was raised, the rate of flow of the Colorado River, draining to the south, was increased. Laden with rubble and sediment, the water abraded the soft sedimentary rock, carving a gorge. Rock exposed on either side of the ever deepening cut was further eroded by wind, rain and frost. Erosion continues today, and the Grand Canyon has reached 18 miles wide and a mile deep in places.

The rim of the Grand Canyon is far above its floor, accounting for major climatic differences between the top and bottom of the canyon. The North Rim averages about 8,000 feet above sea level, the South Rim, 7,000 feet. The higher elevations on the rim have a cool climate, with trees such as subalpine fir (*Abies lasiocarpa*) of the mountain coniferous variety, and even some northern coniferous vegetation. Winter snow can pile up for several feet and temperatures can drop below 0°F in places.

Between 4,000 and 7,000 feet, the forest on the rim is dominated by the pinyon pine (*Pinus edulis*), a low growing tree typical of mid-altitude mountain slopes in arid regions. The floor of the canyon has a hot, dry climate, and vegetation similar to that of the Sonoran Desert. In terms of vegetation and climate, descending to the bottom of the canyon is not unlike traveling from central Canada to southern Arizona.

The Grand Canyon also bears testimony to millions of years of geological changes. Over the ages, the Colorado River has cut through the upper sedimentary rock layers into much older rocks, some dating back 2 billion years. The walls of the Grand Canyon show the layers of rock which have built up over time. The oldest rocks, at the bottom, contain no fossils. Just above them are rocks with fossils of single celled organisms. Above this layer are fossils of mollusks and other sea creatures that lived when the sediments that comprise the middle layer of rock of the plateau were being deposited. Near the rim of the canyon are the fossilized remains of land plants.

ABOVE: *Ponderosa pines (*Pinus ponderosa*) are dusted with snow on a wintry day in Utah's Bryce Canyon National Park. Bryce Canyon is not a true canyon, which is a steep valley eroded by a river. It is like a natural amphitheater and has been hollowed out of the rock by rain, snow and ice. Higher elevations in the canyon are subjected to more severe winter weather than those down below.*

RIGHT: *Rock formations called the Brahma and Zoroaster Temples can be seen from Rainbow Point in Bryce Canyon National Park. Vegetation on Rainbow Point is cool-climate mountain coniferous forest. At the park entrance, 1,000 feet lower in elevation, plant life is desert scrub.*

CAVES

North America has two of the most remarkable examples of caves in the world. One of these is Mammoth Cave in Kentucky, the longest cave on earth. The other is Carlsbad Caverns, in New Mexico, which reach more than 1,000 feet below the surface. Both lie within national parks.

The mapped passageways of Mammoth Cave stretch for more than 300 miles, and there are others as yet unrecorded. No other known cavern is nearly as long as Mammoth Cave. The second longest cave in the world is Optimistitscheskaya, at just over 91 miles long in the Soviet Union, followed by Holloch, which is nearly 90 miles long, in Switzerland.

Mammoth Cave is located in karst landscape – terrain underlain by rock that is soluble in water, usually limestone. Other karst areas include parts of Yugoslavia and Puerto Rico. (The word karst is derived from the Karst Plateau in Yugoslavia, where limestone formations are conspicuous.) The limestone in which Mammoth Cave lies is several hundred feet thick and is situated under a surface of sandstone. The caverns developed as the limestone dissolved in underground water coming from springs and the subterranean Echo River. As the limestone dissolved, caverns were formed. Upper passages of the cave, which are now dry, were hollowed out thousands of years ago. Below these lie newer passages, deeper down, still being carved out of the limestone by erosion.

Sink holes are a hallmark of karst landscape. They are depressions, which can in extreme cases measure more than a mile across, that form when the ground surface above an underground hollow formed by the dissolution of limestone collapses.

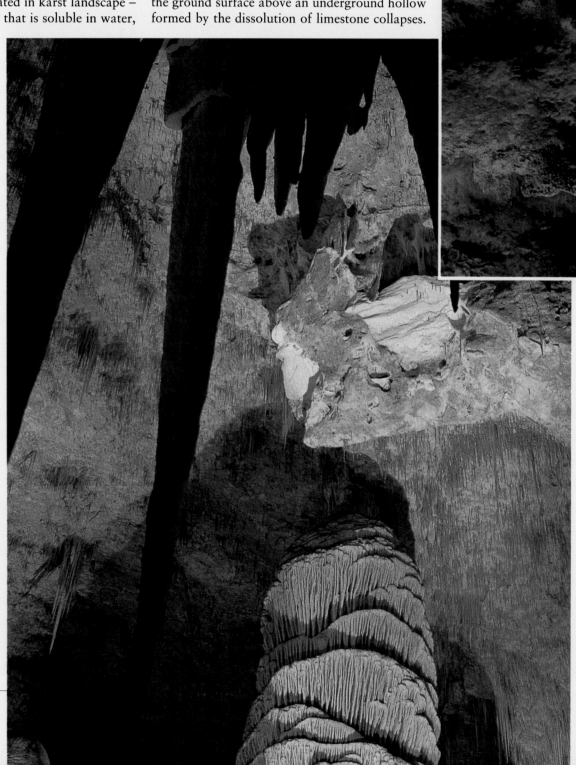

The interior of Carlsbad Caverns in New Mexico stays at a constant 57°F even when the desert sun broils the landscape above. Visitors can tour the cavern to a depth of 829 feet below the earth's surface. The Main Corridor of the Caverns is a quarter mile long and has ceiling heights of more than 200 feet.

Many sink holes have formed in the sandstone that caps the limestone of Mammoth Cave. Ground water seeping down through the sink holes has created immense vertical shafts in the limestone. Most impressive of these are Mammoth Dome, which is 192 feet deep at the Bottomless Pit, at 105 feet deep.

The creation of Carlsbad Caverns, in the Guadalupe Mountains, began 250 million years ago. A horseshoe shaped coral reef, 400 miles long, was created in an inland sea before the Guadalupe Mountains were formed. Eventually, the sea retreated leaving the coral reef partly buried in sediment and partly exposed. Coral reefs consist of lime secreted by corals and other invertebrates, and after a period of time the coral becomes limestone. Ground water from rain which flowed through cracks in the reef began eating away at the limestone. Some geologists believe the fresh ground water mixed with salt water from the ancient sea which was trapped underground, to form sulfuric acid, and it was the sulphuric acid that fostered the consumption of the limestone. By about half a million years ago, most of the

Carlsbad Caverns had been hollowed out of the ancient reef, the exposed surface of which became part of the Guadalupe Mountains.

Carlsbad Caverns and Mammoth Cave are wonderlands of underground rock formations, such as stalactites and stalagmites. These formed as drops of water penetrated the cave from above. As the drops passed through the limestone, the water absorbed the mineral calcite. Once the drops entered the cave they evaporated, and the calcite was deposited as crystals. Little by little, the crystals built up into stalactites, stalagmites, and other oddly shaped formations. Stalactites are formed like icycles on the cave ceiling. When drops of water do not evaporate until they reach the cave floor, stalagmites grow upwards. Sometimes they join, making a column reaching from the ceiling to the floor.

Both Carlsbad Caverns and Mammoth Cave were used as shelters by prehistoric Indians. Indian artifacts dating as far back as 4,000 years have been found in Mammoth Cave, and a number of drawings were left on the walls of Carlsbad Caverns about 1,000 years ago.

The longest cave in the world, Mammoth Cave in Kentucky, has passages still to be explored. The first major explorations of the cave occurred in the mid-1800s when Stephen Bishop, a self-educated black slave, pushed deeper and deeper into its recesses. He began guiding visitors through the cave at the age of 17, in 1838.

BIRD MIGRATION

From the time prehistoric people watched great flocks of migratory birds arrive and depart with seasonal changes, bird migration has been an intriguing mystery. Today, scientists still have only theories to explain why birds migrate, although how they do so has been more clearly defined.

Among the theories about the origin of bird migration is the idea that birds were first driven south by the advancing ice sheets of the Pleistocene era and returned as the glaciers melted. After the ice ages, the impetus to migrate continued on a seasonal basis. Most other theories assume that birds have migrated since before the Pleistocene.

Another theory is that the disappearance of insects and other food in fall prompts birds to move to areas where food remains plentiful. However, this does not explain why birds leave southern areas where food is abundant and head north in spring. Yet another suggestion is that birds are imprinted with the location of their place of origin and they return there every spring just as salmon return to their native streams to breed.

Perhaps the reason for migration lies in a combination of such theories. No one is certain. However, scientists have learned about some of the factors that contribute to triggering migration. Some species of birds that winter in the southern part of the temperate zone are affected by the increasing number of daylight hours as spring approaches. The longer day length stimulates the production of hormones in birds' bodies and brings them into a breeding condition. A restlessness and tendency to flock sets in before the migration north is undertaken. It should also be mentioned that many North American migrants winter in tropical American rain forests, and the forests must be preserved if these species are to survive.

WATERFOWL FLYWAYS AND NESTING AREAS

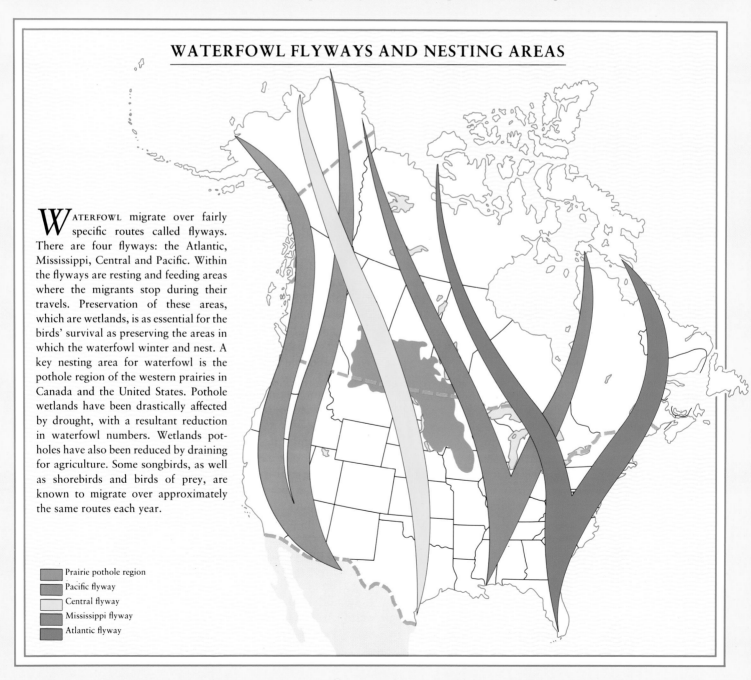

WATERFOWL migrate over fairly specific routes called flyways. There are four flyways: the Atlantic, Mississippi, Central and Pacific. Within the flyways are resting and feeding areas where the migrants stop during their travels. Preservation of these areas, which are wetlands, is as essential for the birds' survival as preserving the areas in which the waterfowl winter and nest. A key nesting area for waterfowl is the pothole region of the western prairies in Canada and the United States. Pothole wetlands have been drastically affected by drought, with a resultant reduction in waterfowl numbers. Wetlands potholes have also been reduced by draining for agriculture. Some songbirds, as well as shorebirds and birds of prey, are known to migrate over approximately the same routes each year.

Prairie pothole region
Pacific flyway
Central flyway
Mississippi flyway
Atlantic flyway

ENDANGERED AND THREATENED
SPECIES AND SUBSPECIES

The following species and subspecies are threatened (T) or endangered (E) within all or
part of their range.

The lists are taken from the USA *Endangered and Threatened Wildlife and Plants,
Fish and Wildlife Service, United States Department of the Interior,* and the Canadian
*List of Species with Designated Status, Committee on the Status
of the Endangered Wildlife in Canada.*

CANADA

COMMON NAME	SCIENTIFIC NAME	STATUS
MAMMALS		
Bison, wood	*Bison bison athabascae*	T
Caribou, Maritime woodland	*Rangifer tarandus caribou*	T
Caribou, Peary	*Rangifer tarandus pearyi*	T
Cougar, eastern	*Felis concolor cougar*	E
Marmot, Vancouver Island	*Marmota vancouverensis*	E
Pine marten, Newfoundland	*Martes americana atrata*	T
Wolverine	*Gulo gulo*	E
BIRDS		
Curlew, Eskimo	*Numenius borealis*	E
Falcon, American peregrine	*Falco peregrinus anatum*	E
Falcon, Arctic peregrine	*Falco peregrinus tundrius*	T
Hawk, ferruginous	*Buteo regalis*	T
Owl, burrowing	*Athene cunicularia*	T
Owl, spotted	*Strix occidentalis caurine*	E
Plover, mountain	*Charadrius montanus*	E
Plover, piping	*Charadrius melodus*	E
Prairie-chicken, greater	*Tympanuchus cupido pinnatus*	E
Shrike, loggerhead	*Lanius ludovicianus*	T
Sparrow, Baird's	*Ammodramus bairdii*	T
Sparrow, Henslow's	*Ammodramus henslowii*	T
Tern, roseate	*Sterna dougallii*	E
Warbler, Kirtland's	*Dendroica kirtlandii*	E
Whooping crane	*Grus americana*	E
REPTILES		
Turtle, leatherback	*Dermochelys coriacea*	E

USA

COMMON NAME	SCIENTIFIC NAME	STATUS
MAMMALS		
Bat, Gray	*Myotis grisescens*	E
Bat, Indiana	*Myotis sodalis*	E
Bat, Mexican long-nosed	*Leptonycteris nivalis*	E
Bat, Ozark big-eared	*Plecotus townsendii ingens*	E
Bat, Sanborn's long-nosed	*Leptonycteris sanborni*	E
Bat, Virginia big-eared	*Plecotus townsendii virginianus*	E
Bear, brown or grizzly	*Ursus arctos*	T
Bison, wood	*Bison bison athabascae*	E

_____ USA _____

COMMON NAME	SCIENTIFIC NAME	STATUS

MAMMALS _____

COMMON NAME	SCIENTIFIC NAME	STATUS
Caribou, woodland	*Rangifer tarandus caribou*	E
Cougar, eastern	*Felis concolor cougar*	E
Deer, Columbian whitetail	*Odocoileus virginianus leucurus*	E
Deer, key	*Odocoileus virginianus clavium*	E
Ferret, black-footed	*Mustela nigripes*	E
Fox, northern swift	*Vulpes velox hebes*	E
Fox, San Joaquin kit	*Vulpes macrotis mutica*	E
Jaguar	*Panthera onca*	E
Jaguarundi	*Felis yagouaroundi cocomitli*	E
	Felis yagouaroundi tolteca	E
Manatee, West Indian (Florida)	*Trichechus manatus*	E
Margay	*Felis wiedii*	E
Mouse, Alabama beach	*Peromyscus polionotus ammobates*	E
Mouse, Anastasia Island beach	*Peromyscus polionotus phasma*	E
Mouse, Choctowhatchee beach	*Peromyscus polionotus allophrys*	E
Mouse, Key Largo cotton	*Peromyscus gossypinus allapaticola*	E
Mouse, Perdido Key beach	*Peromyscus polionotus trissyllepsis*	E
Mouse, salt marsh harvest	*Reithrodontomys raviventris*	E
Mouse, south-eastern beach	*Peromyscus polionotus niveiventris*	T
Ocelot	*Felis paradalis*	E
Otter, southern sea	*Enhydra lutris nereis*	T
Panther, Florida	*Felis concolor coryi*	E
Prairie dog, Utah	*Cynomys parvidens*	T
Pronghorn, Sonoran	*Antilocapra americana sonoriensis*	E
Rat, Fresno kangaroo	*Dipodomys nitratoides exilis*	E
Rat, giant kangaroo	*Dipodomys ingens*	E
Rat, Morro Bay kangaroo	*Dipodomys heermanni morroensis*	E
Rat, Stephens' kangaroo	*Dipodomys stephensi*	E
Rat, Tipton kangaroo	*Dipodomys nitratoides nitratoides*	E
Seal, Guadalupe fur	*Arctocephalus townsendi*	T
Shrew, Dismal Swamp south-eastern	*Sorex longirostris fisheri*	T
Squirrel, Carolina northern flying	*Glaucomys sabrinus coloratus*	E
Squirrel, Delmarva Peninsula fox	*Sciurus niger cinereus*	E
Squirrel, Mount Graham red	*Tamiasciurus hudsonicus grahamensis*	E
Squirrel, Virginia northern flying	*Glaucomys sabrinus fuscus*	E
Vole, Amargosa	*Microtus californicus scirpensis*	E
Vole, Hualapai Mexican	*Microtus mexicanus hualpaiensis*	E
Whale, blue	*Balaenoptera musculus*	E
Whale, bowhead	*Balaena mysticetus*	E
Whale, finback	*Balaenoptera physalus*	E
Whale, grey	*Eschrichtius robustus*	E
Whale, humpback	*Megaptera novaeangliae*	E
Whale, right	*Balaena glacialis*	E
Whale, Sei	*Balaenoptera borealis*	E
Whale, sperm	*Physeter catodon*	E
Wolf, gray	*Canis lupus*	E
Wolf, red	*Canis rufus*	E
Woodrat, Key Largo	*Neotoma floridana smalli*	E

BIRDS _____

COMMON NAME	SCIENTIFIC NAME	STATUS
Bobwhite, masked (quail)	*Colinus virginianus ridgwayi*	E
Caracara, Audubon's crested	*Polyborus plancus audubonii*	T
Condor, California	*Gymnogyps californianus*	E
Crane, Mississippi sandhill	*Grus canadensis pulla*	E
Crane, whooping	*Grus americana*	E
Eagle, bald	*Haliaeetus leucocephalus*	E
Falcon, American peregrine	*Falco peregrinus anatum*	E
Falcon, Arctic peregrine	*Falco peregrinus tundrius*	T
Falcon, northern aplomado	*Falco femeralis septentrionalis*	E
Falcon, peregrine	*Falco peregrinus*	E
Goose, Aleutian Canada	*Branta canadensis leucopareia*	E

_____ U S A _____

COMMON NAME	SCIENTIFIC NAME	STATUS

BIRDS

Jay, Florida scrub	*Aphelocoma coerulescens coerulescens*	T
Kite, Everglade snail	*Rostrhamus sociabilis plumbeus*	E
Parrot, thick-billed	*Rhynchopsitta pachyrhyncha*	E
Pelican, brown	*Pelecanus occidentalis*	E
Plover, piping	*Charadrius melodus*	E
Prairie-chicken, Attwater's greater	*Tympanuchus cupido attwateri*	E
Rail, California clapper	*Rallus longirostris obsoletus*	E
Rail, light-footed clapper	*Rallus longirostris levipes*	E
Rail, Yuma clapper	*Rallus longirostris yumanensis*	E
Shrike, San Clemente loggerhead	*Lanius ludovicianus mearnsi*	E
Sparrow, Cape Sable seaside	*Ammodramus maritimus mirabilis*	E
Sparrow, dusky seaside	*Ammodramus maritimus nigrescens*	E
Sparrow, Florida grasshopper	*Ammodramus savannarum floridanus*	E
Sparrow, San Clemente sage	*Amphispiza belli clementeae*	T
Stork, wood	*Mycteria americana*	E
Tern, California least	*Sterna antillarum browni*	E
Tern, least	*Sterna antillarum*	E
Tern, roseate	*Sterna dougallii*	E
Towhee, Inyo brown	*Pipilo fuscus eremophilus*	T
Vireo, black-capped	*Vireo atricapillus*	E
Vireo, least Bell's	*Vireo bellii pusillus*	E
Woodpecker, ivory-billed	*Campephilus principalis*	E
Woodpecker, red-cockaded	*Dendrocopos borealis*	E

REPTILES

Alligator, American	*Alligator mississippiensis*	T
Boa, Virgin Islands tree	*Epicrates monensis granti*	E
Crocodile, American	*Crocodylus acutus*	E
Lizard, blunt-nosed leopard	*Gambelia silus*	E
Lizard, Coachella Calley fringe-toed	*Uma inornata*	T
Lizard, Island night	*Xantusia riversiana*	T
Rattlesnake, New Mexican ridge-nosed	*Crotalus willardi obscurus*	T
Skink, blue-tailed mole	*Eumeces egregius lividus*	T
Skink, sand	*Neoseps reynoldsi*	T
Snake, Atlantic salt marsh	*Nerodia fasciata taeniata*	T
Snake, Concho water	*Nerodia harteri paucimaculata*	T
Snake, eastern indigo	*Drymarchon corais couperi*	T
Snake, San Francisco garter	*Thamnophis sirtalis tetrataenia*	E
Tortoise, desert	*Gopherus agassizii*	T
Tortoise, gopher	*Gopherus polyphemus*	T
Turtle, Alabama red-bellied	*Pseudemys alabamensis*	E
Turtle, flattened musk	*Sternotherus depressus*	T
Turtle, green sea	*Chelonia mydas*	T
Turtle, hawksbill sea	*Eretmochelys imbricata*	E
Turtle, Kemp's ridley sea	*Lepidochelys kempii*	E
Turtle, leatherback sea	*Dermochelys coriacea*	E
Turtle, loggerhead sea	*Caretta caretta*	T
Turtle, Plymouth red-bellied	*Pseudemys rubriventris bangsi*	E
Turtle, ringed sawback	*Graptemys oculifera*	T

AMPHIBIANS

Salamander, Cheat Mountain	*Plethodon nettingi*	T
Salamander, desert slender	*Batrachoseps aridus*	E
Salamander, Red Hills	*Phaeognathus hubrichti*	T
Salamander, San Marcos	*Eurycea nana*	T
Salamander, Santa Cruz long-toed	*Ambystoma macrodactylum croceum*	E
Salamander, Shenandoah	*Plethodon shenandoah*	E
Salamander, Texas blind	*Typholomolge rathbuni*	E
Toad, Houston	*Bufo houstonensis*	E
Toad, Wyoming	*Bufo hemiophrys baxteri*	E

BIBLIOGRAPHY OF FIELD GUIDES
AND FIELD BOOKS

The following field guides and field books follow the order in *Books in Print*.

Field Book: Yellowstone Park and Absaroka Range, Orrin H. Bonney and Lorraine G. Bonney, 1989, Bonney.

Field Guide: Coastal Southern California, Robert P. Sharp, 1978, Kendall-Hunt.

Field Guide: Northern California, John W. Harbaugh, 1975, Kendall-Hunt.

Field Guide: Northern Colorado Plateau, J. Keith Rigby, 1975, Kendall-Hunt.

Field Guide: Southern California, Robert P. Sharp, 1976, Kendall-Hunt.

Field Guide: Southern Colorado Plateau, J. Keith Rigby, 1976, Kendall-Hunt.

Field Guide: Southern Great Lakes, Rodney M., Feldmann, 1977, Kendall-Hunt.

Field Guide: The Middle Rockies and Yellowstone, Willard H. Parsons, 1978, Kendall-Hunt.

Field Guide to Acadia National Park, Russell D. Butcher, 1977, Acadia Publishing Co.

Field Guide to Coastal Wetland Plants of the North-eastern United States, Ralph W. Tiner, Jr., 1987, University of Massachusetts Press.

Field Guide to Dangerous Animals of North America, Charles K. Levy, 1984, Greene.

Field Guide to Eastern Birds: A Field Guide to Birds East of the Rockies, Roger T. Peterson, 1984, Houghton Mifflin.

Field Guide to Eastern Forests, John C. Kricher, 1988, Houghton Mifflin.

Field Guide to Eastern Trees, George A. Petrides, 1988, Houghton Mifflin.

Field Guide to Geology, The Diagram Group and David Lambert, 1988, Facts on File.

Field Guide to Hawks, William S. Clark and Brian K. Wheeler, 1987, Houghton Mifflin.

Field Guide to Orchids of North America, John G. Williams and Andrew E. Williams, 1983, Universe.

Field Guide to Pacific States Wildflowers, Theodore F. Niehaus, 1976, Houghton Mifflin.

Field Guide to Reptiles and Amphibians of Eastern and Central North America, Roger Conant, 1975, Houghton Mifflin.

Field Guide to Seabirds, Peter Harrison, 1987, Greene.

Field Guide to the Birds: A Completely New Guide to all the *Birds of Eastern and Central North America*, Roger T. Peterson, 1980, Houghton Mifflin.

Field Guide to the Birds of North America, Shirley L. Scott, 1983, National Geographic

Field Guide to the Cascades and Olympics, Stephen R. Whitney, 1983, Mountaineers.

Field Guide to the Grand Canyon, Stephen Whitney, 1987, Morrow.

Field Guide to the Mammals, William H. Burt, 1976, Houghton Mifflin.

Field Guide to the Nests, Eggs and Nestlings of North American Birds, Colin Harrison, 1984, Greene.

Field Guide to the Whales, Porpoises and Seals of the Gulf of Maine and Eastern Canada: Cape Cod to Labrador, Steve Katona and David Richardson, 1983, Scribner.

Field Guide to Western Reptiles and Amphibians, Robert C. Stebbins, 1985, Houghton Mifflin.

Field Guide to Wildlife Habitats of the Eastern United States, Janine M. Benyus, 1989, Simon & Schuster.

Field Guide to Wildlife Habitats of the Western United States, Janine M. Benyus, 1989, Simon & Schuster.

Field Guide Guide to Your Own Backyard, John H. Mitchell, 1986, Norton.

Field Manual of the Ferns and Fern-Allies of the United States and Canada, David B. Lellinger, 1985, Smithsonian.

INDEX

Page numbers in **bold** refer to illustrations

PUBLISHER'S ACKNOWLEDGMENTS

The publishers would like to thank the following for the photographs in this book:

The position of illustrations on each page is indicated by the letters after the page number:

T = top, B = bottom, C = centre, L = left, R = right.

1 Charles Gurche. 2–3 Leonard Lee Rue III. 4–5 Imagery. 6–7 Arthur Morris. 8 Ed Cooper. 10 Larry Ulrich. 12 Imagery. 14 L Neal and Mary Jane Mishler; R John J Smith. 15 Ed Cooper. 16 T Charles Gurche; B Imagery. 17 Larry Ulrich. 18 Janelco. 18–19 Charles Gurche. 19 Ed Cooper. 20 T Mark Warner; B Jack Olson. 21 T Robert Perron; B Charles Gurche. 22 Arthur Morris. 23 T Janelco; B Neal and Mary Jane Mishler. 24 Ed Cooper. 26–27 Erwin and Peggy Bauer. 28 L, R Imagery. 29 Art Gingert. 30 Larry Ulrich. 32 T Larry Ulrich. B Erwin and Peggy Bauer. 33 Leonard Lee Rue III. 36–37 T Leonard Lee Rue III; B Erwin and Peggy Bauer. 38 Arthur Morris. 39 Leonard Lee Rue III. 40 Leonard Lee Rue III. 41 Art Gingert. 42 Leonard Lee Rue III. 42–43 Erwin and Peggy Bauer. 44–45 Erwin and Peggy Bauer. 45 Erwin and Peggy Bauer. 46 Tom Mangelsen. 47 Erwin and Peggy Bauer. 48–49 Mark Warner. 50 Imagery. 51 Janelco. 52 Ed Cooper. 53 Leonard Lee Rue III. 54 Leonard Lee Rue III. 55 Leonard Lee Rue III. 56 Erwin and Peggy Bauer. 57 Erwin and Peggy Bauer. 58 T Erwin and Peggy Bauer; C Erwin and Peggy Bauer; B Art Gingert. 59 T Neal and Mary Jane Mishler. 60 Erwin and Peggy Bauer. 61 L Leonard Rue Jnr; R Art Gingert. 62 T S C Fried; C Leonard Lee Rue III; B Imagery. 63 Art Gingert. 64–65 Larry Ulrich. 66 John J Smith. 67 T Erwin and Peggy Bauer; B Leonard Lee Rue III. 68–69 Charles Gurche. 70 B Neal and Mary Jane Mishler. 70–71 Larry Ulrich. 71 B Larry Ulrich. 72 Larry Ulrich. 73 Larry Ulrich. 74–75 Larry Ulrich. 77 Larry Ulrich. 78 Charles Gurche. 79 T, B Mark Warner. 80–81 Leonard Lee Rue III. 82–3 Leonard Rue Jnr. 82 B Leonard Lee Rue III. 83 T Arthur Morris. 84 Leonard Lee Rue III. 85 T Mark Warner; B Arthur Morris. 86 Leonard Rue Jnr. 87 T, B Imagery. 88–89 Mark Warner. 89 T, B Mark Warner. 90–91 Erwin and Peggy Bauer. 92 Larry Ulrich. 94 T Ed Cooper; B Larry Ulrich. 95 T Ed Cooper; B Robert Perron. 96–97 Robert Perron. 97 Mark Warner. 98 B John J Smith. 98–99 Charles Gurche. 99 Larry Ulrich. 100 T Erwin and Peggy Bauer; B Art Gingert. 101 Erwin and Peggy Bauer. 102 T Neal and Mary Jane Mishler; B Art Gingert. 103 Erwin and Peggy Bauer. 104 Larry Ulrich. 105 Charles Gurche. 106 Jack Olson. 107 T Erwin and Peggy Bauer; C Neal and Mary Jane Mishler; B Leonard Rue Jnr. 110 Leonard Lee Rue III. 111 Larry Ulrich. 112–113 Larry Ulrich. 114 T Neal and Mary Jane Mishler; B Art Gingert. 115 Neal and Mary Jane Mishler. 116 Larry Ulrich. 116–117 Art Gingert. 118 T Leonard Lee Rue III; B Erwin and Peggy Bauer. 119 Erwin and Peggy Bauer. 120–121 Erwin and Peggy Bauer. 122 L Neal and Mary Jane Mishler; R Erwin and Peggy Bauer. 123 Neal and Mary Jane Mishler. 124–125 Art Gingert. 127 TR Erwin and Peggy Bauer; C Leonard Lee Rue III. 126–127 Leonard Rue Jnr. 128 T Art Gingert; B Erwin and Peggy Bauer. 129 Neal and Mary Jane Mishler. 130 Leonard Lee Rue III. 132–133 Neal and Mary Jane Mishler. 133 L Art Gingert; R Neal and Mary Jane Mishler. 134–135 Ed Cooper. 136 Charles Gurche; 138 E R Ricciuti. 139 Leonard Lee Rue III. 140 Erwin and Peggy Bauer. 140–141 Larry Ulrich. 141 Larry Ulrich. 142–143 Larry Ulrich. 144 Larry Ulrich. 145 T Leonard Rue Jnr; B Imagery. 146 Ed Cooper. 147 T Tom Mangelsen; C S C Fried; B Larry Ulrich. 148 T, C, B Larry Ulrich. 149 Larry Ulrich. 150 Erwin and Peggy Bauer. 152–53 Robert Perron. 154 L Robert Perron. 154–155 Ed Cooper. 156 Robert Perron. 156–157 Ed Cooper. 157 Charles Gurche. 158 T Charles Gurche; B Art Gingert. 159 Mark Warner. 160 T Neal and Mary Jane Mishler; B Arthur Morris. 160–161 Arthur Morris. 161 T, B Mark Warner. 162–163 Erwin and Peggy Bauer. 165 Leonard Rue Jnr. 166 T John J Smith; B Mark Warner. 168–169 Erwin and Peggy Bauer. 170 Erwin and Peggy Bauer. 171 Mark Warner. 172 Leonard Lee Rue III. 173 Tom Mangelsen. 174 Robert Perron. 175 Mark Warner. 176–177 Leonard Lee Rue IV. 177 Mark Warner. 178 T, B Mark Warner. 179 Mark Warner. 180 T, BL, BR Mark Warner. 181 Mark Warner. 182 Mark Warner. 183 T, B Mark Warner. 184 T, B Mark Warner. 185 T, R Mark Warner. 186 Mark Warner. 187 T, R, B Mark Warner. 188 Arthur Morris. 189 T Leonard Lee Rue III; B Mark Warner. 190–191 T Leonard Lee Rue III; B S C Fried. 192–193 Imagery. 194 Mark Warner. 195 T Leonard Lee Rue III; L Larry Ulrich; R Leonard Lee Rue III. 196–197 Lee West. 198 Neal and Mary Jane Mishler. 199 T Tom Mangelsen; B Mark Warner. 200 Robert Perron. 201 T Arthur Morris; BL Leonard Lee Rue III. 206–207 Imagery. 208–209 Larry Ulrich. 210 Larry Ulrich. 211 Larry Ulrich. 212 Jack Olson. 213 Jack Olson.

Grateful thanks to the following for acting as consultants:

Peter Brazaitis, David A. Breen, Lauren Brown, John Van Couvering, Jay Pitocchelli, Gordon W. Schuett.